Willie Miller's
ABERDEEN DREAM TEAM

WILLIE MILLER'S
ABERDEEN DREAM TEAM

WILLIE MILLER
WITH ROB ROBERTSON

BLACK & WHITE PUBLISHING

First published 2011
by Black & White Publishing Ltd
29 Ocean Drive, Edinburgh EH6 6JL

1 3 5 7 9 10 8 6 4 2   11 12 13 14

ISBN: 978 1 84502 352 2

A CIP catalogue record for this book is available from the British Library.

Typeset by Iolaire Typesetting, Newtonmore
Printed and bound by MPG Books Ltd, Bodmin, Cornwall

CONTENTS

ACKNOWLEDGEMENTS

Writing this book would never have been possible without sports writer Rob Robertson of the Scottish *Daily Mail*, who I have known for many years and who helped me considerably. Also Aberdeen historian Kevin Stirling, who has encyclopedic knowledge of the club, kept us right with all the facts and figures. Aberdeen fan, Mark Walker did a great job giving the book the once over while Mike Murphy did a fantastic proofreading job and George Cheyne was a great help throughout.

Hearing the Dream Teams selected by well-known Dons fans, which are also published in the book, gave me plenty to think about when I was making my own choices. Top entertainer Buff Hardie of *Scotland the What?* and journalist and broadcaster Jack Webster, as well as Jim Naughtie, have been watching Aberdeen all their lives, and their suggestions of players from the past for possible inclusion were invaluable.

Other welcome contributors include former Open champion Paul Lawrie who has been a great supporter of myself and the club through the years and knows his football, as does Scotland rugby star Chris Cusiter who was a regular at Pittodrie in his younger days with his family and still gets back to cheer on the team when his sporting commitments allow.

Everyone knows that Richard Gordon of BBC Radio Sportsound is a lifelong Dons fan who has been one of the most knowledgeable commentators on Scottish football for many years now. Ally Begg was a former member of Bad Boys Inc. who had hits all over the world before he went on to forge a successful media career, first with Manchester United television, then Setanta before he moved to Singapore to become one of ESPN's main worldwide sports presenters.

Can I thank all who helped produce this book, including our publisher Black & White, and I hope every Aberdeen fan enjoys reading the stories about our great players from past and present and also enjoys debating my Dream Team selection.

Willie Miller

FOREWORD
BY ALEX MCLEISH

Who better than Willie Miller to select an Aberdeen Dream Team? Easily the greatest player to ever play for the club, Willie is a living legend.

As a footballer he had no equal. Sir Alex Ferguson described him as the greatest penalty box defender he had ever seen – sorry Gaffer, that tells just part of the story.

Willie is the most influential captain, most consistent player and best one on one defender – in any area of the park – that I have ever seen.

He had this uncanny knack of being able to psyche out the man he was marking and work out what he was going to do even before his opponent did. It was that footballing sixth sense that helped make him such an outstanding defender.

Although he was captain, Willie never wasted his words on shouting for the sake of it but when he did speak people listened. Although he was a pretty laid-back gent off the park if anyone crossed him he had a number of killer one-liners designed to cut them down to size that always allowed him the last word.

Apart from his snoring that used to keep me awake for hours when we roomed together I can't think of anything bad to say about him and I really tried, believe me!

For twelve years we played together in the centre of defence for

Aberdeen and Scotland and I can only remember one heated exchange. It came against Dundee United when we had each other by the throat before we realised we were being daft and dissolved in laughter.

For a central defensive partnership who lived in each others pockets for so long, to never really get on each others nerves speaks volumes for our friendship and the respect we had for each other as professional footballers.

Although Willie is just three and a half years older than me (yes, I know he looks much older) I always looked up to him when I first started out as a young player at Pittodrie. The first time I saw him in action was when I was sitting in the Pittodrie main stand watching the first team for the umpteenth time and trying to work out how the bloke with the big, black moustache could play so consistently week after week.

His ability to keep up such a high level of performance in every game proved to be a real source of inspiration to me and drove me on to try and reach the high standards Willie had set in my own game.

When I first broke into the team we became, I like to think, equal partners in a defence that didn't lose that many bad goals. We became, and remain, good friends which allows me to criticise his snoring and tell you that I can comment on it so authoritatively because I have never seen anybody sleep as much as Willie.

It was incredible the amount of time he spent with his eyes shut. Whatever the occasion, be it before a big game when other players were nervous, or waiting in an airport lounge before going abroad he always liked to get some kip.

When we played away against either Celtic, Rangers or Partick Thistle we always stayed at The Excelsior Hotel at Glasgow Airport the night before as it was a wee bit out of the city which meant we got some peace.

As a rule we used to arrive at four o'clock on the Friday afternoon and everybody used to go for a walk to stretch their legs, apart from Willie who used to check in and go straight to bed before we even had our evening meal.

Before he dozed off his last words to me before I left the room were always, 'Hey big man, bring me back a present from your walk.' So for years and years every time I went out I had to take a detour by the petrol station at Glasgow Airport to get a chocolate treat for Sleeping Beauty.

When he was awake he was a class act. In fact, the one word I would use to describe Willie more than any other is classy. Away from the action he was always a sharp dresser. His jacket was always expertly made to measure, his shirts were always perfectly creased, his trousers well-pressed and his shoes polished until you could see your face in them. He had an aura about him that he hasn't lost to this day.

I feel privileged to have been asked by Willie to do the foreword for his Aberdeen Dream Team book as I have huge respect for him, both as a man and a footballer.

I hope you all enjoy the book and Willie, I hope I made your Dream Team because if I didn't there will be trouble!

Yours in sport,
Alex McLeish

PICKING MY DREAM TEAM

Putting together my Aberdeen Dream Team has been a really tough but ultimately rewarding task. Although I have been associated with the club for more than thirty years I did not want to forget the players who came before and after me in my deliberations.

I spent long hours with my co-author Rob Robertson evaluating players from every era and the further I delved into the history of the club the more I wanted to make this book a celebration of all the great men who gave their all for Aberdeen.

Whether you agree with my Dream Team selections or not I like to think you will be as fascinated as I was by the stories of all the great players who proudly wore the red – and in the early days the black and gold – of Aberdeen.

Of course many of the European Cup Winners' Cup players of 1983 figured in my Dream Team thoughts and I think you will agree that was only right and proper. But there were other great sides jam-packed with top players who deserved to be looked at closely.

For instance, who can forget the Aberdeen squad that brought the Scottish League flag to Pittodrie for the first time in our history in 1954/55? Or what about the side that brought the Scottish Cup home to Pittodrie for the first time in 1947? Or the fantastic team put together by Eddie Turnbull that won the Scottish Cup in 1970?

Also let's not forget the brave souls who helped pull Aberdeen through the Northern League into the second division and then into the top league within three years of their formation back in 1903.

Through the years there have been very special Pittodrie characters, and not just the ones you all know about like big Doug Rougvie or wee Joe Harper. Can you imagine any modern day Aberdeen player rushing out of the church after his own wedding in his morning suit to play against East Fife at Pittodrie on a Saturday afternoon then getting back in time for his own reception like Billy Smith did in the early 1950s?

Or for a goalkeeper to have the audacity to regularly put up an umbrella and chat to fans behind the goal like Rab MacFarlane did way back in the early 1900s. And what about full-back Don Emery who supposedly had such a vicious shot that he once broke a crossbar and left one opposition goalkeeper in so much fear he refused to face his penalty kick?

Also what about Alex Jackson, whose career was going nowhere fast until he signed for Aberdeen? His time at Pittodrie transformed his fortunes and four years later, after a big money move to Huddersfield, he was scoring a hat-trick for the famous Scotland team dubbed 'the Wembley Wizards' who beat England 5-1 in 1928.

My aim was to pick a Dream Team starting eleven and a full bench plus a manager, a full backroom staff and a club chairman. I am sure my choices will stimulate debate to say the least and I am sure some you will agree with strongly, others you won't.

MILLER'S MILESTONES

June 1969 – Signs on schoolboy forms for Aberdeen as a fourteen-year-old striker and makes regular trips to Pittodrie during holidays for training.

July 1971 – Signed on a professional contract by Eddie Turnbull but immediately farmed out to Peterhead where he finishes as the club's leading goalscorer for season 1971/72 with twenty-three goals.

December 16, 1972 – On the advice of Teddy Scott, plays his first game as a central defender in a reserve game against Rangers reserves at Pittodrie.

April 28, 1973 – Despite now being a central defender, makes his Aberdeen first-team debut against Morton at Cappielow on the left wing after Arthur Graham picks up an injury.

September 19, 1973 – Makes his European debut in a UEFA Cup first round tie against Finn Harps of the Republic of Ireland, at Pittodrie.

March 13, 1974 – First appearance for the Scotland Under-23 team against England at St James Park at Newcastle where he plays right back.

June 1, 1975 – Makes his full Scotland debut playing in midfield against Romania in Bucharest.

December 4, 1975 – Replaces Bobby Clark as Aberdeen captain under manager Ally MacLeod.

November 6, 1976 – Picks up his first trophy as captain as he leads Aberdeen to an extra-time League Cup victory over Celtic.

February 26, 1977 – Makes his 200th first team appearance in a Scottish Cup fourth-round tie against Dundee at Dens Park.

November 11, 1978 – Clocks up 300 appearances in a red jersey in the match against Motherwell at Fir Park.

May 7, 1980 – An easy win over Hibs at Easter Road gives Aberdeen their first League championship title since 1955.

May 21, 1980 – Scores Scotland's only goal in a 1-0 Home Championship win over Wales at Hampden Park.

August 30, 1980 – Willie makes his 400th appearance for Aberdeen in the League Cup second leg tie against Berwick Rangers at Shielfield Park.

August 16, 1981 – Awarded a testimonial match against Tottenham Hotspur.

April 17, 1982 – 500th appearance against Morton at Cappielow, the ground where he had made his debut nine years earlier.

May 22, 1982 – Leads Aberdeen to the first of three successive Scottish Cup triumphs with a 4-1 extra-time victory over Rangers.

June 18, 1982 – Wins his 18th Scotland cap in a World Cup match against Brazil in Spain which beats Bobby Clark's Aberdeen record for full caps.

September 1, 1982 – Scores his first European goal in the second leg of the Cup Winners' Cup preliminary round tie against FC Sion of Switzerland.

May 11, 1983 – Captains Aberdeen to European Cup Winners' Cup victory over Real Madrid in Gothenburg.

May 21, 1983 – Picks up the Scottish Cup after a 1-0 win over Rangers at Hampden.

June 12, 1983 – Given the honour of captaining Scotland for the first time during a tour of Canada.

November 2, 1983 – Plays his 600th game for Aberdeen in the second leg of the Cup Winners' Cup second round tie against Beveren of Belgium at Pittodrie.

December 20, 1983 – Picks up another European trophy as captain when SV Hamburg are beaten in the final of the European Super Cup.

May 12, 1984 – Despite a final day defeat to St Mirren at Love Street, Aberdeen are crowned Scottish Champions five years since Willie picked up his first championship medal.

May 1984 – Voted Player of the Year by both The Scottish Football Writers' Association and the Scottish Professional Footballers' Association.

May 11, 1985 – Willie picks up his third and final Scottish League championship medal after the final game of the season, which Aberdeen won 2-1 against Morton at Cappielow.

April 27, 1985 – Willie overtakes Bobby Clark as he clocks up a club record 698 appearances when he takes the field against Celtic at Pittodrie.

March 5, 1986 – Willie makes his 50th European appearance in the first leg of a European Cup quarter-final against IFK Gothenburg at Pittodrie, where he scores his second European goal in a 2-2 draw.

June 8, 1986 – Picks up his 50th cap for Scotland against West Germany in the World Cup finals in Mexico which gains him entry into the SFA Hall of Fame.

May 17, 1988 – Wins his 60th cap against Colombia in a Rous Cup game at Hampden.

October 22, 1989 – Lifts his final trophy as captain of Aberdeen after they beat Rangers in the Scottish League Cup final.

November 15, 1989 – Wins his 65th and final Scotland cap as he helps his country draw with Norway and qualify for the 1990 World Cup.

August 21, 1990 – Willie plays his 923rd and final game for Aberdeen in a 2-1 Scottish League Cup win over Queens Park at Hampden.

December 4, 1990 – Granted a further testimonial match against a World Select including Bryan Robson and Mark Hughes at Pittodrie.

January 1991 – Officially named as part of Alex Smith's coaching staff.

February 1992 – Takes over from Alex Smith as Aberdeen manager and finishes runners-up to Rangers in the Scottish League and Scottish Cup in first season.

February 1995 – Is sacked as Aberdeen manager and replaced by his assistant Roy Aitken.

June 2004 – Returns to Aberdeen board as director of football.

June 2011 – Takes over as director of football development.

1

THE KING OF THE BOSSES

Aberdeen have had many top managers in their history. In the early days there was Jimmy Phillip, before Paddy Travers took over and then Dave Halliday who brought the first league championship to Pittodrie in the 1954/55 season.

During the golden era of the 1970s and 1980s, when I played, there were figures like Eddie Turnbull, Ally MacLeod and of course Sir Alex Ferguson. Even when my playing career was drawing to a close Alex Smith with Jocky Scott at his side lifted the League Cup and Scottish Cup.

Researching my Dream Team book has shown me that a high number of inspirational men have sat behind the manager's desk at Pittodrie over the years. Every single one of them, in their own way, has helped the club. Some, like myself, didn't succeed as much as they would have liked but you could never question their commitment.

Before I share my thoughts with you on the merits of previous Aberdeen managers can I say I was never one of those players who they took an instant liking to in training. Even Sir Alex had major doubts about me when he took over.

Part of the reason was that I never went out of my way to bust a gut out on the training field. It was a necessary evil for me, something to be tolerated rather than enjoyed.

When I played I knew exactly how to get myself match-fit and peaking on Saturday afternoon at three o'clock. To me, that was the only time that mattered. By the way, for those of you reading this who are much younger than me that is when all our games kicked off back then.

Because my first impressions may not have always been good ones it meant I had to prove myself every time a new manager was appointed. That meant I hated whenever someone left or got sacked. I know that is the same for every player, but it was something I used to dread more than most as they would take one look at me training and think I was a lazy so-and-so.

The number of times trainer Teddy Scott had to explain to the new coach – whether it was Jimmy Bonthrone, Ally MacLeod, Sir Alex, Alex Smith and Jocky Scott or Ian Porterfield – that was just my way must have driven him to distraction.

The fact that I kept my place under five management teams suggests that any misapprehension they had about me in training did not last for long after they saw me play. Looking back I like to think I eventually enjoyed very good relations with them all, which at the very least resulted in us having a mutual respect for each other.

Out of all the categories for my Dream Team picking our all time greatest manager, as you would expect, took me the shortest period of time. Maybe I'm a wee bit biased but can I say you get no prizes for guessing who it is.

As I explained in my introduction, I don't want to simply dismiss the less well-known Aberdeen managers who put in so much effort over the years into trying to turn the club into a major force in Scottish football. So before I go on to talk about the managerial ability of a certain man from Govan with a bit of a temper let me roll back the years and salute others who served.

Our first ever manager, albeit a part-time one, was the fascinating character Jimmy Phillip who cut a dash round Pittodrie with his big moustache, bowler hat and authoritarian style that meant his players were kept on a tight leash.

He had been a wood-cutter by trade and was the first and only true Aberdonian to manage the club until Jocky Scott was given the co-manager's role with Alex Smith. Jimmy was also a qualified referee who officiated at the Olympic Games in Stockholm in 1912, and by all accounts was so single-minded even I could not have influenced his decisions.

Aberdeen Football Club was officially formed on April 14, 1903 and Jimmy was appointed on July 1, 1903. He was the man who led the Dons into their first competitive match against Stenhousemuir on an overcast but historic day at Pittodrie on August 15, 1903 that ended in a 1-1 draw. There was huge local interest with 8,000 fans turning up to see the new team. The first ever goal scored for Aberdeen came in that game and captain Willie MacAulay got it.

That day they wore white and it was only in the next season that the more familiar black and gold outfit that led to the nickname 'the wasps' was introduced. The forward line of the time hated the black and gold strips because opposition fans used to taunt them that they did not deserve to be nicknamed 'the wasps' because they had no sting in their play.

For that first season they played in the Northern League, which was a regional league that took in teams as far down as Perth. What fascinated me about those early days is the way that managers appear to have been getting it in the neck even back then. Letters to the *Aberdeen Evening Express* called for Jimmy's head because early results had not been very good. There were also accusations that players had been seen 'dawdling' about town rather than training all the time. Small beer indeed compared to what some of the present day players allegedly get up to on their days off.

Jimmy obviously realised early that signing a few decent players gets the fans interested and Bert Shinner, who he brought from Middlesbrough, was the first real Aberdeen idol. Bert played on the right wing and provided the ammunition for inside forward Willie MacAulay who top scored with thirteen goals in that first season in the Northern League. They finished a creditable third behind league winners Montrose and runners-up Arbroath.

They were moved up to the Scottish Second Division and when

3

the First Division was extended from fourteen to sixteen teams Jimmy lobbied the SFA strongly for their inclusion. He put up such a strong case that Aberdeen topped the poll of the clubs who won admission in the 1905/06 season. With Aberdeen now in the top Scottish league the Aberdeen board decided to back date Jimmy's pay, and handed him £116 3shillings and 4d for his first fourteen months in charge.

To strengthen his team he also brought greats like Jock Hume, Willie Lennie and Charlie O'Hagan to Pittodrie. He brought Aberdeen a long way in a relatively short space of time and took the club to their first ever Scottish Cup semi-final on March 21, 1908, where they lost to Celtic in front of Pittodrie's first ever 20,000-plus crowd. He was also proud of the fact that left winger Willie Lennie became the first Aberdeen player to win a Scottish cap. Jimmy was the first Aberdeen manager to win against Rangers home and away when his team beat them twice in the 1910/11 season.

He was a man who had big ambitions and had a real pioneering spirit to the extent that, rather than go on a pre-season tour to England in 1911, he took his team on a tour of central Europe where he visited Bohemia and Moravia, which are now part of the Czech Republic, and also to Poland where they played eight games in two weeks with a squad of just twelve. They must have been a really special group of players because remarkably, although they lost the first match they won the next seven on the bounce. Jock Hume, who was a full-back, was forced to play up front during the tour and scored eighteen goals.

Out of the thirty-three Aberdeen players and officials who served in the First World War eight of them died and it was a tribute to Jimmy that he managed to pull the club together when league football resumed at Pittodrie on August 16, 1919 with a game against Albion Rovers.

Throughout his time in charge Jimmy was a passionate defender of anything to do with Aberdeen and appeared to fall-out on a regular basis with the SFA. Nothing has changed on that score, Jimmy, people still fall out with the SFA!

He was also the manager of the club for a famous game of which I must confess I knew precious little about until now. It was our record 13-0 Scottish Cup win over Peterhead on February 10, 1923 which I assumed was simply us having a good day. Not so.

It appears the third round Scottish Cup tie was originally to be played in Peterhead but their directors, who knew they would get a bigger pay day away from home, agreed to switch the tie to Pittodrie. The Highland League club got £250 to change the venue and Aberdeen also met the travelling expenses of their players and directors.

The Peterhead players, quite rightly, were furious at the deal done behind their backs. They thought they had little chance of winning away from home and to be bloody-minded said they would not play unless they were paid £10 each. The Peterhead board said no, which led to a players' strike which meant they had to field a side without eight first team regulars and including two Aberdeen University students to get eleven players out on the pitch.

The game was played in dreadful conditions which although didn't help Aberdeen's passing style didn't stop them being 5-0 up at half-time. Midway through the second half two Peterhead players, Buchan and McRobbie, had to go off suffering from exposure. No wonder they were beaten 13-0. Ironically only 3,241 people turned up paying £181 8s 11d to watch the goal fest which left Aberdeen out of pocket.

Jimmy finally stepped down in 1924 after a tour of Germany after twenty-one years in the job, during which time he had brought Aberdeen through the leagues and turned them into a respected and well established club side. He also made the first move to bring Alex Jackson, who went on to be a member of the Wembley Wizards who beat England 5-1 at Wembley in 1928, to the club. He left with good grace and went on to be a club director so he could continue his fights with the SFA within the corridors of power on behalf of Aberdeen. He had turned into a real top-class administrator when he was tragically killed in a road accident in Belfast in 1930.

Paddy Travers took over Jimmy's good work and he also had a

great pedigree as a former player with Celtic and Aberdeen. He had been part of the Aberdeen team that finished runners-up to Rangers in the 1910-11 championship race and had also managed clubs in Norway. He returned to Scotland to take over at Dumbarton before he took up the manager's role at Pittodrie.

He put together a worldwide scouting network in places as close as Ireland and as far afield as America and South Africa, which brought players like Billy Strauss, Charlie McGill and Steve Smith to the club. His team were the nearly men of the late 1920s and despite having the only unbeaten record in British football in the 1929/30 season were beaten to the league title by Rangers. He was an ardent timekeeper and when internationalist Alex Cheyne was a few minutes late turning up at Pittodrie before a match he found he had lost his place. No doubt Alex was never late again.

His time was tainted by an alleged bribery scandal in 1931 called 'The Great Mystery' involving five of his best players that damaged the club badly. Pat tried to cover it up but Benny Yorston, Frank Hill, Jimmy Black, David Galloway and Hugh McLaren were all sold pretty quickly after the allegations broke.

Although no charges were brought and the club tried to dismiss what was happening as 'domestic trouble' it was clear all was not well in the dressing room.

It appears that a group of players had placed fixed-odd bets with a local bookmaker that Aberdeen would be drawing at half-time and winning at full-time in a number of matches in the first few months of the 1931/32 season. The alleged illegal betting scam only came to light when the group tried to get outside left Adam McLean involved when he joined the club. The former Scotland and Celtic player wanted no part and turned whistleblower.

It was a difficult position for Travers to recover from, at the time there were suggestions that he had lost control of the dressing room, but the fact he immediately got rid of the players he thought were involved suggests to me he was strong and handled the situation very well. Once the controversy had died down things improved for Aberdeen.

On the positive side Paddy took the club to their first ever Scottish Cup final against Celtic in 1937, which was played at Hampden in front of a huge crowd of 146,433 but ended in a 2-1 defeat. He left in 1938 to join Clyde, with Dave Halliday being appointed out of 100 applicants for the job.

Dave had been born in Dumfries and played on the left wing for Queen of the South before signing for St Mirren, Dundee and Sunderland – where he scored 153 goals at the rate of just under one a game. Arsenal snapped him up for £6,000, which was a lot of money back in November 1929, but he struggled to find the net, with half of his tally coming in one game when he scored four goals in a 6-6 draw against Leicester City in 1930. Further moves to Manchester City and a team called Clapton Orient (now Leyton Orient) followed before he became player-manager of non-league Yeovil and Petters United in 1935.

Yeovil and Petters United may have been non-league but they were professionally run and it was a good starting point for Halliday's managerial career. They competed in the English Southern League which was at the time the most senior division outside of the Football League. A lot of their players were semi-pros and worked at the Petters factory in Yeovil that made petrol and diesel engines for export to the British in India, which meant he had his players on his doorstep every day.

His last game for them as player-manager was in an FA Cup tie against Manchester United at Old Trafford before he joined Aberdeen as manager on January 5, 1938. In one of the few interviews I found researching the book, Halliday told *The Sunday Post* back in 1957 how his move came about.

'In the 1937/38 season Yeovil could do little wrong and our run in the FA Cup had the place buzzing,' Halliday told *The Sunday Post*. 'We had already beaten Walsall and Ipswich to progress to the fourth round. Then we were drawn against Manchester United at Old Trafford so we were set for Yeovil's greatest game. I was beginning to enjoy being manager, especially being able to pick myself in the team.

'In the run-up to the Manchester United game I saw the Aberdeen job advertised in the sports section of a newspaper in the dressing room. To my surprise I was given an interview and met at Aberdeen station by George Anderson (an Aberdeen director) and taken round the side streets so nobody would see me at Pittodrie.

'They were keen to keep my visit a secret so I told nobody. I must have impressed them because they offered me the job a few days later but I told them I wanted to stay until Yeovil had played Manchester United at Old Trafford. We did okay and lost just 2-0 and after that I was on my way to Aberdeen.'

He only had a year before the outbreak of the Second World War so he had no time to build a team. By his side was Dave Shaw, the former Hibernian captain, who was the first team trainer. He brought in voluntary afternoon sessions for first team players and the fact hardly anybody missed one shows how important they were in ensuring Aberdeen became one of the fittest teams of their generation.

Reading about Halliday gave me the impression he was a confident manager who never seemed to talk much about the opposition. I think he must have been in the mould of Liverpool's Bill Shankly, who always used to assume his team was good enough to beat anybody. As long as his own side was in order then there was nothing to worry about.

Dave was the Aberdeen manager when the team changed from their old black and gold colours to red on March 18, 1939 in a game against Queen's Park. It remains a mystery as to why the change took place. Even Aberdeen historian Kevin Stirling, who has an encyclopedic knowledge of everything related to the club, has yet to come up with a definitive answer to that one. According to Kevin the best theory is that the team changed to reflect the red in the official City of Aberdeen coat of arms.

When the Second World War broke out in September 1939 two directors, Charles B. Forbes and George Anderson, both former players, took over the management reigns while Dave did his bit for the war effort, but thankfully the basic fabric of the immediate pre-war side was still around when the boss returned to resume his duties at Pittodrie.

I was fascinated to see that unfortunately one airman from Lossiemouth who had guested for Aberdeen during the Second World War wasn't among the players who remained at Pittodrie when peace broke out and Dave regained control.

He was the legendary Stanley Mortensen who scored a hat-trick in the famous 4-3 win by Blackpool over Bolton Wanderers in 1953 which gave the equally legendary Stanley Matthews his first FA Cup winners' medal. Of course Stan would have gone straight into my Dream Team based on what he achieved in football, but I am basing my starting eleven on what they did for Aberdeen which means Stanley doesn't make the cut. The fact that fans at Pittodrie actually saw him in action in Aberdeen colours will always give him a special connection with the club though.

Stan was at Pittodrie, on and off, for two years from 1942, averaging about a goal a game. His most famous match, on May 22, 1943, was when Aberdeen were playing the British Army, which had top players like Stan Cullis of Wolves, Tommy Lawton of Everton and Jimmy Hagan of Sheffield United in their ranks. The Army side were winning by four goals to one at half-time with the Aberdeen goal coming from Mortensen. Just after half-time, the Army scored again before Mortensen scored four of his own and nearly snatched the unlikely draw for Aberdeen. I wonder what Dave Halliday would have given for having Stan in his team in the long term?

After the war the 1945/46 Southern League Cup competition – on paper a war trophy, but in reality a full blown fore-runner for the League Cup competition itself – saw Halliday's Dons march to a Hampden final appearance against the mighty Rangers. On the way there they beat Hibernian, Ayr United and Airdrie. On the memorable spring afternoon of May 11, 1946 in front of 135,000 people Aberdeen came of age, winning a thrilling game 3-2 thanks to a last minute winner from George Taylor.

For me the unsung hero of that game has to be Alec Kiddie who was a St Andrews University science student at the time and also a keen athlete who wanted to retain his amateur status until he graduated three years later. As an amateur he was not allowed to take any financial reward for bringing the first ever cup of any significance to Pittodrie. Instead the Aberdeen directors presented him with a watch which I am told by his son Paul, who is now the head of communications at Heart of Midlothian, he always wears with pride.

The following year, 1947, Dave took his team back to Hampden in both the League Cup final, which they lost 4-0 to Rangers, and in the Scottish Cup final itself two weeks later, when they lifted the trophy with a 2-1 win over Hibs in front of 82,140 fans. That day they were inspired by George Hamilton, the Dumfries lad that Halliday had brought to Pittodrie with him back in 1938.

Match reports all praise his display and it was his goal from a tight angle nine minutes from half-time that laid the foundations for a famous victory. Stan Williams scored the other and although George had a penalty saved by Hibs goalkeeper Jimmy Kerr he was still voted man of the match. The Scottish Cup win meant everything to the Dons fans who turned out in their thousands in the pouring rain to cheer the team on their open-top bus ride around the city.

Not surprisingly, with a side containing many pre-war names, Dave was faced with a major rebuilding job within months of the Scottish Cup triumph. After two seasons spent flirting with relegation with his young team, the manager's new-look side came of age and went on to lose successive Scottish Cup finals in 1953 and 1954, before realising their full potential and landing the ultimate prize, the Scottish League Championship in 1955.

With sixteen clubs in the Scottish top division, the league programme consisted of thirty games, and with three left Aberdeen had forty-five points, five more than Celtic and ten ahead of Hearts who had three games in hand. In the first game of the run-in Dave's Aberdeen side came up against Clyde who were managed by Pat

Travers, the former Aberdeen boss who, a full eighteen years earlier, had brought him to the club.

Aberdeen's target was to take three points from their final three games to guarantee the title. A win at Shawfield would make the championship arrive quicker, as if other results went their way it would take their main challengers Celtic out of contention. Hearts would need to win all of their final games to give them forty-seven points, and their only hope was for Dave's team to slip up which would allow them to pip Aberdeen on goal difference.

As it turned out no worrying scenarios were played out for the Dons as other results all went their way on the day. The hero was Archie Glen who held his nerve to score a first half penalty that beat Clyde in that vital game. Earlier in the season Glen had missed two penalties, the last one at Pittodrie against Clyde, and after a crisis of confidence had been replaced by Jackie Allister as the main place kicker.

But Jackie missed the Clyde game through injury which meant the responsibility fell yet again to Archie. Showing no sign of nerves he fired his penalty high into the net, inches under the crossbar giving Clyde goalkeeper Ken Hewkins no chance. Aberdeen goalkeeper Fred Martin was twice called upon to secure the lead, his most vital save coming from Tommy Ring when he dived full length to stop a goal-bound shot.

What fascinated me about this game on April 9, 1955 was the heroic role played in proceedings by Jackie Hather who picked up a leg injury. In those days when substitutes were not allowed it was common practice for injured players to limp their way through the rest of the game regardless of the seriousness of their injury. Jackie got injured early in the second half but kept going out on the wing to provide nuisance value to the opposition defence.

There was always a worry over him at the best of times as he played an entire career with one kidney. He had even put off an operation to make sure he was available to help Aberdeen in their title run-in. Granted he had to go off in the last few minutes when his body simply gave up on him against Clyde, but it was a superhuman effort for him to play seriously injured, especially as this was a man who had been struggling with his kidney complaint plus his leg problem. You don't get more dedication than that.

The players did not know when they first came off the pitch that they were Scottish League champions for the first time in the history of Aberdeen Football Club. Celtic won 1-0 at Dundee but their goal difference was such they had no chance of overtaking them. When they got into the dressing room they were told Rangers had beaten their other rivals Hearts and the title had been won.

Nowadays winning the title is the top domestic prize. Back then, remarkably, it was cup competitions that took pride of place which meant that not many Dons fans were at Shawfield to celebrate such a historic moment.

To put things in perspective, when Celtic played Aberdeen in the 1954 Scottish Cup final there was a massive 130,060 people in the Hampden crowd that day with 20,000 Dons fans making the trip to Glasgow from the city alone. Less than a year later only 400 Aberdeen supporters were in the crowd of 15,000 to see them secure the league title at Shawfield.

When the team arrived back at Aberdeen Joint Railway Station around midnight only thirty fans, although some have even suggested just ten as the rest were people waiting for other people on the train, had bothered to turn up to welcome them home. Imagine how many would be lining the streets of Aberdeen if League Championship success came the way of the team nowadays?

Also think of how many acres of newsprint and internet message boards would be full of discussion about the match. Back then the late edition of the *Green Final* gave the title win a mention under the headline: 'Hail, the Dons champions' although the one I liked best was 'Cocks o' the North and Scottish Champs – Fa's like us?'

Despite the low key reaction to the League Championship win, it was a defining moment in the history of the club. They had won the title with forty-nine points from thirty games, three ahead of runners-up Celtic. Interestingly, maybe it was because it was not a central belt team that won the title, there was not much praise for the way Aberdeen played.

Some newspapers of the time said they were too defensive and dull to watch. Well, can I say the statistics don't back up that accusation. Dave Halliday's team scored forty-one goals at home, one less than top scorers Celtic. Away from Pittodrie thirty-two goals were scored, with only Hibernian with thirty-six and Celtic with thirty-four getting more. Defensively they had a record that would have made myself, Alex McLeish and Jim Leighton proud. Only twenty-six goals conceded in all matches: a fantastic achievement.

What was also of interest was how much the players got for bringing the first League Championship trophy to Aberdeen. The money came directly from the Scottish League and the £1,000 the club received was divided up into eleven equal parts, but the club had used nineteen players that season. That meant there was £91 available for each position, which had to be sub-divided among all the players who had played in that position during the season.

For instance, goalkeeper Fred Martin, who had been in great form all season, had missed two games which meant his pay packet was reduced, with Reg Morrison, who played in the other two games, getting the rest, for helping win the league title. Compare that to the riches available to players nowadays. You would think the Aberdeen board would have made up the difference in Fred's case at least as a gesture of good will.

The Championship trophy hardly had time to gather dust in the Pittodrie boardroom before Leicester City had tempted Dave south to take over at Filbert Street on July 1, 1955. Publicly he said he was going because he needed a new challenge.

Privately it seems he felt sickened, not by the lack of cash given to his players for winning the league, but by the fact that the SFA, who had the power to propose Aberdeen as Scottish League champions as candidates for the new 'European Champions Club Cup' instead chose Hibernian. Looking back it looks like Harry Swan, the Hibernian chairman who was President of the SFA, had put forward his own club rather than Aberdeen, which makes it easy to see why

Halliday got disillusioned. At Leicester, Halliday guided City to the First Division in his second season in charge, but met with mixed fortunes thereafter.

For all the work he did for Aberdeen Football Club and the fact he brought them their first Scottish League title plus a Scottish Cup Halliday thoroughly deserves my consideration as one of the top managers in the history of the club, and if it had not been for one other certain person could have managed my Dream Team.

Dave Shaw had been the Aberdeen trainer under Dave Halliday and knew from day one he had a tough act to follow when he took over in the 1955/56 season. The fact the board was split on his appointment didn't help his case. The chairman at the time, William Mitchell, told him in no uncertain terms he had been given the nod against Mitchell's wishes.

To think you have your chairman against you from day one must have been tough for Dave to come to terms with. He probably knew he was fighting an uphill battle to make his time at Pittodrie a long and fruitful one.

To be fair to him he had the best possible start and no doubt the fans would have loved him after his side beat Rangers in the semi-final of the Scottish League Cup to set up a meeting with St Mirren at Hampden.

Unfortunately the League Cup that year didn't capture the imagination of the Aberdeen fans, at least when it came to travelling to the final, although their homecoming more than made up for that. Maybe the fact the team had won the Scottish League title a few months earlier gave the supporters the impression success would occur on a regular basis. Either way only 44,104 fans in total bothered to turn up to watch a game that led to more silverware heading to Pittodrie.

In what appears to have been a scrappy game, Aberdeen went ahead after Jimmy Mallan put through his own goal before Bobby Holmes equalised for the Paisley club. Although they were stuck in their own half for most of the second period, with eleven minutes left Graham Leggat mis-hit a shot that Jim Lornie in the St Mirren goal misjudged in the wind and to Graham's surprise – and Jim's embarrassment – he had just scored the winning goal in the Scottish League Cup final. Even Dave Shaw admitted his team had been lucky to win but the 15,000 supporters who turned up at the railway station in Aberdeen to welcome them home didn't care that it had been a fortunate victory.

That legendary author and journalist, life-long Dons fan Jack Webster, was a young reporter on the *Press and Journal* at the time, and in his excellent dispatch he described how 'a miniature Hampden Roar nearly lifted the roof of the station as team captain Jimmy Mitchell stepped from the train and was lifted shoulder-high, carrying the cup. A large cordon of police had to clear a way as the players were chaired, with great difficulty, through the seething mob to the bus waiting inside the station building.'

Although Jack was to witness first-hand Aberdeen winning many more trophies through the years, for Dave Shaw that was unfortunately the only moment he had to cheer about as Aberdeen manager. From champions in 1954/55 under Dave Halliday the team finished second the following year, but then dropped to fifth and then eleventh. In 1959 they were a lowly thirteenth, two places off the bottom.

With the pressure mounting Dave had a chance of redeeming himself after he steered Aberdeen to the Scottish Cup final of 1959 against St Mirren, the team they had beaten in the League Cup final three years earlier. His side was never at the races as they were beaten 3-1.

On November 17, 1959, he was demoted to his previous role as trainer with Tommy Pearson, who had been coaching the youth team and the reserves part-time, taking over.

Tommy was a former Aberdeen player who had become a sports writer with the *Scottish Daily Mail* after he hung up his boots in 1953. Such was his popularity as a writer and former Pittodrie footballer he was invited back to coach the youth team and reserves but had to abandon his journalistic career in November that year when he was promoted to the manager's chair.

Tommy had it tough and lost important players like Jack Hather, Jim Clunie and significantly Archie Glen who picked up a serious injury against Kilmarnock that virtually ended his career. He tried to replace him with up and coming players but the gamble failed to pay off. The only light that shone on his first season at Pittodrie came in the shape of the newly installed floodlights that were switched on in October 1959 that allowed evening games to take place on cold, dark, north-east nights. It was not a fruitful period for the club and in a six-year period under Tommy there was not a hint of success. With no cup finals and no serious league challenges Tommy had no choice but to fall on his sword and he resigned on February 13, 1965.

The man who took over excited the Aberdeen fans and no wonder. Eddie Turnbull was a football superstar during his time as a member of 'The Famous Five' at Hibs and a man who demanded respect. He didn't suffer fools gladly and was one of the toughest guys I had ever met, albeit only briefly as I will explain.

Eddie had been coach of Queen's Park where he caught the eye of the Aberdeen board a year earlier after his amateur team had forced the Dons to a replay and extra-time in a second round Scottish Cup tie.

When he arrived he made it clear things would be done his way. He wanted control of everything and really was the first modern manager the club had ever had in that he took training, picked the team and made all the big decisions.

Eddie, a bit like Jock Stein, was ahead of his time. He travelled the world looking at coaching techniques and was a disciple of Helenio Herrera, the South American coach of Inter Milan who took them to three successive European Cup finals.

He came to Aberdeen at the same time as Jock went to Celtic, and as Eddie will tell you, there was no love lost, on his side at least. Eddie always felt he was Jock's equal and the success that Jock had at Celtic acted as a spur to Eddie to match him domestically.

When I was talking to some of the older guys at Pittodrie when I first came to the club they used to joke that Eddie had arrived at Pittodrie with all the strength of a force ten gale coming off the

North Sea. Within a month he had handed out no less than seventeen free transfers and made it clear he thought the club was an absolute shambles. He got rid of all the backroom staff apart from the legendary trainer Teddy Scott and chief scout Bobby Calder.

Within those first few months in charge he had transformed the dressing room and taken Aberdeen into the 1967 Scottish Cup final against Celtic. They lost 2-0, but remember this was against exactly the same Celtic starting eleven that won the European Cup later that season so it was no disgrace.

The fact that Eddie was ill and couldn't go to the game had an impact on the result as not having him yelling in their ear from the touchline and keeping them right would have affected his players, of that I have no doubt. He had missed taking training for most of the week and made it to the pre-match overnight stay at the Gleneagles Hotel before accepting he was too ill to travel any further and I am sure that would have been a huge frustration for him at the time.

Eddie made some great signings like goalkeeper Bobby Clark from his old club Queen's Park and some other top young players like Frank Munro, Jimmy Smith, Tommy McMillan and Jimmy Whyte, with the best of the lot being Martin Buchan.

As I wrote earlier Eddie travelled the globe trying to pick up coaching ideas, and embraced a plan from American soccer bosses who invited teams like Aberdeen, Stoke City, Wolves and Hibs to become the adopted teams of major cities in the USA in a tournament held over there. The Dons were christened the Washington Whips and won the Eastern section before losing to Wolves who won the Western section in the final. During the tour Aberdeen became one of the first Scottish teams to play on synthetic turf in venues such as the Houston Astrodome and the Los Angeles Coliseum, and Eddie came back making it clear it would be good to train on such an indoor surface near Pittodrie. Unfortunately it never happened but it showed Eddie was thinking of the future of the game all the time.

Slowly but surely Eddie put together a top-class Aberdeen side and of course the game that cemented his place in Aberdeen history was the Scottish Cup win over Celtic at Hampden in front of 108,434 fans on April 11, 1970. Celtic had just won their fifth championship in a row and were about to play Feyenoord in the European Cup final. Aberdeen had finished in eighth place after winning fourteen matches out of thirty-four.

For those of a certain vintage who still love to hear details of the famous game, Aberdeen took the lead through a Joe Harper penalty after Bobby Murdoch had handled. With seven minutes left Derek McKay, the former Highland League player, made it 2-0 before Bobby Lennox pulled one back. Just as the Aberdeen nerves were starting to get a bit frayed Derek scored the third to make the game safe. Martin Buchan lifted the trophy and the whole of Aberdeen celebrated long into the night.

I had signed on schoolboy forms for Aberdeen in June 1969 and had been up at Pittodrie a few times and it was a great period to be associated with the club.

I had caught the eye of a number of football clubs both north and south of the border at that time and was not sure who to sign for. Eddie and his scouting team noticed me when I was playing up front for Eastercraigs, the famous Glasgow boys club. My profile raised even further when I played for Glasgow Boys against London Boys at White Hart Lane, alongside a certain young man called Jimmy Calderwood who was to figure in the history of Aberdeen at a later date.

Bury and Bristol City had both offered me terms but after Aberdeen's legendary scouts Bobby Calder and Jimmy Carswell visited me on behalf of Eddie I was sure my future lay at Pittodrie. They were great guys who convinced my parents that they would look after their little boy. They were true to their word and Aberdeen had a great set-up under Eddie. I was put up in the Brentwood Hotel in Crown Street every time I came up to train at Pittodrie during the summer holidays with Eddie making sure every one of us young lads was well looked after.

I must have done okay because I was offered and signed an

apprenticeship contract put together by Eddie after I left school, but there was a last minute hitch that nearly killed my Aberdeen career stone dead before it had even started.

Eddie may have been manager but he didn't bother himself with such things as paperwork involving the apprentices and left that to the administrative staff. Unfortunately whoever it was had forgotten to send my forms to the SFA which meant I had not been officially registered with them.

That meant that technically I was a free agent and other teams could come in and poach me away. Celtic had been following my progress closely with Eastercraigs for nearly a year and when they got wind of the registration error they were straight in for me.

Although Eddie didn't know much about me he was a proud and competitive man who didn't want one of his youngsters being snatched from under his nose by one of his rivals. He got Bobby Calder and Jimmy Carswell to woo me all over again.

Eddie and his scouting team were pushing at an open door in their attempts to sign me all over again. My parents had instilled in me a sense of right and wrong and it would have been very wrong for me to walk out on a club that had really looked after me. To be honest I had decided I wanted to leave behind the religious bigotry that affected the city of Glasgow at the time and make a fresh start.

Moving to Aberdeen under Eddie was that fresh start, although he gave me a rude awakening on my first day on the ground staff as to how hard a slog I was facing to make the first team. He called me into his office for what I thought was going to be a warm welcome and a pat on the back.

Instead he told me where the brooms were kept and that I had to sweep the terraces. Once I had finished I had to clean the boots of the first team. It was Eddie's way of keeping my feet on the ground as clearly he could see on my face that I naively thought I would be fighting it out for a place in the first team before very long. He gave me a signing on fee of £250 and told me it was up to me to show him I deserved to make the reserves. He didn't even mention the first team.

I was a bit in awe of Eddie, especially when I watched him training the first team. He was a tough task-master who didn't let anyone step out of line, whether the player involved was one of his stars like Joe Harper or a youngster like me. Talking to people I respected at the club about Eddie in later years it became evident how much of an innovator he had been.

For instance, he was big mates with Tommy Docherty when Tommy was manager at Chelsea and on a visit to Stamford Bridge he noticed that the Doc had a special podium built high in the stand so he could get a bird's-eye view of proceedings. Eddie followed suit and whenever I came to watch Aberdeen play when I was an apprentice Eddie would be up in the stand rather than down by the touchline where the view he got was limited.

He also had an eye for a player, and I'm not talking about me here, and knew a good coach when he saw one, which was why he made such good use of Teddy Scott who I will talk about later.

The few times that Eddie worked with the youngsters I was impressed by his desire for us to use the ball as much as possible. When he was in charge of Queen's Park he made it clear every player had their own personal football at training and they had to keep it with them everywhere. It was the same at Aberdeen and every time we trained we had a ball each, which I enjoyed.

Just as I was settling into my new life at Pittodrie I was shocked one morning in July 1971 when I walked in for summer training to be told Eddie had resigned and was heading back to be manager at his old club Hibs. It was a big shock to the senior players who were walking about the stadium ashen-faced. It was an equally big blow to teenagers like me who had been signed on as apprentices by Eddie. It would mean I would have to prove myself all over again to whoever got the job.

That moment proved to be a test of character for me. It made me realise at the tender age of sixteen that you could never take anything for granted in football or in life. I was only as good as my last tackle and could never afford to stop working hard.

The fact that Aberdeen promoted Jimmy Bonthrone, who was Eddie's assistant, to the job eased my anxiety a bit. 'Better the devil you know', as they say, and Jimmy was anything but a devil. He was a very nice bloke, the good cop to Eddie's bad.

He clearly felt that Eddie had made a good decision to sign me as an apprentice and soon after he took over he offered me full-time football. I took up his offer but my first-team debut was still a long way off.

Jimmy farmed me out to Peterhead in the Highland League for a season to toughen me up. I was still playing centre forward back then and it was Jimmy who turned me into a centre-back with a bit of help from Teddy Scott.

An injury crisis at the club meant I played my first game in the centre of defence for Aberdeen reserves against Rangers reserves and did so well that it became my position from that moment on. Just as I was coming to terms with playing in defence Jimmy gave me my debut against Morton at Cappielow on April 28, on the last day of the 1972/73 season which I remember to this day. To my horror he played me in attack in place of Arthur Graham of all people, who was a speedy left winger! I played in many different positions during my career but if you had given me a choice of starting positions the number eleven jersey is one I would never have wanted to take.

Then again it was my debut and needs must as Arthur had picked up an injury. It was an important game as only a win would secure us fourth position in the league, and UEFA Cup football the following season.

Arthur came off injured with thirty-five minutes left and on I trotted to play out wide with the instruction to supply crosses to Barry Mitchell in the middle. I like to think I did okay and helped set up our equalising goal for Willie Young, and when Drew Jarvie scored the winner I could not have been happier.

Granted I was a tad confused that I had gone from a recognised reserve team centre back to first team outside left in the blink of an eye. Jimmy Bonthrone told me later he wanted to give me a run but did not think I was experienced enough to play in the centre of defence in such a big game.

The following season after Henning Boel picked up a knee injury early in our League Cup campaign, and because Martin Buchan had moved to Manchester United the previous year, I started to get a few games at number six alongside Willie Young in the centre of defence. That would turn out to be my breakthrough year and although I have a lot to thank Jimmy for, he did not enjoy the happiest four years at Pittodrie.

The fact that big Willie Young took off his jersey and threw it in Jimmy's general direction after being furious at being substituted against Dundee United had not helped Jimmy's hopes of remaining manager. That incident was an embarrassment to Jimmy who had real integrity and who didn't like to see such public shows of insubordination. Feeling he might have lost the dressing room, or at least Willie's respect, he fell on his sword early in the 1975/76 season after we got off to a poor start to our league campaign. Willie Young always knew that he was attracting interest from top English clubs and the conspiracy theorists suggested at the time he was keen to get a move away and that incident at Dundee United sped up the process.

When Jimmy quit it had a bigger impact on me than when Eddie Turnbull left. I hadn't played first-team football when Eddie was there and although he signed me he left for Hibs before my break-through. It was Jimmy who had really helped my game, realised I should play in defence, and I had gained confidence from realising I was part of his long-term plans.

To this day I believe players must shoulder some of the blame when a manager is sacked and I felt that emotion and feeling of guilt when Jimmy left. It was a sad day for me when he walked out the door.

The man who replaced him was a different kettle of fish. Jimmy had been a bit reserved. Ally MacLeod was full on and full of ideas, some good, some crazy.

I feel Ally deserves a mention in the candidates for my Dream

Team for the sudden impact he had on Aberdeen. It is no secret he was an acquired taste as a coach and a taste that myself and many of the first team players never really came to terms with.

To those of you who only remember Ally from his time with Scotland and his boasts that we would win the 1978 World Cup you might think it strange that I rated him as a manager. I think you have to make the differential between manager and coach. He could motivate players on the day superbly as a manager although he was eccentric to say the least and on the training field as a coach he could drive me to distraction.

The first time I met him was on the day he was appointed in November 1975 and I could not get a word in edgeways. It was like being in a wind tunnel and having someone pushing you back all the time with his words.

He was so excited about becoming Aberdeen manager I thought he was going to internally combust. He walked in with a big smile on his face and to be honest he wore it most of the time he was at Pittodrie. The eternal optimist, he was one of the few men I have never really been able to fathom or get to the bottom of what made him tick.

He took over a team in transition and guided us to a League Cup victory before he left to take over as Scotland manager and he deserves praise for that. To be fair he got on my nerves more than any other manager for his madcap ways in training, like changing the score in bounce games when it suited him. He was like an overgrown schoolboy who loved what he did. Although he was never a great tactician he made you want to win for him. It was Ally who made me Aberdeen captain for the first time when he took the captaincy off Bobby Clark and gave it to me ahead of a game against Ayr United.

Every manager I played under was a strict disciplinarian but Ally dished out punishments in the most bizarre ways. While Sir Alex Ferguson would give you the hairdryer treatment Ally would make you do something daft. For instance, he had not been happy with the attitude of Willie Garner and a few other players at training and told them to report to Pittodrie that night for what they thought was an extra session.

It was an extra session all right but one carried out in complete darkness as Ally didn't put the floodlights on. Willie and the lads walked down the tunnel and heard a voice from the stand shouting at them to run round the pitch. They looked round and couldn't see Ally who was wearing a dark tracksuit and blended right in to the surroundings.

All they heard was his booming voice telling them to run round the pitch. Just when they thought their punishment was over the voice from the back of the stands would tell them to do press-ups or sprint. He never even acknowledged the players presence and left the stadium leaving them all standing on the track wondering what exercise they would be ordered to do next.

On another occasion he fined Alex McLeish, who was in the reserves at the time, for drinking a glass of cola in an Aberdeen hotel *after* a game because he didn't like his young players having fizzy drinks.

For all Ally's crazy ways he knew a good player when he saw one and it was he who brought Stuart Kennedy and midfielder Dom Sullivan to the club, as well as Joe Harper who returned to Aberdeen from Hibs.

He also won us our first trophy since Eddie Turnbull's side famously lifted the Scottish Cup by beating Celtic back in 1970. Our successful League Cup campaign started with decent performances in our group, although I missed the first few games through injury.

We opened our League Cup campaign with a win over Kilmarnock on August 14, 1976 when a familiar face took the armband in my place with Joe Harper captaining the side and scoring the first of our two goals. My knee injury kept me out of an away win over St Mirren and a home victory over Ayr United, so clearly I had to get fit quickly because this team was going great guns without me. I got the captain's armband back for an easy four-goal win over St Mirren and a draw and a loss to Ayr United, although we still topped our qualification group with nine points, three more than the Ayrshire outfit.

In the quarter-final Ally was starting to get excited as he felt we could win the competition. If players think they play too many games nowadays that was nothing compared with our schedule. After our group games we had a two-legged quarter-final against Stirling Albion. We won the first leg 1-0 at Pittodrie thanks to a Joe Harper goal but they beat us by the same scoreline on their patch. There was no extra-time in those days, which meant we had to go to a third match at the neutral venue of Dens Park where we won 2-0. After that game we had to pick Ally off the ceiling as he was now adamant our name was on the cup.

The fact we were due to play Rangers in the semi-final didn't dampen his enthusiasm which increased our own confidence we were going to beat them. That semi-final is one of my abiding memories of my time in an Aberdeen strip.

Ally had us incredibly fired up before kick-off to the extent he just had to point us in the direction of the tunnel and we were away. We went out there snarling like an American Football team does on its way out onto the pitch at the Superbowl.

I have to say we played the near perfect game. Rangers didn't have a chance and a hat-trick from Jocky Scott and one each from Joe Harper and Drew Jarvie helped us to an easy 5-1 win. I can remember vividly Ally rushing out onto the pitch at the final whistle jumping up and down like a crazy man. He kept saying to us in the dressing room that it had been a great game to watch and we had to see it again. Then he got it into his head we had to see it there and then so we all headed off to the BBC television studios in Queen Margaret Drive to watch a replay of the game.

Nowadays such enthusiasm by a manager at the semi-final stage may be frowned upon. After all we had won nothing and could have been heading for a fall. For most people, apart from Ally and our team, we were the underdogs going into the final against Celtic.

This was our first appearance in the League Cup final since 1955. This was going to be Celtic's thirteenth consecutive appearance in the final. November 6, 1976 is the date that will live long in my memory.

Ally had all but written his victory speech before kick-off but he was taking no chances. He was always a very superstitious man and had worn the same blue suit to every League Cup match. He also got it into his head if he got a haircut we would be beaten so when he walked out at Hampden he was looking slightly disheveled in a well-worn suit and hair that hadn't seen a brush for a couple of days.

From my point of view I was a nervous twenty-one-year-old who tried to savour every moment of the cup final because, as Bobby Clark had told me in the dressing room beforehand, I may never be playing in one again. History will show that wasn't Bobby's best prediction but he didn't know that at the time what would unfold in my career.

As things turned out my first trophy as Aberdeen captain was secured in a rip-roaring game. First Celtic went ahead after Kenny Dalglish scored with an early penalty before Drew Jarvie equalised from an Arthur Graham cross to put us level. The game went into extra-time and within two minutes of the first period Davie Robb put us ahead again, and although we had to do some desperate defending near the end I had won my first trophy as Aberdeen captain.

I had a few pictures taken of Ally and myself with the trophy and at the after-match dinner we had at the Station Hotel in Perth he reminded me of a conversation we had at the start of the season. He had told me we would definitely win a trophy that year, but to be honest I dismissed his thinking as just more optimistic talk from the most optimistic man on the planet. What I didn't realise is that he really did think his positive thinking had had a bearing on the outcome of the League Cup final.

The next day I did one of my first proper television interviews when Scotsport, hosted by the great Arthur Montford, came live from Pittodrie where a crowd of 25,000 had turned out to watch the League Cup being paraded round the stadium.

What wasn't in doubt was the affect the win had on Ally's career. His star started to rise even more to the extent that, after just eighteen months at Aberdeen, he was appointed Scotland manager in place of Willie Ormond who had returned to club football with Hearts.

During his time at Pittodrie he gave us all confidence and made Aberdeen get that 'cup-winning feeling' again that had been lacking for so many years. Yes, he only won one trophy and left far too early but he was like a breath of fresh air around Pittodrie.

I accept hype is a word associated with Ally but he had a good heart. He had the ability of making the most extravagant claim sound plausible and the daftest idea workable. I believed in Ally MacLeod and that is what you need to do in your manager.

Interestingly I was told years later that there was a three-man short list to replace Ally. Alex Stuart of Ayr United, who was the rank outsider, was on it along with a certain Alex Ferguson of St Mirren and Billy McNeill who was at Clyde.

As it turned out big Billy got the nod. Now if I thought Ally didn't hang around Pittodrie much then I wasn't prepared for the short time that Billy McNeill stayed with us. Big Billy is a legendary figure in Scottish football history and quite deservedly so, but left after just a season with us to go back to his beloved Celtic.

In that time he took us to the Scottish Cup final where we lost to Rangers and he also brought some important players to the club like Gordon Strachan and Steve Archibald, as well as giving Alex McLeish his debut against Dundee United, albeit only because Willie Garner had broken the pre-match curfew.

He convinced me to sign a new contract for not much extra money. I was haggling with the club over a new deal and I remember Billy calling me aside soon after he had joined, putting his arm around my shoulders and taking me for a stroll round the running track. By the time we had done one lap he had convinced me to re-sign for just an extra fiver a week. Looking back I must have been daft but such was the aura he had it was difficult to say no to him.

Big Billy was an instant hit with the fans and he did well in his brief spell with us. We finished second in the league to Rangers and he clearly had the fans on his side as 10,000 turned up to cheer us home after we lost the Scottish Cup final to Rangers which was a touching moment for Billy and all the players. It made me desperate to reward the fans with some silverware the next time we returned home from Hampden.

Unfortunately Billy didn't stay around long enough to help make that happen as the pull of taking over as Celtic manager in place of his mentor, the legendary Jock Stein, proved to be too strong. As things turned out his decision to go paved the way for a gentleman who would have a huge influence on my footballing career and who would transform the fortunes of Aberdeen Football Club.

Back when he was just plain Alex Ferguson, rather than a Knight of the Realm, he was our third manager in just over two and a half years. My initial thoughts? To be honest it was another coach I had to prove myself to. Would he keep me on as captain? Would he even give me a game? All these thoughts ran through my mind.

I was right to worry as he had early, serious doubts about my commitment. He thought I was not a very good trainer but, as I mentioned earlier, he wasn't the first manager to make that observation. Running round the pitch or on Aberdeen beach was never fun.

What helped my cause was that Teddy Scott yet again convinced the gaffer to give me a chance. When Alex questioned my application Teddy told him – like he had done with previous managers – to wait until three o'clock on a Saturday afternoon to see the real Willie Miller in action.

With that mild panic over I went back to try and fit in with the gaffer's plans. He was certainly different to the other managers I had worked under. He was just thirty-five years old when he was appointed, and while Eddie Turnbull had been tough, Jimmy Bonthrone quiet, and Ally MacLeod eccentric, Alex Ferguson was strong-willed, enthusiastic and more driven that the rest. Also he had confidence in his own ability. If he had a plan he stuck to it. Nothing made him waver. You were either with the gaffer or against him.

In the early days we did have a few differences of opinion which he always won. The first was over whether I defended too deep during games. The gaffer thought I did and told me so in no uncertain terms.

Now I knew he was right but I also knew my own game and the limits of my body. If I had gone pushing the team out every time he yelled at me I would be knackered by half-time. I liked to play at my own pace and felt by the time he arrived at the club I had the experience to marshall the defence on my terms. In the age-old tradition, sometimes when Alex shouted instructions at me from the touchline I pretended not to hear him and would carry on my merry way which made him furious.

Years after he had left Aberdeen we discussed, with the benefit of hindsight, whether I had in fact played too deep or not. He told me the reason he wanted me to push up was that he felt I underestimated myself and I had the mental sharpness to play further up the pitch and dictate games more than I did. He also felt I was fitter than I thought and I didn't have to sit way back. Looking back he was probably right, but at the time I felt knowing my limitations benefited the team. Certainly our defensive system worked and as I joked to the gaffer he would never have been able to call me the best penalty box defender he had worked with if I had always pushed up my defence.

Through the years working with the best British manager ever I found that he was never stuck in his ways. One of the things that made him such a great manager was his ability to embrace change. He was always open to ideas and I felt I could suggest things to him. He would always listen and although he might not always agree with me he wasn't the great dictator that some people make out.

As well as teaching the players a lot I feel he refined his managerial talents at Pittodrie. It could be said that the gaffer was still learning his trade when he took over and maybe we helped him in some small way through the way we reacted to his teachings.

For instance, I think he learned it was never terribly clever to compare players to those from a previous club when you take over at a new one. He had this dreadful habit of comparing me to Jackie Copland who he used to coach at St Mirren before he came to Pittodrie. Like me, Jackie was a former striker who had been turned into a defender. In those early days he would go on about how Jackie would have played that pass better than me, that Jackie would have read that situation better than me, that Jackie would have . . . well you get the picture.

It was quite frankly driving me demented and not doing my confidence any good. I knew I was a better player than Jackie, sorry Jackie but it is true, so to be compared to him one training session after another was a real source of anger.

I summoned up the courage to go into the gaffer's office and have it out with him. We had a 'frank exchange of views' I think they call it, and although he didn't back down or apologise the name of Jackie Copland was never mentioned again within my earshot out on the training field. I'm not entirely sure I would have had such a fair hearing from Alex if I had not been the captain because you had to win his trust and some players in those early days simply didn't have it.

From day one I was impressed by the ability of the boss to prepare everything perfectly. In his first pre-season he took us to Gordonstoun, the top private school where Prince Phillip and Prince Charles were educated. Although a staunch socialist the gaffer liked the idea of getting away from it all and getting us to bond as a team away from any distractions.

It was here that I first encountered the fire of Alex Ferguson when it came to his self-belief and his desire to succeed. He sat us all down in the big school dining room one evening and gave us a great speech that centred round the fact that he felt that we could make history and challenge the Old Firm.

Other teams had challenged them through the years he said like

Hibs, Kilmarnock and Dunfermline but we were better than they had been. We could break the Old Firm monopoly.

He was more eloquent in the words he used compared to other managers I worked under. He had a much wider vocabulary, and I don't mean by that he swore a lot, although clearly he could let rip with some industrial language when required. He had a way with words that made you listen. His doctrine at the time was simple. Work hard, listen to what he was saying and all pull together and we would have success.

He could bring you down a peg or two with just a few of his choice phrases. One of his best known was 'I've seen more life in a dead slug', which he used time and time again if he thought you weren't trying. My favourite through the years was when a hapless striker would try and make an excuse for being tackled before he got his shot in. Invariably the player in question would claim he felt he had time and didn't think he had anyone near him, to which the reply would be: 'Where do you think you were, the Sahara Desert?'

For me the moment I realised the high standards Sir Alex had set came just five games into his first season in charge. On September 16, 1978, we came away with a 1-1 draw against Rangers at Ibrox. Was Alex happy? Not a bit of it.

All the players were pleased with the result but he felt we should have won. The way some of the guys celebrated in the dressing room after the result really got up the gaffer's nose. He pulled us up for a lack of ambition and being too negative in our outlook. I was told as captain I had to show my team mates that I was never happy with a draw, regardless of how well we had played. Wherever the game was played, Aberdeen Football Club under Alex Ferguson wanted to win. Nothing else mattered.

It was a pivotal moment of his time in charge. I remember looking round the dressing room that day and the penny dropped to us all. A team with the likes of Jim Leighton, Stuart Kennedy, Steve Archibald, Joe Harper and John McMaster in the starting line-up and with Alex McLeish and Gordon Strachan on the bench should fear no one.

What I came to learn through the years was that he was a shrewd judge of character. He knew exactly how to deal with every individual player. Some he put his arm round, some he left alone and others he would give the hairdryer treatment. Ah yes, the hairdryer treatment. I was lucky that it never happened to me but it was a scary experience to watch. His face would be red with anger and he didn't miss when he was in full flow.

I remember one famous incident when we played Arges Pitesi of Romania in the UEFA Cup in the 1981/82 season. Now I had watched Alex kick anything he could find in his dressing room when he was angry. Kit hampers was one of his favourites and to this day I have no idea how he did not break a toe or two.

At half-time in Romania we were having a nightmare and I think Gordon Strachan had said something nippy. That was the catalyst for Alex to set his sights on a set of tea cups and a big tea-urn on a table. He punched the huge tea urn with his fist thinking it would tumble down, and you could see the pain in his face when it didn't move an inch. Although we were playing badly and knew it was not a laughing matter we all struggled to stop giggling. He didn't want to show weakness and gave his angry team talk while at the same time grimacing in pain at his injured hand which had a burn mark on it. He did have the last laugh when midway through his rant he then vented his anger on the tea-cups that went flying all over the dressing room with us players diving for cover.

His early prediction that we had nothing to fear from any other team in Scottish football came true when we won the Scottish League championship in 1979/80, which was the first time Aberdeen had won the title since 1955.

It was a significant and character-building championship win in that we made a late charge to the title and the way we won it gave us great self-belief. With six games to play we were three points behind Celtic but beat them at Parkhead in the run-in. We beat St Mirren 2-0 at home, drew 1-1 with Dundee United at Tannadice and knew a win over Hibs at Easter Road coupled with a St Mirren draw at home to Celtic would give the club the title.

We fulfilled our part of the bargain with a 5-0 win over Hibs thanks to two goals from the mercurial Ian Scanlon and one each from Mark McGhee, Steve Archibald and Andy Watson who was making a rare first team start. News then came through from Love Street that St Mirren's match against Celtic had finished all square and all hell broke lose.

I remember the boss running onto the park and the players all running to the end of Easter Road where the Aberdeen fans were to celebrate. Sir Alex had made his first major breakthrough and that title win remains my most fulfilling domestic honour. The next day I found myself making a speech in front of 20,000 people at Pittodrie before handing the microphone over to Bobby Clark who had fulfilled his dream of winning the league title with his beloved Aberdeen.

Scottish Cups and League Cups were to be won along the way and the confidence of everyone at Pittodrie was sky high under Sir Alex. In my case, maybe I was getting a bit too big for my boots as in the third game of the 1981/82 season I had a dressing room argument with Sir Alex which not surprisingly I lost. I stupidly had a head to head with him during half-time of a game against Partick Thistle that I thought was not going well for us. Now remember I said earlier that he came to respect the decisions I made on the park which was true but I think the way I made my point that day was a bit over the top.

When I suggested we had to change from playing five at the back he reacted badly. Very badly. As captain I felt I had to speak up because we were struggling to cope with the Thistle attack using the formation the gaffer had put out and were lucky to still be drawing 0-0. He disagreed with my assessment and told me to shut up or I would be substituted. Suffice to say I didn't hold my tongue and had an early bath. From memory that is the only time in all the years I worked with Alex that I questioned his authority and paid the price.

That row was a defining moment for me. I knew I had crossed the line. I could make points to the gaffer privately in my role as captain but never ever in the dressing room, especially at half-time of an important match in front of the rest of the team.

The only other time I had the guts to question his authority was when I was nearly dying through hypothermia. We had won despite the fact we had played badly against St Mirren. Being his old club the gaffer always wanted to beat them well.

We had been playing in monsoon conditions and into a biting wind in the second half. I couldn't feel my face and ran quickly off the park at the final whistle to get into the warmth. I was probably moving faster than I did in the game, it was that cold.

The gaffer had got to the dressing room before me and was waiting in an angry mood. He sat us all down to give us a telling off. With my teeth chattering I had been sitting there for fifteen minutes and he was still getting stuck into the right back. As captain I would have a go at me last, if at all, and I couldn't wait until then as I was freezing already.

I stood up and said to the boss, 'Sorry, but I have to go into the bath to get my circulation moving again so if you want to speak to me you'll get me in there.' There was a deadly hush because the rest of the players were not sure how he would react. Luckily for me he saw wee Gordon Strachan going white and even big tough Doug Rougvie looked ill so he said, 'Right the rest of you, into the bloody bath, but I'm not finished with you yet.' Unfortunately he was true to his word and he sat giving us a hard time on the edge of the bath and also on the bus journey back to Aberdeen.

As I said I never really fell out with the gaffer for longer than five minutes but I must admit there was a bit of tension during the summer before we started out on our winning European Cup Winners' Cup run in 1983.

That was because I was weighing up an offer, albeit briefly, to move to Rangers. The gaffer took me aside and told me I would win more trophies at Pittodrie and I would be crazy to move. To be honest I knew that was the case and he was pushing at an open door when he asked me to stay at the club.

He told me he would not play me until I made up my mind which meant I missed Drew Jarvie's testimonial match against Ipswich Town on August 7, 1982 which I deeply regretted. I knew I would be daft not to stay at Aberdeen but did so for football reasons alone and through my respect for the boss. I wanted an extra £20 a week to take me up to £220 but got that knocked back and I accepted a £10 a week rise instead. Little did I know that would prove to be the best decision of my life. If I had not stayed at Pittodrie I would have missed out on the greatest day of my professional career when we won the European Cup Winners' Cup final against Real Madrid. On our way there we had beaten Sion of Switzerland easily, struggled against Dinamo Tirana of Albania then beat Lech Poznan of Poland.

The quarter-final was when Alex and the whole Aberdeen team started to get noticed internationally. As everyone knows we were drawn against the mighty Bayern Munich who had great players like Paul Breitner and the pin-up boy of West German football at the time Karl-Heinz Rummenigge in their ranks.

In the first leg on March 2, 1983 we came away from Munich with a goalless draw which gave us a great chance of qualifying. At Pittodrie two weeks later there was an incredible atmosphere inside the stadium that I had never experienced before or since. The place was packed and the minute we walked out the 24,000 capacity crowd made an incredible noise.

In saying that we did not start well and Klaus Augenthaler gave them the lead after just ten minutes although we equalised through Neil Simpson just before half-time. In the dressing room Alex and his assistant Archie Knox gave us one of their best team talks ever.

Alex was not always a shouter in the dressing room and as I said earlier had a knack of capturing the mood of the moment and tailoring his teamtalks accordingly. He realised we were all wound up like a coil after our tricky first half so he was calm and focused. He sat us all down and told each and every one of us what our role would be in the second half and made it clear to us who would win. He expertly diffused the pressure of the moment and we ran out in the second half feeling incredibly positive, like a new set of players if you like.

Alex's influence wasn't finished yet. On the hour mark Hans Pfluger put Bayern ahead and we were on the back foot until the gaffer made a tactical switch that changed the game. John Hewitt replaced Neil Simpson and John McMaster came on for Stuart Kennedy. McMaster was given the job of sitting in the centre of midfield and trying to run the show. Neale Cooper was moved to left back to stop Karl Del Haye while the taller Rougvie moved from left back to right back to stop Pfluger.

With fourteen minutes left John and Gordon Strachan were at the heart of a set-piece free-kick we had practiced so much in training. They gave the impression they had a mix-up over who would take the kick before Gordon put over an inch perfect free-kick that big Alex McLeish headed home. That still wasn't good enough because a 2-2 draw would mean Bayern would go through on the away-goals rule. As the tension mounted a strike from John Hewitt won us the match. We had taken one of the biggest scalps in European football and suddenly the names of Alex Ferguson and Aberdeen Football Club were known throughout Europe.

After the tight game against Bayern Munich the semi-final proved to be a walk in the park for us with a 5-1 win over Waterschei in the first leg at Pittodrie making the second game across in Belgium a formality. Although we lost 1-0 we were never in danger of not making the final. The down side of that 1-0 defeat was that it turned out to be the last game played for Aberdeen by Stuart Kennedy who picked up a knee injury which was a real tragedy.

The gaffer was a man who did his homework on the opposition to the extent that before the second leg against Waterschei he had booked a flight from Brussels to Madrid to watch the other semi-final in Spain between Real Madrid and Austria Vienna anticipating we would be in the final. Although he was much too professional to tell us beforehand he had come clean a few weeks later and admitted that he had booked the flights the day after we had won the first leg 5-1. He was able to make the journey because our semi-final was on the Tuesday evening and the other game was held the following night in Madrid.

When he returned he was full of confidence we could beat the mighty Real Madrid in Gothenburg in what was three weeks time. As always his preparation for the big game was thorough and he left no stone unturned to make sure all the players had to concentrate on was the football match.

He knew the media spotlight would be on us like never before and wanted no distraction. He tried to take the pressure off us as best he could, or at the very least deflect it onto himself in the run-up to the game. He wanted not a single person getting in the way of things. Not even our wives and girlfriends.

Being a clever man the gaffer tried a bit of humour to get them onside. He got his secretary to invite all of our partners to a meeting at Pittodrie to discuss their travel arrangements to the final. No doubt they all turned up thinking they would be treated like VIPs, flown across in style and put up in the best hotel before he sprang a surprise.

He handed each and every one of them a false travel itinerary. They were told they had to gather at five o'clock in the morning at Pittodrie where a bus would take them to Gothenburg. They were ordered just to take a toothbrush, a cup, and some warm clothes but nothing else because it was a very small bus. The gaffer told me the look on all their faces was an absolute picture. When he told them it was all a wind-up and they would be flying across and staying in a very good hotel the relief among the group was evident.

There had been a serious point to be made in his rather unorthodox approach. After having a bit of a laugh with the girls over their travel arrangements he told them all that in the days before the game they should not attempt to contact their respective partners. Any problems they had in the run up to the match they had to deal with themselves or seek help from a designated Aberdeen official. Most of them took it well, even the poor wife of Doug Bell who was pregnant at the time, although unfortunately Doug missed the final through injury.

Keeping everybody away from the players and ensuring we were relaxed continued to be important for the gaffer. It certainly worked because, hard as it may be to believe, I never felt more relaxed than I ever did in the run up to such a big game.

Back then, being a young manager, Alex was learning all the time and had no problems taking advice from more experienced coaches. He had one of the best with him when he went to Gothenburg and the legendary Jock Stein turned out to be a great sounding board. They had lots of private meetings together and the strategy that Alex adopted after long talks with Jock was that they should try and lull the Real Madrid management team into a false sense of security.

It went against the grain a bit for the gaffer who was a proud man but he knew it made sense. Giving the Spaniards the impression that Aberdeen were a bunch of country bumpkins to try and lull them into a false sense of security was a masterstroke.

Jock suggested that Alex go even further and take a trip round to the Real Madrid hotel and present their manager Alfredo di Stefano, the legendary footballer, with a bottle of whisky and try his best to give the impression he was in awe of him. That would not have been an easy act for the gaffer but he went through with it and played his role to perfection. In major matches like this even having the smallest psychological edge beforehand can make a difference, and making Real Madrid think we were only there to make up the numbers certainly did us no harm.

The gaffer kept the pressure off us as best he could even on the eve of the big game when he held a quiz, although it nearly ended up in a brawl. Alex was such a competitive animal we had banned him from taking part as we knew if he took part there would be fireworks regardless of the outcome.

The quiz master was Alan 'Fingers' Ferguson – no relation to Alex – who was the Aberdeen press officer for the final. Things were going fine with me being captain of one team and Gordon Strachan being the other leader.

It was all good-natured stuff until after the final question the scores were tied and we needed a tie-break question. I remember that bloody question to this day; 'What Scottish football team has the most number of letters in its name?' asked Fingers. We guessed nineteen with Hamilton Academicals and thought we were right. Indeed so did Gordon's team who had admitted defeat. Then, to our astonishment, Fingers said we were wrong and passed it over to Gordon's side who looked puzzled before knocking off the final 's' from Academicals and guessing eighteen letters. They were right and we were furious. I shouted that I thought it had been a general knowledge, not a spelling quiz.

There wasn't quite a riot but there was a lot of wind-ups going on in the wake of the result. By the time we had finished the quiz it was well past midnight and all of us had forgotten we were due to play the biggest match of our lives the next day. That was the desired affect the gaffer wanted and fair play to him for keeping our minds off the game.

Next morning after breakfast Alex wandered round having quiet words with each player in the hotel before we set off for the stadium in the pouring rain. We were not intimidated by Real Madrid in any shape or form and the gaffer gave a little smile when he mentioned to me that he had tried to give the false impression to di Stefano that we were just happy to make up the numbers.

The Ullevi Stadium wasn't a great setting for such a major cup final, and when we got there the pitch was in poor condition after such heavy rain. That didn't bother us at all, in fact it may have worked to our advantage as Sir Alex had us in top condition so we all knew we were fit enough to battle it out if the game went to extra-time.

In the dressing room before the game the gaffer and his assistant Archie Knox went over what he wanted us all to do. He told us this could be the greatest match of our careers and to cherish every minute and not let ourselves down.

We started superbly well and gave them a real shock when Eric Black scored from an Alex McLeish knock down of a Gordon Strachan corner just seven minutes into the match, which was just the start the gaffer wanted. They equalised from the penalty spot in fourteen minutes, after a pass-back from Alex McLeish to Jim Leighton got caught in the muddy pitch which forced Jim to bring

Santillana down in the box. After Juanito scored from the spot we lost our shape pretty badly. It was our worst period of the game but with the gaffer shouting instructions from the touchline we managed to regain our composure which allowed us to go in at half-time all square.

He must have been pretty pleased at how we were performing because at the break there were no rants, nor hairdryer treatments just calls for us to up the tempo a bit, keep the ball more and not to lose our composure like we had for part of the first half. He asked Peter Weir to take more risks and push further forward to take the pressure off the midfield. It was a great tactical move with Peter revelling in his new more forward role.

All our hard training on Aberdeen beach during dark winter days also paid dividends for us as we were the fitter team as the match went into extra-time, which was testament to the training regimes of the gaffer and Archie Knox.

With tension high I felt we should have had a penalty when Neale Cooper was brought down by Isidro and Doug Rougvie was unlucky not to score during the first period of extra-time.

Twelve minutes into that period we got our just desserts as Peter glided past two Real Madrid defenders before giving the ball to Mark McGhee whose cross from the left was met perfectly by substitute John Hewitt to score the winner. At the end José Antonio Salguero nearly equalised with a free-kick that I gave away on the edge of our box, but when it narrowly went wide of the left-hand post I knew we were home and dry.

At the final whistle our reserve goalkeeper Bryan Gunn ran out of the dugout so fast he knocked the gaffer over. Normally he would have got a bollocking for that but even Alex had a smile on his face as he picked himself up and, covered in mud, gave me a big hug.

That evening the gaffer had a few drinks and like the rest of us enjoyed the greatest moment of his career up to that date. He was a young manager who had retained me as captain and now helped me become part of an Aberdeen team that had won the European Cup Winners' Cup. I couldn't even call it a dream come true because as a boy growing up in Glasgow I never thought I would ever lift a European trophy. My early dreams revolved around simply making it as a professional footballer, nothing as grand as lifting a European trophy for a great side like Aberdeen. Thanks to the gaffer we had made history.

When we arrived back in Aberdeen the scenes were incredible. I remember him meeting former Dons player W.K. (Stonewall) Jackson who was eighty-three at the time and was too ill to even attend matches at Pittodrie, but who had made the effort to come to the ground to welcome the players home.

Not surprisingly Alex was a man in demand after the final and the stories about him leaving Aberdeen came thick and fast. But such was the drive and focus of the man he never let all the speculation over his future get to him. He knew we only had an outside chance of winning the league that year but we were also in the Scottish Cup final and he wanted at least one more trophy that season.

Although Dundee United won the championship after finishing one point ahead of us and Celtic in a tight finish, the gaffer kept at us to finish the season on a high. He was desperate for us to beat Rangers in the Scottish Cup final and an extra-time goal from Eric Black gave us the victory he so coveted.

He was such a perfectionist he made his own headlines after-wards by suggesting that only myself and Alex McLeish had performed to our full potential during the game. That angered some of the other boys who had performed heroics through a long hard season and who ran their socks off in that cup final.

I already had total respect for Alex and what he did after he made those comments made me realise he was a man of true integrity. Some people go on about him never backing down which is true in the main but he always knew the difference between right and wrong. He had made those comments about the team in the heat of the moment when a television microphone was thrust under his nose.

The day after our Scottish Cup winning party at St Andrews, which was a bit of a subdued affair under the circumstances, the

41

gaffer called the team together and apologised to them for suggesting only me and big McLeish had played well against the Rangers. If that wasn't enough a few days later he went on television to make a public apology.

Now I might be wrong but I can't remember the gaffer publicly criticising his Manchester United players very often. Could that all date back to that incident after our Scottish Cup final win? Did he learn a lesson that day? Only Alex can tell you the answer to that one but he may have done.

What I can say is that whole episode left me with even more admiration for him. It takes a strong character to admit you are wrong, especially someone as tough and focused as Alex, but he still said sorry in public.

Even after our European Cup Winners' Cup and Scottish Cup wins he wanted, actually make that *demanded*, more from us. His energy levels were incredible and any thought I had about basking in the glory over the summer was quickly forgotten as he pushed us to build on our success.

The gaffer didn't have to wait long because a few months later during the 1983/84 season I became the first and so far only captain of a Scottish club to lift two European trophies when we won the Super Cup. We beat Hamburg over two legs in a season when the success just kept on coming.

In the first Super Cup game in Germany we managed to secure a no-score draw and in the second leg at Pittodrie Peter Weir kept up his great form by providing a cross that John Hewitt pulled back for Neil Simpson to score. If I do say so myself it was my pass that set up Mark McGhee to score our second. We won the Scottish Cup and the Scottish Premier League by seven points that year as well and that brought a big smile to the face of the gaffer.

In the 1985/86 season we targeted the Scottish League Cup which was the trophy that the gaffer really wanted as he had never won it before. We beat Ayr United, St Johnstone, Hearts, Dundee United and then Hibs 3-0 in the final to give him his clean sweep of domestic honours. After we won the Scottish Cup with a 3-0 win over Hearts the rumours came thick and fast over the gaffer's future.

He had rejected approaches from, among others, Rangers and Tottenham Hotspur in his years at the club, but when Manchester United came calling he could not say no, and who could blame him.

In my eight years working under the gaffer we enjoyed great success and for that I will always be eternally grateful to him. Also, and hard as it may be for some of you to believe, we had a lot of laughs along the way.

Of course he had a temper but he enjoyed himself big-time as well. He enjoyed a glass or two of wine, horse racing and a variety of other sports and he was also very well read. He loved hearing his players laughing and joking in the dressing room. In his eyes the more that happened the better health the team was in. The more successful the club, the bigger the wind-ups was his doctrine. It was impossible to curb the enthusiasm of a man who gave his all every minute of every day during his successful period at Pittodrie.

Alex also found out at Aberdeen the need for him to have a trusted second in command. He needed a sounding board, something that continued when he went to Manchester United, but it was at Pittodrie when he perfected the 'good cop, bad cop' routine. He also showed back then that if he was unhappy with his number two he would have no qualms about showing him the door.

The first two assistant managers to serve under him at Pittodrie were Pat Stanton and Archie Knox who were great football men in their own right. Pat had been highly respected as a player with Hibs, Celtic and Scotland and was the quiet, level-headed player who balanced Sir Alex's determination and short fuse.

Archie was less of a contrast to the manager than Pat was, and there were some magnificent spats between Sir Alex and Archie. They were both passionate football men. They were both born winners and even wanted to win five-a-side matches. A prime example of the gaffer's competitive spirit came during an Aberdeen versus Dundee United match that the press never reported on or even heard about.

The boss was friendly with Jim McLean when he was Dundee

United manager and had heard that they had a decent five-a-side team made up of the coaches at Tannadice.

He challenged them to a match that was played at Tannadice and was easily won by Jim McLean and his team. The gaffer and Archie took it badly and demanded a re-match at Pittodrie. But when the Dundee United coaches turned up they found Alex and Archie had drafted in the Aberdeen youth goalkeeper and a promising young striker into their five-a-side team. Suffice to say they won at a canter.

The gaffer's decision to move to Manchester United was inevitable as it was clear he wasn't going to stay at Pittodrie his entire career as he was very ambitious. Only a side of the calibre of United could have tempted him away.

When he left it was tough for me to take as we had been close and I knew whoever came in would have a hard act to follow.

The Aberdeen board approached Tommy McLean first but he turned them down. To be honest their next choice, the late Ian Porterfield was unfortunately the wrong guy at the wrong time. Don't get me wrong, Ian was a lovely bloke but following in the shoes of the gaffer was always going to be tough.

One of Ian's problems was that he didn't know much about Scottish football when he arrived from Sheffield United. He had moved from Raith Rovers to Sunderland in 1967 as a player and never played or coached north of the border until he arrived at Aberdeen back in 1986. He didn't help his cause when he appointed Jimmy Mullen as his assistant, who was a great coach but also had never worked north of the border, which meant neither of the two of them had a feel for the demands of Scottish football.

Ian was pretty laid-back, maybe too laid-back for my liking. We went from tough training sessions and emotional team talks under Sir Alex to a more 'do as you please' approach. Maybe that was the way they worked in the English leagues as I remember Kenny Dalglish telling me they did little more than play five-a-sides in training when he was at Liverpool. That may have been okay for some English clubs but at Aberdeen we had been worked long and hard by Sir Alex and expected more of the same.

To be fair to Ian in his two years at Pittodrie he did take us into the Scottish League Cup final where we lost in a penalty shoot-out to Rangers. We also qualified for Europe twice. He also signed Charlie Nicholas from Arsenal for £425,000 which was an inspired piece of business.

He left in 1988 and found a new job at Reading a year later and I was pleased that he went on to manage teams like Chelsea before having a globetrotting career that saw him manage the national sides of Zambia, Trinidad and Tobago and Armenia. As I said he was a very nice man and I was deeply saddened to hear of his death through cancer at the age of just sixty-one in 2007.

He was replaced by the management team of Alex Smith and Jocky Scott who went on to win a League Cup with me and a Scottish Cup without me. Both were fantastic for the club and deserve to be ranked among the most successful managers in the history of Aberdeen Football Club.

Alex was the senior partner, highly respected in the game, particularly on the coaching side. He was like a father figure and was the front man for the club in its relations with the media and he also handled negotiations with players over their contracts. He occasionally took training but that was mainly the domain of Jocky Scott. Between the pair of them they hammered out the tactics for a Saturday. They also had Drew Jarvie in their backroom staff whose main responsibility through the week was working with the reserves but he also had input in first team affairs on match days with Teddy Scott taking the reserves in his place.

Alex and Jocky had no problems mentioning time and time again how they wanted to continue the success that the gaffer had brought to the club. They wanted to emulate Sir Alex's deeds but found it was impossible because the financial balance of power had shifted away from Pittodrie. The Rangers revolution under Graeme Souness was under way, Celtic were spending huge money to keep up and the Aberdeen fans demanded our board did the same but the money wasn't there.

Alex and Jocky went down a different route and tapped into the overseas market in Holland to sign Theo Snelders, Peter van de Ven, Willem van der Ark, Paul Mason, Theo ten Caat and Hans Gillhaus. They came to Pittodrie because they believed they could further their careers, win trophies and compete in Europe. Not many managers could have taken the risk of bringing unknown players from Holland but Alex Smith's astute signings made a huge difference.

Gillhaus, who cost £600,000, was the pick of the bunch and had just won the European Cup with PSV Eindhoven. All six were magnificent footballers and if Mason had been a Scot rather than a Scouser, I'm sure he would have amassed more than fifty caps. There were ten internationals players in Alex and Jocky's Aberdeen squad and just thinking back, it still excites me how that team played at its peak.

Although I had been struggling with a knee injury that would subsequently end my career I was fit enough to play in our run to the League Cup final of 1989/90. Along the way we beat Albion Rovers, Airdrie and St Mirren before a goal from Ian Cameron beat Celtic in the semi-final. In the final we were due to play Rangers and it was a game I was desperate to win.

They had beaten us in the last two League Cup finals and I was aware I didn't have long to go in my career and wanted at least one more success. Alex Smith was a cool customer in the run-up to the game but I could tell he was as keen as I was to get one over on Rangers.

They may have been red-hot favourites but we took the lead through a Paul Mason header before Rangers equalised after referee George Smith made an absolute howler when he awarded a penalty. Ally McCoist was backing into me but he gave the decision against me, much to my horror, and Mark Walters scored from the spot. The game went to extra-time and there was poetic justice when Paul Mason proved to be our match winner with a fine goal. Unfortunately it was to be my last final at Hampden for Aberdeen.

Playing for Scotland against Norway a few weeks later my knee buckled under me and I was out for five matches. What kept me going was my aim to be fit for the 1989/90 Scottish Cup final against Celtic. Two games before the Hampden showdown I returned to the side against St Mirren in my first home game for six months and felt I played well in our 2-0 win. Granted I was thirty-five years old and not getting any younger but felt pretty fit and did okay in the final league game of the season against Celtic at Parkhead which we won 3-1.

Unfortunately Alex Smith didn't see it like that and although I travelled to Glasgow with the team for the Scottish Cup final I was told the night before I would not be playing. I won't pretend that was easy to take as I had always been a first pick throughout my career up until that final injury affected season. This time round I had to sit in the stand and watch the team beat Celtic 9-8 in a penalty shoot-out. Ironically it was Brian Irvine, my replacement in the starting eleven, who scored the winning penalty, but there was no bad feeling from me towards the rest of the lads and I was delighted with their success.

I did play at Hampden again under Alex Smith but it was only against Queen's Park in a Scottish League Cup tie the following season on August 21, 1990, which turned out to be my final competitive match as I had to hang my boots up through age and injury.

I was made part of Alex and Jocky's backroom staff and ended up taking over from him as Aberdeen manager in 1992.

I was in charge for three years and as it is my Dream Team I will let others judge whether my time in the hot seat was a success or otherwise. After an admittedly poor start to the 1994/95 league season I was replaced by Roy Aitken who led the team to Scottish League Cup six months after he was appointed.

Goals from Billy Dodds and Duncan Shearer, both of whom I brought to the club, beat Dundee in the final on November 26, 1995.

Roy signed Paul Bernard who became the first £1m Aberdeen player and Dean Windass was brought in from Hull City for a £750,000 fee with Jim Leighton and Eoin Jess returning to the club.

When Roy left in November 1997, Alex Miller had a couple of

years at the helm and when he left Paul Hegarty was in charge for nineteen games in the 1998/99 season. Next up was Ebbe Skovdahl who everybody has their own particular views on. Me? I can't quite understand how he never got more stick after some dreadful heavy defeats, and to be frank I felt he got more credit than he deserved over his three years in charge.

I accept he was a bit of a cult figure among the fans because of his colourful use of language and outlook on the game and I also have to acknowledge he was an entertaining character. He was our first foreign coach and although he took us into two domestic cup finals the way his teams played never really did it for me and I shed no tears when he left.

Steve Paterson lasted just one season before Jimmy Calderwood steadied the ship and brought much needed consistency to the club over a five-year period and took us into Europe.

I have to put my hands up and accept that the next appointment of Mark McGhee, which I had a major say in, did not work out and it was disappointing to see my former team mate leave after less than two years.

His replacement Craig Brown may be old in years but has the enthusiasm of a much younger man and I am hoping he can bring the good times back to Pittodrie along with his deputy Archie Knox. I accept that it will be nearly impossible for Craig to emulate the Ferguson years at Pittodrie but you can but dream.

Out of them it is Sir Alex Ferguson who I appoint as my Dream Team manager although can I also salute all the other men who were in the hot seat at various times at Pittodrie and gave their all for the club.

2

THE BACK ROOM BOYS

One of the keys to the success of Sir Alex Ferguson was the fact he always surrounded himself with good people. His backroom staff were important to him and he would always recognise the help they gave him through the years.

After picking the gaffer as my Aberdeen Dream Team manager I cast my mind back over the years to all the great men he worked with. Some, like Pat Stanton, did not stay at Aberdeen long but made a big impression.

I know who I want to appoint as my Dream Team assistant manager and also chief scout but the first name on my backroom staff list is the man who would provide the glue to hold them all together.

I could never have put together an Aberdeen Dream Team without naming the legendary Teddy Scott among my backroom staff. Teddy was the unsung hero of many a Pittodrie team, especially the ones that Sir Alex Ferguson put together. In total he served under fifteen of the club's managers, including me, in a variety of roles.

He was a player, reserve team coach, trainer, physiotherapist, kit man and also trained the local Aberdeenshire referees who thought highly of him for giving up his time. There is nothing he would not do for the football club; on one occasion when I was manager I had to send him down to the North Sea shoreline to check if the tide was out before we made plans to train on the beach.

I owe Teddy a huge debt as he was a very important influence on me throughout my career, including during my time as manager. When I first came to Pittodrie he was coaching the reserves and provided valuable support and advice. He taught me discipline and made sure I learned good habits from the start.

He was a father figure to the young boys and throughout his career at Aberdeen always took care of them. He made sure none of them got above their station if they were getting a bit too cocky too soon.

He brought a calmness and sensibility to the club and cut through all the nonsense that football can sometimes bring. It was Teddy, when he was reserve team coach, who moved me from centre forward back to defence as he had a hunch I would do well dropping back. I wasn't sure at first but thank goodness I listened to Teddy's advice.

Some of his training sessions were legendary as they were really tough, right out of the army training ground where Teddy learned them himself during National Service.

He loved his family, Aberdeen Football Club and cricket, in that order. He would do absolutely anything for the players or the club. He idolised Sir Alex and the gaffer respected him hugely.

He was born and bred in Ellon and lived there all his life. He didn't learn to drive for years and sometimes if he had missed the last bus home he would sleep on the Pittodrie snooker table.

For more than fifty years Teddy worked for Aberdeen and was down as 'kit manager' when he retired. The description on his payslip at the end of each month should really have read 'the heart and soul of Pittodrie'.

He turned a room next to where the strips were washed near the home dressing room into his very own den where he would have his fags, a cup of tea and talk to anyone who wanted a natter. Liverpool had the boot room. At Aberdeen we had 'Teddy's Room'. You went into Teddy's Room through the front door and you could go out the back straight into the home dressing room.

It was an incredible place that was a real Aladdin's cave of football memorabilia. Every nook and cranny was filled with international caps given to him by Aberdeen players, framed shirts, medals, posters, trophies, scarves, pennants, programmes and even empty man of the match champagne bottles. He also kept a diary of his time at Aberdeen and had a multitude of scrapbooks and cuttings from his years at the club.

He was a humble man and although he was given a plaque by UEFA for being one of the longest servants to the one club he kept it tucked away at the back. Teddy was more interested in showing off club honours won by his boys than any personal mementoes. He was a huge cricket fan, could tell you anything about the sport, and he proudly kept a cricket bat, signed by Ian Botham and Allan Lamb, in his den. There was always a kettle on the boil and enough teabags to keep a Women's Guild going for months.

Teddy was one of the most honest men I have ever met, the sort of straight talking soul that you need at a football club. If you had a bad game he would tell you and you came to trust his opinion.

He joined Aberdeen way back on March 3, 1954 and was obviously a lucky charm as the year after he signed the League championship flag was flown over Pittodrie for the very first time. Teddy used to joke he didn't have much to do with that success as he didn't play at all that season, mainly because Alec Young and Jim Clunie were ahead of him in the race to get the centre half jersey. At five feet seven inches he wasn't the biggest defender but he assured me he had the ability to time his headers like Eric Black used to do.

Indeed he only ever played one first team game and that was in a 2-0 away win the following season over Stirling Albion on February 25, 1956 before he was loaned to Brechin City and following a free transfer moved to Elgin City in the Highland League.

He was quickly brought back into the coaching set up by Dave Shaw and every new manager found him indispensable until the very idea of Pittodrie operating without him became unthinkable. When Sir Alex Ferguson once jokingly threatened to fire him for packing the wrong socks Gordon Strachan replied: 'And where will you get the ten people to replace him?'

Gordon also tells the story of how he had complained in passing to Teddy about having a sore bum a few days before setting off to the World Cup in Spain in 1982. When he hooked up with the Scotland squad in their hotel in Glasgow before setting off, he opened his bag with his boots and shin guards that Teddy had packed for him before he left Pittodrie, and in there with them was a special brand of extra-soft toilet roll. Told you Teddy would stop at nothing to make sure his players were well looked after.

Through the years Teddy kept adapting to the changes in the game which made him so important to the club. He could automatically detect when some of the younger players were trying to take the easy option in training. On one of the long runs we used to do I swear he used to hide behind trees to keep an eye on players. Whenever anyone was tempted to walk or take a short cut he would jump out in front of them and tell them in no uncertain terms to get back on the right track.

His stories were always fascinating as he still remembered the days when a trainer used to run onto the pitch with a spray to take away the pain and a 'magic sponge'.

He also used to tell tales of the days when the team always traveled by train to away games and Eddie Turnbull used the sauce bottles and salt and pepper shakers in the dining car to illustrate what he wanted his players to do out on the pitch.

He even used to say that to soothe pre-match nerves players were sometimes offered a quick whisky before kick-off to give them a bit of 'Dutch courage'. As I said he worked under fifteen managers. Out of the lot of them I think the only one he struggled to get to grips with was Ally MacLeod who he found a bit too eccentric for his liking but then again he wasn't alone.

He was hugely impressed by Billy McNeill but not as much as he was impressed by Alex Ferguson. The pair were to become exceptionally close over the gaffer's eight years in the north. Even when he left he would regularly phone Teddy for a quick chat and a catch up.

To Teddy it was obvious from day one that he had the ability and determination to bring trophies to Pittodrie. He used to say that Sir Alex was a winner in everything he did, whether it be football or horse racing. Some people may have doubted the gaffer's chances of success at Manchester United but they were quickly slapped down by Teddy. The thing that Teddy noticed, which I agree with wholeheartedly, is that the gaffer always paid great attention to detail.

He surrounded himself with the right sort of people like Teddy and took care of all the little details, which paid off when it came to the bigger picture of running the football club like clockwork. What impressed Teddy, who was a real man of the people, was that Sir Alex looked after not only the players but all the office workers, down to making sure that the cook got tickets for the big matches. That sort of attitude from the top down helped create a tremendous spirit about Aberdeen and Teddy Scott was impressed as much with Sir Alex Ferguson the man as Sir Alex Ferguson the football manager.

It was fitting that the gaffer brought a full strength Manchester United team including David Beckham and Ryan Giggs to Pittodrie in January 1999 for Teddy's testimonial. It was a great night in front of a packed crowd who were all there to cheer a very special person. Aberdeen won 7-6 on penalties after the match had ended 1-1. The penalty shoot-out defeat was United's last before they went on to win the treble of the English League title, the FA Cup and the Champions League.

Four years later, at the age of seventy-four, Teddy retired from the club in August 2003 – forty-nine years after he first walked through the door of Pittodrie. It was a sad day for Aberdeen Football Club and marked the end of an era. He was a great football man.

In the bad times at Pittodrie he would always give you good advice. During the good times he would pass on his knowledge but in either circumstance he would never be too high or too low. He would always use the same measured tones. That was Teddy Scott. That is why he will always be revered.

I am sure Archie Knox, my choice as my Aberdeen Dream Team

assistant manager, would have no problems being mentioned after Teddy as he had the same high opinion of him as the rest of us.

Coaching manuals always tell you the best managerial partnerships at football clubs have a good cop, bad cop set up. That wasn't quite the set up with Sir Alex and Archie at Aberdeen. Most of the time one would kick you hard then the other would kick you harder.

Working for the pair of them wasn't for the faint-hearted. Now, don't get me wrong. Once you had their respect you realised their bark was worse than their bite. Both were hard task-masters and both pretty loud, and Archie could never be described as the silent partner in any managerial relationship.

He used to laugh at the public's perception of him as being the sort who frightens players into giving of their best. He was more stick than carrot in his approach but there was a lot more to Archie than just shouting at the players. He had a great football brain and lived for the game. He was a clever man who did his homework on the opposition and left no stone unturned to ensure we were all prepared for every game.

On our first night in Gothenburg to prepare for the European Cup Winners' Cup final we spent hours pouring over the dossier that Archie had prepared on Real Madrid. It was an excellent piece of work and gave us valuable pointers on what to expect from different players. Archie accepted that he did a fair bit of shouting and bawling but he was nothing like that as he set out what he had found out about the Spanish giants. He was cool, calm and perfectly reasoned as he went through the dossier step by step. I'm not saying it was the only reason we won that match but we all knew, thanks to Archie's dossier, everything about our opposite number and that came in very useful.

Ryan Giggs described Archie as a man's man and that sums him up perfectly. He was totally committed to making us all better players. He used to get the younger guys like Neil Simpson, Neale Cooper and John Hewitt back in the afternoon to work on crossing, passing and touch. At times they weren't that enthusiastic about going back but they didn't have a choice and all that extra work made them better players. His coaching sessions in general were always imaginative and bright and there always was value in them.

Also I don't think Archie was a threat to any of the bosses he assisted which is not always the case. Some assistants have an eye on the manager's chair but Archie was always a trusted lieutenant and never actively thought to take over at a club apart from his time as manager in his own right at Dundee.

The only time I saw Archie lost for words was during a training break in Spain when for a laugh we tossed him into the swimming pool. He had always said he couldn't swim and within a few horrifying seconds after we threw him in the deep end we realised he had been telling the truth. He went down but never came back up and I remember Alex McLeish leading the rescue party. Usually Archie had a quick reply ready for any occasion but this time he was so genuinely scared that he was lost for words for once.

Anyone taking a look at Archie's CV will realise how many managers have relied upon him for advice and appointed him their number two. He was a player with Forfar Athletic, St Mirren, Dundee United and Montrose.

He was player-manager at Forfar in 1976 and came to Aberdeen under the gaffer in 1980. Three years later he joined Dundee as their manager before reuniting with Sir Alex at Aberdeen and being his right-hand man at Manchester United where he stayed from 1986 until 1991.

He returned to Scotland to become Walter Smith's assistant at Rangers and stayed with him when he moved south to join Everton. A spell helping Scotland under Craig Brown was followed by assistant roles at Millwall under Mark McGhee and with Eric Black at Coventry City. He was Richard Gough's assistant at Livingston before joining up with the Scotland squad again and then becoming the national Under-21 coach in July 2006.

From there it was to Bolton Wanderers under Sammy Lee and Gary Megson before moving to Blackburn Rovers under Paul Ince. On December 29, 2009, he was appointed as the assistant manager to Craig Brown at Motherwell before returning to Aberdeen. Archie isn't the sort of chap to get all sentimental talking about his career but to work at such a high level for so long shows the quality of the man as a coach.

Now that we have the best manager, assistant and trainer we need a top scout and an assistant to find us the best players for our Dream Teams of the future. Look no further than the pair that signed me up along with scores of others like Alex McLeish, Joe Harper, Tommy Craig, Willie Young, John McMaster, Charlie Cooke and Arthur Graham.

Bobby Calder was the chief scout when I was at Aberdeen and he takes that role in my Dream Team with Jim Carswell who was the west of Scotland scout being his Dream Team assistant. They were a perfect double act in that Jim would do all the leg work in the west of Scotland to find a quality player in the first place. Then in would breeze Bobby to charm the parents and convince them their boy would be well looked after at Pittodrie which, based on personal experience, he always was.

It is more of a family team effort nowadays with parents being able to transport their son to matches or maybe take them up to Pittodrie under their own steam for training camps during the summer. Back then the onus was on the football club to bring the youngster north, chaperone him all the time, find him a nice family to stay with in Aberdeen over the summer months and look after him very well. Aberdeen did that superbly well and had a youth set-up that was second to none.

On occasion, if a set of parents were swithering between sending their boy to Aberdeen or another club, Bobby would turn up at their door and turn on the charm. He would have a bottle of whisky and cigars for the father and a box of chocolates and some flowers for the mum.

Once he had your signature he looked after you very well. In my case Bobby used to meet me at Queen's Street Station in Glasgow to take me up to Aberdeen. He was a charming man but he had a tendency to tell you the same football stories over and over again. The first time they were fascinating, maybe even the second and third time. By the time you had heard them the tenth time on the train you were praying Aberdeen wasn't far away.

Like anybody in football, or indeed life, Bobby didn't just become a top scout by chance. He was a former top-class referee who took charge of the 1947 Scottish Cup final between Aberdeen and Hibs. He made the transition into coaching and went on to be manager of Dunfermline and even had a spell as a soccer ref in the USA before being asked by Aberdeen chairman William Mitchell to look out for players for the club. He made such a great job of it in the 1950s that Rangers tried to poach him away but he stayed loyal to Aberdeen.

Jimmy Carswell was the man who first spotted me and did a lot of the ground work before Bobby came on the scene to sign the deal and convince me, not that I took much convincing, to sign for Aberdeen rather than Celtic or one of the clubs down south that had been tracking me.

In terms of success the one man to run my Dream Team has to be Dick Donald. Aberdeen had its greatest successes under him. The present chairman Stewart Milne took over the club at a difficult time and he is driving it forward well and I predict a bright future for us as a club.

But in terms of bringing silverware to Pittodrie nobody comes close to Dick, who played for the club in the late 1920s and came onto the board twenty years later before being appointed chairman in 1970. He was very supportive of me as a player and even more so as a manager. He appointed me to the role and never once interfered. Even when I left I had no hard feelings towards him.

He was a very down to earth man who had a great financial brain. He made money in property, theatres like His Majesty's in Aberdeen and also through a chain of picture houses including the Astoria and the City cinema in George Street. The players used to get free passes to the cinema and my son and daughter used to get 50p off him for no reason when he met them at the club. He always had a bag of sweeties for the kids – and also the players when I think about it. He used to bring Kit-Kats on the bus and hand them out.

Perhaps his biggest legacy was spotting the managerial talent of

Sir Alex Ferguson. When Billy McNeill left Pittodrie for Celtic it was Dick who identified the gaffer as his successor. It was an astute move and Aberdeen would not have gone on to the success we had if anyone other than Sir Alex had been appointed. Dick laid the foundations for the glory days and after having a sixty-five-year connection with the club it was fitting that the Richard Donald Stand was built in his honour as a permanent memorial to a great man.

3

THEY SHALL NOT PASS

Down the years Aberdeen have been blessed with some of the best goalkeepers in the business. Some were great shot-stoppers, others fantastic at dominating their area, all brave as lions. Some of the best known were so talented that they even played outfield for the first team! The majority were real characters, although the man that makes my Dream Team was probably the quietest of the lot.

It was no foregone conclusion that my number one would be the man I mostly played alongside for club and country. I am not going to name him just yet to allow you to hear about some of the other great goalkeepers who were considered for my Dream Team.

First up has to be a man who was a huge influence on me when I first broke through into the Aberdeen first team. Bobby Clark is an Aberdeen legend and quite rightly so. He was one of the most articulate, clever men in football and a wise, calming influence in the dressing room. He was nicknamed Clark Kent because when he took off his ordinary clothes and put on his goalkeeper's jersey he became superman.

He was a cool customer and I can only remember him once losing the rag. He took real exception at something Stuart Kennedy had said and chased him all over the Pittodrie car park. Because Stuart was one of the quickest players in Scottish football there was never any chance of Bobby catching him. By the time the pair met again in the dressing room things had cooled down and the urbane Bobby had resurfaced. In fact I am sure Bobby apologised to Stuart, rather than the other way round. That was Bobby. He was such a gentleman he didn't let things bother him too much.

He was Eddie Turnbull's first signing and had been his former goalkeeper at Queen's Park. Bobby, who was born on September 26, 1945 became first choice between the sticks at the age of just twenty with the departure of John 'Tubby' Ogston to Liverpool in 1965.

Bobby was a solid, non-showy type of goalkeeper who owed more to good anticipation and positioning than to athletic dives through the air to get to the ball. He did lose his first team place to Ernie McGarr in the 1969/70 season, and quite remarkably rather than play for the reserves in goals he played at centre half in two first team games. It was no real surprise in Bobby's eyes as, like a lot of goalkeepers I played with, he always fancied himself as an outfield player.

His move came about early in the season because Aberdeen were a bit short of central defenders and Bobby had initially been drafted in to play at number five for the reserves. He did so well for the second team he was promoted to the first team squad for a Scottish League game on September 2, 1969 against no less a side than Rangers. He was named on the bench and had hoped to play at the back that day but an injury to striker Jim Forrest saw him playing up front at Ibrox. We lost 2-0 but Bobby said the defeat was not his fault. He was too busy trying to score goals than save them. Three weeks later he actually started, wearing the number six jersey against St Johnstone where we lost 3-1.

Once the outfield injury crisis was over Eddie Turnbull realised he was better suited between the sticks but he struggled to get a game in his favoured position for the rest of that season.

You always knew where you stood with Bobby as he was straight down the line and had an honest approach that I always appreciated, but it sometimes backfired on him.

I think the best way to illustrate that is for me to tell you about one incident that went down in Aberdeen folklore. Despite there being a lot of mutual respect Bobby had a few run-ins with Eddie Turnbull during his time. One came when Eddie told him he was being brought back into the first team after losing his place to Ernie McGarr during that 1969/70 season.

Now Eddie wanted to drop Ernie for one game for breaching club discipline over something that never became clear. It was most definitely not for football reasons and more to teach Ernie a lesson. He expected Bobby to be delighted to be recalled so imagine his dismay and anger when Bobby said he wasn't going to play.

Bobby said that Ernie had been playing better than he had been and it would be folly just to drop him for disciplinary reasons. Bobby told Eddie for the good of the team he was refusing to play and that Ernie should retain his place. Faced with a goalkeeper who didn't want to play for the first team Eddie had no choice but to eat humble pie and keep Ernie in the team. Not before he had given him a tongue-lashing mind you.

Ernie did finally lose a bit of form and a lot of Aberdeen fans may have forgotten that Bobby had fallen so far behind him that he played between the sticks just the once that season up until a home match against Ayr on February 25, 1970.

That is significant as it would have been a crying shame for Bobby not to play in the Scottish Cup final winning team of 1970 and to enjoy the moment he so deserved. I, for one, was pleased that Bobby won his place back and played in that famous game as he contributed so much to Aberdeen through the years. Apart from Ernie he saw off a number of other goalkeepers through the coming years like Andy Geoghegan and John Gardiner.

Only twice was he tempted to leave Pittodrie. First Rangers and then Stoke City tried to sign him but he turned them down. He went on to set new appearance records for the club at the time and won a League Cup winners medal in 1976. In his final season he won a League championship medal in 1979/80 which was the icing on the cake of his tremendous career. He did go to Clyde for a while and then became involved in the emerging African football scene before moving to the USA.

I can't praise Bobby highly enough and although he didn't make my final Dream Team he came close and deserves a place on the bench. When I made my debut for Aberdeen in April 1972 against Morton he was first choice goalkeeper and elder statesman and a man I looked up to and had huge respect for from day one.

As I started to become a regular it was good to know I had a goalkeeper as talented as Bobby behind me. He was captain at the time and kept that role until Ally MacLeod was appointed manager. It was no secret that Ally's ways took a lot of getting used to and Bobby struggled with them more than most.

A lot of the time I had to just grin and bear it as his antics drove me mad but Bobby, who as I said was a very intelligent man, struggled to hold his tongue especially during five-a-side games when Ally would make up the score as he went along.

Bobby's team may be winning a game by four goals against my team in training, but Ally would swap the scores round to keep things interesting. He drove us all crazy when he did that as we were all competitive guys and wanted to win even five-a-side matches. Bobby decided to take the law into his own hands and every time somebody scored a goal in training would drag his studs behind his goal to keep proper score and used to shout out the correct score when Ally bellowed out his made-up one.

I don't think Bobby had too much time for Ally's ways in general but it was still a surprise when he took the captaincy off him and gave it to me in rather unorthodox fashion. Ally called me in one day and said he was giving me a special wedding present. I thought it might be a set of cut-glass decanters or maybe a few bob extra in my pay packet but I was very wrong.

Ally, in his infinite wisdom, said he was giving me the Aberdeen captaincy to mark my wedding day. It was a big shock and a huge privilege to be captain but I would have much rather he said he was giving it to me because he felt I was a born leader. He announced he was making me captain to the press a few days later and thankfully had changed his story a bit by saying he wanted an outfield player to have the armband rather than a goalkeeper.

In the dressing room the day before my elevation was publicly announced by Ally to the players I felt a bit awkward standing there in front of Bobby but he was great with me. He congratulated me on the appointment and made it clear he would back me all the way. It was an indication of his professionalism that Bobby took that attitude. He was the ultimate professional and someone who helped me out when I first took over as captain. There was no bad feeling on his part and he was such a team player that he actually felt Ally had made the right decision. He told me he felt the game was changing and Aberdeen needed an outfield player as captain and I fitted the bill.

Although Bobby and Ally never saw eye to eye such was his importance to Aberdeen that even after he had chipped a bone in his thumb the week before the Scottish League Cup final of 1976 he was still picked to play. We tried to keep his injury secret but we need not have bothered as he was in magnificent form in that 2-1 win over Celtic. Although Drew Jarvie and Dave Robb got the goals you can't forget that Bobby made some great saves along the way. It was my first trophy as Aberdeen captain and nobody was more pleased for me than Bobby. I may have taken the armband from him but he did not bear any grudges.

I always liked having Bobby in the dressing room as he was an interesting guy to listen to and I remember once he sparked a debate about nuclear war. Who says footballers never talk about anything serious? At the end of the discussion Bobby suggested that he might build a nuclear bunker under his house and I think it was Stuart Kennedy who said he should take training cones in with him so he could continue doing coaching sessions. Quick as a flash Bobby replied: 'I'd also like to take a gun in there with me because if any of you lot came knocking on the door of my nuclear bunker begging to be let in I would shoot you.'

On a serious note, Bobby was always around to offer me advice from the moment I joined the club until the moment he left. For instance when I first joined Aberdeen he always encouraged me to do extra training to improve my game. You need players like that in your life when you are growing up and developing. He gave me the perfect lead to follow.

Also in the days before sports psychologists Bobby's belief in Aberdeen Football Club was infectious. The first time I met him he told me Aberdeen could win the League that season. I didn't have the heart to tell him that Celtic was running away with it as that would have shattered his illusion.

When we finally won the Scottish League in the 1979/80 season he was in goals for all but two matches, and we lost one against Kilmarnock and drew the other against St Mirren without him. I was more pleased for Bobby than anyone else in the team when we won the title because winning it had always been his dream.

It also thankfully brought an end to me having to listen to him going on about how Aberdeen could win the league. We had actually done it, so he could shut up. He played in thirty-four of the Premier Division games that season and lost just eighteen goals which helped us pip Celtic to the title by a single point.

Another man who was equally as significant a figure as Bobby, albeit to a different generation of Aberdeen fans, was Carnoustie-born Fred Martin who was the final line of defence in the famous team that won Aberdeen their first Scottish League championship in the 1954/55 season. Fred recorded eleven shut-outs in twenty-seven appearances and was a major reason why the trophy came to Pittodrie.

He joined from Carnoustie Panmure in October 1946 not as a goalkeeper but an inside forward. There you go again, another Aberdeen goalie thinking he can play outfield! He even turned out as a centre forward for Woolwich Royal Artillery during his National Service.

When he returned to Pittodrie he still had illusions he could play outfield but occasionally used to play in goal during bounce games in training and went from an inside forward to first choice goalkeeper under Dave Halliday, which I must admit I still struggle to get my head round.

Can you imagine say Alex McLeish coming back from Scotland

duty and saying to Alex Ferguson, 'I've been playing pretty well in goals during Scotland training so how do you fancy letting me play in goals against Rangers on Saturday?' You would have to stand well back as the hairdryer treatment would be the order of the day.

Fred made the transition from inside forward to goalkeeper well and newspaper reports from the time suggest he had a great ability to command his area. Because he was such a big man who stood well over six foot tall and was very broad as well he wasn't the sort of player you would push around. In 1952 he gained his first representative honour with the Scottish League and two years later was capped at international level.

He was also Scotland's goalkeeper in their first appearance in the World Cup finals of 1954 that were held in Switzerland. In general terms Fred didn't have the best of luck in a Scotland jersey and in that World Cup he was in goals when Scotland lost 7-0 to Uruguay and was also in the team that were destroyed 7-2 against England at Wembley in 1955. Fred also played in three losing Scottish Cup final sides in 1953, 1954 and 1959 during his eleven seasons with Aberdeen. He remains in the pantheon of Aberdeen greats quite simply because of his performance in that league-winning season and also because of the great unblemished service he gave the club.

My greatest ever foreign Aberdeen goalkeeper has to be Theo Snelders who was no household name when he arrived at Pittodrie from FC Twente in 1988 for £300,000. By the time he left he had become a real cult figure. The fact that Theo had been one of the men that Alex Ferguson thought about signing when he took over at Manchester United speaks volumes for his talent.

I was at an SFA coaching course with Alex Smith, who was Aberdeen manager at the time, on the day he heard Theo had agreed to sign. My first concern was whether he spoke any English to which Alex replied not very much. Playing alongside a Dutchman who didn't understand the language filled me with deep concern so the first thing I said to Alex was: 'As long as we can get him to understand the words "stay on your bloody line" then we should be fine.'

He made his debut at the age of twenty-four in a 1-1 draw away to

Dundee on August 13, 1988 and conceded just twenty-five goals in thirty-six Premier Division matches which was the best goalkeeping record that season. Off the back of such impressive form he was named the Scottish PFA Players' Player of the Year and started his acceptance speech with the line 'fit like' which showed he had embraced the north-east dialect and culture very quickly.

Theo really commanded his penalty-box and he was very brave when it came to taking cross balls, although I still didn't like to see him stray too far off his line. He was in such inspired form at Pittodrie he even won a call-up to the Dutch national team, albeit for just one cap in a friendly, but that was still no mean feat considering the other goalkeeping talent the Dutch had at the time who were playing for more fashionable clubs than Aberdeen.

In 1989/90 he helped Aberdeen to beat Rangers 2-1 in the Scottish League Cup final and played a major role in the penalty shoot-out win over Celtic in the Scottish Cup final. It was Theo's save from Anton Rogan in the shoot-out that gave Brian Irvine, who was playing instead of me, the chance to score from the spot and bring the trophy north.

Foreign goalkeepers in general had a soft centre to them in those days but that wasn't the case with Theo. I remember on one occasion he dived at the feet of Ally McCoist and had his cheekbone shattered in the challenge.

He was an unbelievable professional. He wasn't terribly fun but then again he was Dutch. The Dutch must have a sense of humour but in my experience it is hard to find. He may not have been the life and soul of the party but he was a player you could really trust in the dressing room. He liked things done properly and was disciplined and well organised.

There have been other goalkeepers who were real characters through the years and deserve mention, one of whom I played against earlier in my career when he was coming to the end of his. John 'Tubby' Ogston, who I mentioned earlier, was in goals for the Banks O'Dee when they won the Scottish Junior Cup in 1957 and was signed by Aberdeen soon after.

He spent three seasons in the reserves before he took over from Fred Martin in 1959, a position he held up until 1965 when he moved to Liverpool in August of that year. Although a fine shot-stopper he was kept out of Bill Shankly's team by Tommy Lawrence and his young understudy Ray Clemence, which was no disgrace. In 1968 he signed for Doncaster Rovers and it was three years later that yours truly came up against him after he had moved back to the north-east of Scotland and was winding down his career playing for Deveronvale.

I was on Aberdeen's books as a budding centre forward but had been farmed out to Peterhead to get some experience and to toughen me up in the Highland League. One of my first memories as a young striker was playing against Ogston as a raw seventeen-year-old.

He was a big imposing figure but whether it was the arrogance of youth or foolhardiness I wasn't scared of him at all. At every corner kick I positioned myself right in front of him to try and put him off.

By midway through the match it was clear I was getting under Tubby's considerable skin to the extent that after a corner where we both challenged for the ball we ended up falling to the floor together in a heap as play raged up the other end. As both of us slowly got up Tubby noticed the ref's back was turned and the linesmen were both concentrating on the ball. He used that moment to strike. He hit me hard in the ribs with a rabbit punch that hurt like hell. He didn't even speak a word to me as he knew he had got his point across.

I was badly winded and needed treatment straight away. I complained to the ref but realised I was wasting my time. Nobody had seen Tubby's punch. For the rest of the game I was a shadow of myself as I was struggling to breathe but didn't want to go off as that would be me admitting defeat.

The lesson I learned that day was that if I was ever wronged in a match or lost my temper I would get my revenge in the way Tubby had done. He had got even with me behind the back of the referee and no action was taken against him. I was never the type of player who would take players out behind the ref's back during my career but that one occasion showed me that if I ever was to do it I had to be subtle about it as there was no point being sent off for retaliation. It was a good lesson for a young player.

Delving further back into the history books the name George Anderson jumped out at me for all the work he did for the club. He joined us in the summer of 1914 when he signed from Sunderland and was an ever-present between the sticks up until 1922. On his retirement he became a successful north-east businessman and town councillor and in the 1930s he returned to Pittodrie as a director. During the Second World War he kept the club going with the assistance of his fellow director Charles Forbes who was a local schoolmaster.

George and Charles did a power of work for Aberdeen Football Club and George was a flamboyant figure with his bowler hat and carnation. The fact he owned the local sweet factory in Rosemount meant the children of the Dons players never went short of a treat or two.

During the Second World War George worked with players from south of the border who had come up to 'guest' for the club in matches to keep morale high. Those who temporarily wore Aberdeen colours were players of the class of Bobby Ancell of Newcastle United, Alex Dyer of Plymouth Argyle, Joe Harvey of Bradford City and of course Stan Mortensen who was serving at RAF Lossiemouth and who I have also mentioned in the book.

They say you have to be a bit mad to be a goalkeeper and the history books show that one of the most entertaining was Harry Blackwell. The Sheffield-born goalkeeper was signed from Scunthorpe United in 1922 to take over from George Anderson. He was at the club up until 1930 but it was a Scottish Cup match against Peterhead on February 10, 1923 that Aberdeen won 13-0 that earns him a place in my thoughts.

In that game he assumed the role of spectator as play was up the other end on a rain-lashed day at Pittodrie. Bored out of his mind he decided to call for a raincoat to put on and sheltered under an umbrella given to him by a fan. Only he once put down his umbrella to stop Jim Wiseman of Peterhead from scoring. How is that for style!

Another character was Rab MacFarlane who was one of the stars of Scottish football at the start of the twentieth century. He came to Pittodrie in 1904 and was totally unorthodox in his approach. Swapping banter with the fans behind the goal was his trademark, regardless whether they were the home or away support. Imagine a goalkeeper doing that nowadays. His manager would be going mad at him.

There was also Steve Smith who was one of the few native Aberdonians to ever keep goal for the club. He used to sell chocolate and programmes at Pittodrie in the pre-war era and his first club was local junior side Hall Russell's. What fascinated me about Steve was that, like many young men from the north-east of Scotland, he decided to emigrate to America as a teenager to start a new life before he had played for Aberdeen.

He played for nine years in North America, first for two Chicago sides, Thistle FC and the All Scots Club. He also turned out for Brooklyn FC and the Canadian Occasionals of Toronto.

He returned to Scotland in 1930, simply because his Pittodrie boyhood heroes were keen to sign him. He may have been just five feet eight inches tall, which is pretty small for a goalkeeper, but he managed to be an ever-present in the team for seven seasons. When he retired as a player in 1937 he stayed on to coach the reserve team during the Second World War before emigrating yet again to the USA in 1947.

Another great servant was George Johnstone who was the first Aberdeen goalkeeper to pick up a Scottish Cup winners medal when he was part of the team that beat Hibs 2-1 in 1947. A year before he was in the side that won the 1946 Southern League Cup final 3-2 against Rangers, in what was the forerunner for the Scottish League Cup and was a top player of his day.

In that 2-1 Scottish Cup win over Hibs he had the worst possible start when he let a harmless back-pass from George Taylor slip through his fingers and into the net. He made up for his mistake with some fantastic saves to help his team to a famous victory in front of a huge crowd of 82,100. Winning that trophy was a sweet moment for George because a decade earlier he had been part of the Aberdeen side that had lost the Scottish Cup final to Celtic. George spent twelve years at Pittodrie and played more than 200 games before moving to Dunfermline and then Raith Rovers.

There are other goalkeepers who played in more modern times who also caught my eye. Peter Kjaer, who I noticed Buff Hardie of *Scotland the What?* has put in his Dream Team elsewhere in the book, was a good shot-stopper and a top man. He hardly put a foot wrong in his time with Aberdeen but sorry, Buff, he hasn't made my Dream Team or the bench.

Another man who deserves an honourable mention is Bryan Gunn, who although he did not start many matches for Aberdeen, was a great guy to have in the dressing room and on the training pitch and was a part of our European Cup Winners' Cup squad.

He was always upbeat and I remember him having a bit of a laugh at the gaffer's expense – a brave thing to do for a young goalkeeper – during training. Alex Ferguson used to be a centre forward and still played a bit in training games when he first arrived at the club. He was tough as he always was and Bryan used to claim the gaffer used to leave an elbow in here and there when he went up for challenges.

Bryan wanted to get even which was never going to be easy. The challenge he gave himself was to punch the ball clear while catching Sir Alex in the head with his fist in the follow-through. Accidentally of course. Bryan hit his target a few times but to be fair to Sir Alex big Bryan used to say he would never moan and just got on with the game. Only Bryan could have given the gaffer a sare heid and got away with it.

His chances of making a breakthrough at Aberdeen were slim because Jim Leighton, who I will come to, kept him on the sidelines. When Alex Ferguson also brought in the more experienced Belgian

Marc de Clerc I really thought Bryan may be on his way before he had a real chance to show his worth.

Before I go on about Bryan I feel Marc deserves a quick mention for being the only Aberdeen goalkeeper I know to score in open play in a competitive first team match from a kick-out. I was on the park that day on August 30, 1980, when he did it in a League Cup tie and it was an incredible moment. He sent out this huge kick from hand and it sailed over all our heads, deceived the Berwick Rangers goalkeeper much to his embarrassment and ended in the back of the net.

Because Marc had taken his place in the reserves Bryan was relegated to doing the duties of an apprentice like cleaning the boots, baby-sitting the gaffer's children or washing his car in the Pittodrie car park. He always said at least he must have done a really good job on the cars as he was never asked to wash the mini-bus as other apprentices had to do.

Luckily for Bryan in the summer of 1981 Marc left due to the fact he had grown quickly frustrated at playing second fiddle to Jim Leighton all the time and knew there was no chance of getting a first team place. Bryan was given a new one-year contract extension but spent most of his time in the reserves although he did play occasionally when Jim was injured.

Bryan got his first winners medal in the Scottish Cup final win over Rangers in 1983 when he was on the bench and he celebrated a bit too much. I remember Archie Knox telling me how revolted he was – and it took a lot to revolt Archie – when Bryan had one mouthful of his breakfast the next morning and was sick all over the plate in the main dining room at the Gleneagles Hotel where we had held our celebration party the night before.

Even on the night we won the European Cup Winners' Cup there was an incident involving Bryan that is always remembered despite the fact he didn't play.

Now Bryan is a big bloke standing well over six foot tall and was on the bench for the final in Gothenburg. At the final whistle, like the rest of us, he was excited but when he jumped out of the dug-out to celebrate he knocked Sir Alex over in the process as he ran across his path to get onto the pitch.

The gaffer fell flat on his face into a puddle unknown to big Bryan who just kept going, jumping up and down in celebration as he went. The boys tell a great story of how the gaffer went down head-first like he had been shot into the puddle and got up as quick as he could looking disheveled and with his Aberdeen fleece jacket covered in a mixture of water and ash from the speedway track that ran round the stadium.

Bryan always fancied himself as a bit of an outfield player and the other thing that sticks in my memory about Bryan was that, like Bobby Clark before him, he played outfield for Aberdeen, albeit it in the reserves, and even scored a goal in open play.

I believe it came against St Mirren reserves in May 1984 just before the first team was due to play Celtic in the Scottish Cup final of that year. Aberdeen had an injury crisis and Bryan volunteered to play outfield. In fact once the idea was in his head he was badgering Sir Alex to play him days before the game.

I was in the stands at Love Street watching that night and I remember Neil Simpson floating a free-kick into the box and big Bryan who was playing up front headed it home. He then set off on his own over the top celebrations as he ran round the park before stopping in front of the main stand where he knew I was sitting alongside Alex McLeish and Mark McGhee. He milked the applause to death and made sure we all heard about his goal for months to come.

Because Bryan was a bit younger and maybe not on the same money as the rest of us every pound was precious to him which makes me still feel guilty about one incident in particular. If I didn't feel bad enough missing a penalty for Aberdeen, big Bryan rubbed salt in my wounds on the way home claiming I cost him the down payment on a new motor.

We were playing Dinamo Berlin in the European Cup first round in 1984 and I missed a spot-kick, as did Eric Black, in the shoot-out that put us out of the competition. Although Bryan was not playing he would have got the same European bonus as the rest of us if we had won and the minute I shot wide his dreams of a new car were over.

Bryan – or rather his boots – came in useful in our Scottish Cup final win over Hearts in 1986. The kit man had forgotten to pack Alex McLeish's boots and he only found out about it when we were at Hampden and didn't have time to get any others. He had mistakenly put in the boots of reserve striker Andy McLeod, which had the initials AMcL on them – just like big Eck's did, but Andy's were size sevens while big Eck wore a nine-and-a-half.

Big Bryan was on the bench and was a size ten-and-a-half – one size bigger than Eck. As nobody had similar size feet Archie Knox hit on the brainwave of stuffing Bryan's boots with cotton wool and giving them to Eck who would wear two pairs of socks to fill them out a bit more. It seems to have worked a treat as Alex played the entire match and put in a good shift.

Bryan finally left Pittodrie later that year to go to Norwich City where he had great success which I was delighted about as he was a fantastic goalkeeper who deserved to play every week rather than sit on the bench.

The man who kept Bryan and many other goalkeepers in the shadow during the fourteen years he was at the club spread over two terms was Jim Leighton. I have kept the best to last in terms of my goalkeeping Dream Team pick as I believe Jim is an all-time Aberdeen and Scotland great. He was the most consistent goal-keeper I had the pleasure of playing in front of and his play helped us to many trophies through the years.

I have to be brutally honest and admit Jim didn't have a lot going for him as a footballer if you took things at face value. His shape for instance. He was never an athletic shape. Everybody remembers Jim's gap-toothed smile and of course his legs. Some may even have called them bandy – but not me, Jim!

I still have this mental picture of him taking goal kicks with that big trailing leg of his. He could hardly get the ball over the half-way line at the best of times. Whenever he was supposed to hit Mark McGhee with his kick-outs the ball invariably landed on wee

Gordon Strachan's head. There was even one time when we were playing Arbroath at Gayfield, which to be fair to Jim is the windiest ground in the world, when he took a goal kick against the wind which blew back and led to me heading the ball away in the arc of the eighteen-yard box.

He was not the big type of imposing goalkeeper that people like nowadays although he did stand nearly six foot two inches tall. In fact we discouraged him from getting involved too much in the physical stuff. We told him not to come off his line if he could possibly help it as he would just get in the way of myself and Alex McLeish. That suited Jim down to the ground who was comfortable staying on his line most of the time, but that doesn't take away from the fact that he was incredibly brave and picked up many knocks because he always put his body on the line.

What made him stand out was his ability to make world class saves at both club and international level. Club football in Scotland tended to be all action and you had to be concentrating all the time as play raged from end to end and you never knew when you would be called upon next, even in a top side like Aberdeen.

By the same token Jim's club experiences weren't like, say, Alan Rough when he was at Patrick Thistle, who had to pull off top-class saves all the time because the team he was playing for were not as good as Aberdeen. Sometimes I think that can make goalies at clubs that are struggling look a bit better than others because they are involved all the time and grabbing the headlines with one top save after another.

Jim on the other hand had no margin for error. The times he was called upon to make saves for Aberdeen may have been few and far between in some games, but guaranteed any mistake he made would have been magnified. Thankfully for us Jim hardly ever made a mistake.

Jim was such a success with Aberdeen and Scotland as he had incredible powers of concentration. He could be doing nothing for eighty-nine minutes for Scotland and still pull off a top-class save with a minute left.

Jim was always a quiet chap who just got on with things on and off the park. He was not loud, funny or a party animal or part of the dressing room guys who played the pranks. He never got excited about anything which was great for a goalkeeper who you want to be a calm guy rather than someone who gets flustered easily.

He was brought to Pittodrie by Ally MacLeod who gave him the ironic nickname, 'Brendan Foster' in training sessions, not because he was as fast as the 1974 European 5000 metres champion, but because he was so slow.

He made his debut against a team called Kikinda on a pre-season tour to the country then known as Yugoslavia but I remember him making his competitive Scottish Premier League debut against Hearts on a rain-sodden pitch at Tynecastle on August 12, 1978. It was a tough surface to control the ball with your feet, let alone your hands but Jim showed his worth by making some fantastic saves on a greasy surface. At the start of the 1980/81 campaign Bobby Clark hurt his back which put him out of action and ultimately led to him leaving the club.

Once Jim was in the team he was impossible to dislodge. Look at the record books from the time he was at the club from 1980 to 1987. In his first year he played forty-six games, then fifty-eight, fifty-nine, sixty-three in the year we won the European Cup Winners' Cup, forty-three, forty then forty-eight before he moved to Manchester United. A phenomenal achievement.

Jim was part of a young group of players such as Doug Bell, Neale Cooper, Neil Simpson and John Hewitt who all came through the ranks to consolidate places in the first team squad around the same time.

Perhaps the one incident that epitomises the dedication Jim showed to Aberdeen came when we won the Scottish Cup 2-1 against Celtic in 1984. On the Monday before the final Jim had been cutting his grass when he switched off the power in his electric mower to clean the blades. Just at that moment when he had his hand in the blades his three-year-old daughter Claire accidentally flicked the switch on again and sliced open the pinkie on his right hand.

When he told Sir Alex the gaffer called him all the names under the sun before making it clear he still wanted him to play. He told Jim to keep away from Pittodrie because photographers might get a picture of him with his bandaged hand. The fact he wasn't at training still led to speculation, some of it wilder than the next. Jim had lost his fingers, he had electrocuted himself and one of Gordon Strachan's neighbours even heard a rumour Jim had died, but Sir Alex was trying to keep the sad news quiet so not to upset the rest of his squad.

Jim was very much alive and had stitches put in his finger and special strapping on the morning of the game. I don't think anybody noticed he had a problem as yet again he pulled off a string of great saves.

He had a long shift to deal with that day through no fault of his own. We had gone one up through an Eric Black goal then Roy Aitken of Celtic was sent off for fouling Mark McGhee. We should have finished them off after that but instead let them back into the game with a Paul McStay goal four minutes from the end, taking the game into extra-time.

The introduction of Doug Bell by the gaffer during the extra thirty minutes made a huge difference as he was everywhere in the midfield. It was Doug's run and shot that came back off the post that allowed Gordon Strachan to get the rebound and give the ball to Mark McGhee to score the winner.

Jim also made some great saves and that capped one of his best ever seasons as he helped us become the first team outwith the Old Firm to complete the League and Cup double. Even the outspoken Brian Clough described Jim as 'a rare bird – a Scottish goalkeeper that can be relied upon'.

The only time that Jim nearly came a cropper was not when he played for Aberdeen but in the famous World Cup qualifier against Wales at Ninian Park. We needed to get at least a draw to qualify for the play-offs for the 1986 finals and in the first half had been under the cosh. Mark Hughes had put Wales ahead and Jock Stein was going through us like a dose of salts in the dressing room.

Then physio Hugh Allan whispered in his ear and he cut short his rant, much to the relief of everyone, and made his way into the area near the bathroom. I heard a bit of shouting and then Alan Rough came out ready to play, with Jim following sheepishly behind him pulling on his tracksuit top.

As it turned out Jim was having to come off because he had lost one of his contact lenses during the first half and didn't have a spare pair. Now I was shocked to find out we had to change our goalie at half-time in one of the biggest games in Scottish football history, but what stunned me was that Jim wore contact lenses in the first place. He had never mentioned it in all our years together at Aberdeen and must have put them in long before he ever came into the dressing room before a big match, or even training for that matter.

To make matters worse Sir Alex, who was the Scotland assistant manager at the time, also had no idea Jim wore contact lenses. The gaffer thought he knew everything about his players but here was one little secret about Jim nobody knew.

Thankfully things ended well as Alan Rough made some smashing saves for us and a penalty by the late, great Davie Cooper earned us a draw. In the play-off Jim was back between the sticks when we beat Australia.

Knowing Jim wore contact lenses allowed me and Alex McLeish to wind him up mercilessly for years to come. Many a time I joked that I always knew his eyesight was deficient and now I had proof I was right. Jim took it all in his stride, as he did everything in football. He was unflappable apart from the odd cross-ball of course (just joking Jim!) and the fact he remained at the top level for so long shows exactly why he is my first pick for the number one position in my Dream Team.

Also can I say Jim was the most considerate room-mate I ever had. We used to share together on Scotland duty and unlike big Alex McLeish who was on the go from dawn to dusk Jim realised I was a slow-starter in the morning. He used to leave me in my natural habitat away from the pitch – my bed – for as long as I liked and didn't make too much noise.

Also not many people might know this but Jim had the nickname 'Bozo' during his playing days, which was a play I think on the character Gonzo who was in The Muppets. That changed to 'Bozo Bond' in the dressing room after, as a young player, he told us all about his undercover uncle.

We were heading to Majorca for an end of season bonding session when our flight was diverted to the smaller nearby island of Minorca after a huge electrical storm the likes I have never seen before or since.

The storm had knocked out the electrical supply in the hotel we had booked into at short notice so we had to sit around talking by candle light. During the general chit-chat we heard Jim talking about his uncle who was spy. We all stopped completely in thrall of his story.

We started taking the mickey out of him on the grounds that his uncle could not be a very good spy if Jim knew that was his job. Jim was just out of his teens at the time and he was instantly regretting telling us about his uncle who was the spy as the torrent of abuse headed his way. During that holiday whenever anybody saw Jim they would hum the theme tune to the James Bond film *From Russia With Love* and from then on the nickname 'Bozo Bond' was born.

Jim learned some good goalkeeping habits from Bobby Clark in his early days and I think it was partly Bobby's influence that helped him go on to great things. Jim was a real student of the game and would study the opposition team before a game and pick out who he considered the danger men and who had to be watched at corner-kicks. He would also nominate the poor guys to stand in his walls in front of any free-kicks and woe betide anyone who didn't stand where he told them to stand.

His thoroughness extended to his own pre-match preparations and he was always out on the pitch long before the rest of us with one of the substitutes who would provide a variety of crosses and shots for him. Then when the rest of us would come out onto the pitch he would pick some else to hit more balls at him.

Jim used to sit next to Gordon Strachan in the changing room and had to put up with a lot of good-natured banter from Gordon throughout his time at Pittodrie. Jim's hair used to be all over the place in the morning and Gordon used to always ask him if he had had a hard time in his coffin the night before.

Glen Hoddle once told Steve Archibald that he thought Aberdeen were the ugliest team he had ever played against. When Stevie told wee Gordon the news, he replied: 'He must have been looking at Jim Leighton and Doug Rougvie.'

Despite his lack of film star good looks, for me Jim was the best goalkeeper in Europe in the early 1980s and an all-time great of the Scottish game. His natural ability was incredible but he also worked extremely hard in training to remain at the top of world football. With Jim between the sticks my Dream Team would not lose many goals.

4

THE RIGHT CHOICE

I have played with some great right backs during my time at
Aberdeen and looking through the history books I am clearly not
the only central defender to have done so. Through the best and
worst of times at Pittodrie it appears that Aberdeen always had a
decent right back to rely upon.

Don't believe me? Well, have a look at some of the great servants
of the club who pulled on the number two jersey through the years.
One of the men who nearly made my Dream Team is former captain
Jimmy Mitchell who was given the armband by Dave Halliday in
the golden era of the mid-1950s, when he was our first ever League
Championship-winning captain.

Jimmy made his debut against Motherwell at Fir Park in a League
Cup tie on August 9, 1952 where things didn't start well and his
team lost 5-2. Although they finished a lowly eleventh in what was
called 'Division A' back in those days, they did manage to make it
into the Scottish Cup final where they lost to Rangers 1-0 in a replay
at Hampden.

The following year Jimmy's team got their revenge as they
trounced Rangers 6-0 in the Scottish Cup semi-final at Hampden
in front of 111,000 people on April 10, 1954. Unfortunately they
couldn't do an Old Firm double and in the final Celtic beat them 2-1
and in the league they struggled once again finishing ninth.

Over that summer Jimmy made it clear he wanted more effort

from his team who he felt had gained vital experience by playing two, albeit losing, back-to-back Scottish Cup finals and just needed to find a bit of consistency.

The following season, 1954/55, Jimmy got his wish and had his greatest year in an Aberdeen jersey. Four straight wins in their first four league games set them up for a major title challenge as they finally found that consistency he had craved. He was also in top form and missed just one game in one of the most exciting seasons in the history of the club.

For once, Aberdeen had a realistic chance of winning the Scottish League championship for the first time. It was the Holy Grail for Aberdeen who had never won it in their fifty-two year history. After a fantastic run of results they were top of the table with three games left and knew a win over Clyde at Shawfield on April 9, 1955 would bring the title to Pittodrie. With a trip to nearest challengers Celtic at Parkhead the following week and then a final match at home to Raith Rovers, it was very much a case of now or never for Aberdeen as Celtic were snapping at our heels. There was no room for a slip-up.

The omens were not good as five days earlier Clyde had beaten Aberdeen 1-0 in a Scottish Cup semi-final replay with the defeat coming at a cost. Some of the top players at Pittodrie like Jack Allister and Paddy Buckley picked up injuries that they had not recovered from in time to travel to Shawfield, although they were all in the crowd that famous day.

Match reports of the time suggest Jimmy Mitchell led his depleted team superbly, like all good captains should, with the winning, championship-clinching goal coming from the penalty spot as early as the thirteenth minute, scored by Archie Glen.

More success was to come when Jimmy lifted the League Cup later the same year with a 2-1 win over St Mirren in front of 44,106 fans at Hampden. Television was in its infancy back then and there were only so many places players could be interviewed. So captain Jimmy had to go all the way from Glasgow to Edinburgh Castle to be interviewed for a nationwide broadcast by the BBC.

During the interview he took it on himself to invite all Aberdonians to greet the cup-winning side at Aberdeen Joint Station later that evening. Little did he know that 15,000 of them would take up his offer and cheer him and his team mates to high heavens when they walked off the train.

Jimmy also fought hard for his players, and as captain he was the man who was sent in to talk to the Aberdeen board when the players were in revolt over a lack of bonus money for winning the title. He led a delegation made up of fellow players Archie Glen and Fred Martin who had tried earlier in the season to get a better financial deal when it became apparent they were in with a good shout of winning the title.

Now, with the League championship trophy proudly on display at Pittodrie, they thought they would get a fairer hearing. They attended a board meeting in the Caledonian Hotel to try and get extra money but were given the cold shoulder. All the players got was a round figure of £1,000 sent from the Scottish League to the club in recognition of their win, which was money that every side that won the championship received with that figure being divided into eleven parts, and as I mentioned earlier players like Fred Martin didn't get all of that because they had missed a few games.

Although Jimmy didn't make many mistakes there was one game when everything went wrong for him. He was a great raconteur and could tell stories against himself like the time he gave away three penalties, yes three, in the one match against Celtic. Bobby Collins scored a hat-trick from the spot during the match on September 26, 1953 after fouls by Jimmy. We all mistime tackles now and again, but come on, Jimmy! Actually, I blame the ref. I bet none of them were penalties.

In my day I was fortunate to play alongside some top-class right backs but there was only one or two who I played alongside with Scotland. One was Stewart McKimmie who came close to making my Aberdeen Dream Team and when you look at his record you can understand why.

Stewart was another local boy who went on to great things in an

Aberdeen jersey after he signed for the club in 1983 from Dundee, as a replacement for a gentleman called Stuart Kennedy who I will also discuss. Sir Alex spotted his talent and signed him for £90,000 in December 1983 which turned out to be a real bargain.

He made his debut at the age of twenty-one against Hibs and won the European Super Cup after we beat Hamburg in just his second ever game for the club. He would go on to win two Scottish League Championships in 1984 and 1985, three Scottish Cups in 1984, 1986 and 1990 and three Scottish League Cups in 1985, 1989 and the last in 1995 as captain. Along the way he won forty international caps for Scotland, appearing in the 1990 World Cup, the 1992 European Football championship and the 1996 European Football Championship. That is a fantastic track record in anybody's eyes.

Before I come on to Stewart's contribution to Aberdeen I have to mention why he will always be remembered by Scotland fans. Stewart may have scored just one goal for his country but it turned out to be one of the most famous in our history. When I tell you it is the one that beat the then world champions Argentina 1-0 in a friendly at Hampden in 1989 you will understand why.

Stewart's joy at helping Scotland become the first country to beat the Argentines since they won the World Cup three years previous was intensified because he wasn't in the original squad for the game. He was only added at the last minute because Richard Gough picked up an injury. I remember he said to me he expected to start on the bench and I was delighted for him when Andy Roxburgh put him on from the start.

I remember Stewart saying a little bit of quick-thinking – some may say cheating but I would never call it that – by that other Aberdeen top man of the time Alex McLeish helped him score his goal. The ball actually went out of play for a throw-in to Argentina but Alex quickly grabbed the ball and threw it down the line even before the linesman's flag went up.

The ref was also caught unawares and waved play on which allowed play to be worked up the right-hand side and when the ball reached Stewart he just hammered it into the net. Stewart always laughs at the fact that although he won a host of trophies with Aberdeen, he will probably always be remembered by non-Aberdeen fans because of that goal.

Although he did win forty caps which is a creditable total, I always felt he should have been given more. The problem was that with so many great Scottish right backs around early in his career he was never a regular in the national side and the game against Argentina was only his third. In a way his goal against Argentina made people sit up and take notice of his huge talent and he went on to play in the next three major championships with Scotland, which was only fair.

He played against Costa Rica and the mighty Brazil in the World Cup in Italy in 1990 and played in all three group games in Sweden in the European championship in 1992 and in the matches against Holland and hosts England at Euro '96.

What made Stewart such an asset to Aberdeen was the fact that he was so versatile and talented a footballer he could play almost anywhere. Later in his career at Pittodrie he could slot into the centre of defence when required and although he didn't quite make my Dream Team he deserves his place on the bench.

There are other Aberdeen full-backs who deserve a mention that maybe have been lost in the midst of time. One of the most interesting and colourful backstories belongs to Donald Colman, or should that be Donald Cunningham? Confused? Then let me explain. The former Aberdeen full-back was actually born Donald Cunningham in Renton in Dumbartonshire on August 14, 1878. His parents were very strict and had great plans for their son which did not involve football. Donald loved the game but didn't want to offend his parents so registered to play for Glasgow Perthshire under the name of Colman, which was his grandmother's name.

He went on to play for Tontine Athletic, Renton and Maryhill Juniors before his secret finally came out. Where he was telling his parents he was going every Saturday afternoon is beyond me but after they realised their boy was a pretty good footballer and loved the game they allowed him to keep playing. The problem was that the name Donald Colman had stuck and that was what he was known as throughout his career.

Although he was good enough to be a junior internationalist senior sides never really gave him a chance, with Hibs and Sunderland both passing up the chance to sign him. Motherwell took the plunge in 1905 and signed him at the relatively late age of twenty-seven on a two-year deal but, to put it bluntly, he made no impression whatsoever. With his career going nowhere and on the recommendation of his pal, Jimmy Muir, who was an Aberdeen striker at the time he was given a trial by manager Jimmy Phillip.

He clearly made a big impression and was handed his debut on September 21, 1907 in a 1-0 away defeat to Dundee. Over the next two seasons he did not miss a single league or cup match and was playing the best football of his life. Newspapers at the time described him as a top-class right back who was one of the most intelligent players on his generation. He was quick thinking enough to be a step ahead of whatever left winger tried to get the better of him.

Colman became such an influential figure that he became club captain at the age of thirty-three. On top of that he became the oldest Aberdeen player to win a first Scotland cap when he was selected to play for his country against Wales in 1911. He played for the club up until 1920 before leaving at the age of forty-two to combine a summer coaching job in Norway with a post as the trainer of Dumbarton during the regular Scottish season.

Eleven years later, in March 1931, he finally returned to be trainer at Aberdeen under Pat Travers. During his time as a coach at Pittodrie he wrote his name into the history books by becoming the inventor of the dugout. He did so because he spent much of his time and effort working on players' footwork and ideas such as possession football and using space that he wanted a pitch side view of proceedings. He was so convinced of the importance of watching his players' feet from ground level that he devised the dugout where he sat to observe the game as it unfolded. The idea quickly spread throughout Britain and managers came down from the stand to sit in the dugout at the side of the pitch. Examples of dugouts as first pioneered by Donald Colman, or should that be Cunningham, can be seen at football grounds to this day and is a lasting memorial to a true Aberdeen great.

Before I go on to choose my Dream Team right back there are two or three others from the past that caught my eye. I have to mention Bobby Hannah who apparently was one of the toughest tacklers around. Match reports of that era described him as having a 'great but curious two-footed tackle'. Even one attempt to do a two-footed tackles nowadays and Billy would have been given his marching orders. Sounds an interesting player to say the least.

Also, what about Willie Cooper who was a local boy made good? Willie joined Aberdeen in 1927 and occasionally captained the team through his twenty-one years at the club. He played 373 games during his time at Pittodrie which was broken up by his time away during the Second World War.

He was part of the group of nine men such as Frank Dunlop and George Hamilton who returned from the fighting and made a huge contribution to Aberdeen's success in the late 1940s.

He was a real top-class defender who was fast and accurate with his passing. He wasn't the tallest but made up for that with a tremendous physique and of course, that biting tackle. He was seldom troubled by injury and from September 1932 until October 1936 he never missed a league game, setting a club record for the time of 162 consecutive league appearances.

He was also hugely respected by his fellow professionals which earned him plus points in my book. An indication of that came in the 1946/47 season when he had been part of the side that made it into the Scottish Cup semi-final. Willie had been an ever-present in the cup run, but in that win over Arbroath at Dens Park where Stan Williams scored the two winning goals, he pulled a muscle and had to sit out the final at Hampden.

Aberdeen won 2-1 thanks to two first half goals within a nine minute period from George Hamilton and Stan Williams. In the second half, Hibs goalie Jimmy Kerr saved a penalty from Hamilton but thankfully the Dons held on to win.

Willie came down from the stands in his suit at the end of the game to celebrate with his team mates and such was the high regard in which he was held by the rest of the team that Willie Waddell, who was the man who was drafted into the side in his absence and who left soon after to join Kettering Town, offered him his medal. It was a lovely gesture that the other Willie politely declined.

Attempts to honour Willie didn't stop there and there was a public campaign supported by fans from every club in Scotland to get permission from the SFA to present him with a special medal. It hasn't happened before or since but Willie did get that Scottish Cup final medal that he thoroughly deserved in the end after the SFA relented. He was also a member of the Southern League Cup final winning team of 1946 who beat Rangers 3-2 at Hampden to lift the trophy.

As a boy who played for the junior side Mugiemoss in 1927, and because he didn't retire until January 31, 1948 when he played against Falkirk, he was a real local hero. He deserves to be considered for my Dream Team as he was one of the club's greatest servants playing for us for twenty-one years.

Another real character was Jock Hutton who went by the name of 'The Tank' and who was, by conservative estimates, suggested to be at least fourteen stone. Despite his bulk newspaper reports of the time talk of Hutton rampaging up the touchline passing opponents on his way. What it doesn't say is if he ran past them or simply straight through them as he was a big, big guy.

He had been signed as an inside forward by Jimmy Phillip and given his debut in that position against Albion Rovers on August 16, 1919. But Phillip switched him to defence when it became apparent he was never going to be a box to box player. From the right back position he became one of Scotland's best defenders of his time.

He was good enough to be chosen to captain the Scottish League select on four occasions and won his first full cap against Northern Ireland in 1923.

He left us to join Blackburn Rovers where he supposedly performed incredible feats of strength at training including lifting one of his team mates off the ground with just his teeth. Yes, I know, I didn't believe that either, but it appears to be somehow true. He helped Blackburn Rovers lift the FA Cup with a 3-1 win over Huddersfield and is still a cult hero at the English club.

Another top full-back who could also play in the centre of defence was the big Dane Henning Boel who quite rightly was one of the founding members of the Aberdeen Hall of Fame back in 2003.

Henning started out at his local amateur side Ikast FS in Denmark where he became a regular in the Danish national team, earning five Under-21 caps and thirteen of his fifteen full caps from 1965 to 1967. When the professional North American Soccer League was founded in 1968 he played for the Boston Beacons before signing for Aberdeen in 1969 around the same time I joined as an apprentice under Eddie Turnbull.

Now I know a lot of you will remember Henning as a big centre back but really the game everybody remembers is the famous 3-1 win over Celtic in the Scottish Cup final on April 11, 1970. Henning was playing right back that day and you would be struggling to see a better performance against a Celtic team that don't forget had made the European Cup final of that year. He marked John Hughes out of the game and even came across to the other side of the defence at times to keep the legendary Jimmy Johnstone quiet. An injury sustained in a UEFA Cup tie against Borussia Monchengladbach in 1972 signalled the end of his time in Scotland as he found it difficult to regain his place in the Aberdeen side but he made a big contribution when he was here.

Now I can turn my attention to the man who has beaten off all contenders to make my Dream Team right back. Stuart Kennedy is quite simply one of the greatest full-backs Scotland has ever seen.

A lot of people don't realise that the first person to note his potential was Alex Ferguson long before he was manager at Aberdeen. Alex was player-coach at Falkirk under Willie Cunningham when Stewart was starting to show his worth. He was a part-time apprentice at Brockville and worked with Alex when he took the reserves.

The gaffer could always pick out players with the right attitude and he told me that from day one Stuart was among the most competitive players he had worked with. I found that out to be the case as years later when he even took bounce games in training very seriously indeed.

Stuart, who had worked in the Clyde shipyards as an apprentice electrician, moved to Aberdeen in 1976 from Falkirk for £40,000 and was hardly ever out of the team that I played in. Although he had been signed by Ally MacLeod when Alex took over he was delighted to see Stuart already at the club. Throughout his time at Aberdeen he worked like a Trojan from start to finish in every game and won every major domestic honour.

For the record he won the Scottish League title in 1979/80, the Scottish Cup in 1981/82 and the League Cup under Ally MacLeod in 1976/77. In the Scottish Cup semi-final of 1983 he was the victim of a strong tackle by Roy Aitken that hurt his knee which sadly was the start of his injury problems.

Stuart being Stuart overcame that problem and played again the next midweek against Waterschei of Belgium in the second leg of the European Cup Winners' Cup. We had won the first leg 5-1 and were set for the final. Unfortunately Stewart aggravated his knee injury after catching his studs in the turf.

There was no way he would be fit enough to play in the final and like the rest of the team I was gutted for him. For him to come so far and not have the pleasure of playing in the final must have been heartbreaking. In a show of respect for Stuart which the whole Aberdeen squad backed and appreciated, Sir Alex named him among the substitutes so he could pick up a medal in recognition of all he had done for the team. It was the right decision as Stuart had played in nine out of the ten previous ties in the competition and scored in the opening game against Sion of Switzerland.

Some people who don't know Sir Alex would argue that he would never put an injured player on the bench for Manchester United in such a big game but I would argue otherwise. Sir Alex values loyalty and honesty and had great respect for Stuart which is why he named him in the squad for the game in Gothenburg.

Sir Alex has a bit of sentiment about him at times. He is not just fiery Sir Alex all the time. Ironically Stuart twisted his knee leaping out of the dug-out in celebration at the final whistle after our win over Real Madrid and that added to his injury problems. Neither Aberdeen nor Sir Alex gave up on Stuart at any stage and he got the best medical treatment on his injured knee for eighteen months before having to admit defeat and retire.

At international level Stuart experienced the highs and lows of the game and played for Scotland in the ill-fated World Cup of 1978. I was extremely disappointed not to make the squad but after what happened out in Argentina I used to joke with Stuart that maybe it was no bad thing that I missed out. It is hard to believe that during his career he won just eight caps and they were won only between 1978 and 1981. He was up against, amongst others, Danny McGrain and Sandy Jardine, both Old Firm players, so it was never going to be easy.

Off the pitch I was around when Stuart had one of the most exciting moments of his life. It came after we had beaten Rangers 1-0 to win the 1982 Scottish Cup and no, it wasn't lifting the trophy that got his pulse racing. We had booked to stay over at the plush Gleneagles Hotel to celebrate our victory and by coincidence staying there that night was the Hollywood legend Burt Lancaster, who was in Scotland filming the movie *Local Hero*. Stuart was a huge movie buff and when he met Burt Lancaster he was speechless. Burt was one of his movie heroes and although I am sure the Scottish Cup final win was a great moment for Stuart it was equalled for him by meeting such a Hollywood legend.

Throughout our time at Aberdeen Stuart was the epitome of the model professional and the sort of player that made it easier for me to play football. I never really worried too much about who was playing on the opposition left wing as I always knew Stuart would take care of him.

Off the pitch Stuart had the honorary title of the barrack room lawyer for the way he pursued our win bonuses with the board. He was like a union shop steward, always trying to get us the best deal, which was great for the younger players in the squad who maybe didn't have the confidence to tackle such issues head on.

Throughout all my years the only player who gave Stuart any sort of trouble was the South Korean international winger Cha-Bum Kun who he faced in the 1979/80 UEFA Cup first round when we played Eintracht Frankfurt. He scored the German's side goal at Pittodrie that a Joe Harper strike cancelled out but I have never seen Stuart as despondent after a game as I did that night. To make matters worse we lost 1-0 across in Germany in the return leg which put us out of the competition.

What made Stuart so special was that he wasn't one of those defenders who got a nose bleed when he crossed the half-way line. I used to be in awe at the way he used to bomb up and down the right wing leaving defenders in his wake.

Stuart was the quickest player I ever played with or against. He once raced Stevie Archibald, who is no slouch, over 100 yards at a training camp at Gordonstoun School and gave him ten yards start and still beat him. Giving anybody ten yards over 100, especially a fellow professional footballer, and still beating him to the tape shows how fast he was. He was simply electric.

Stuart always fancied himself as a bit of a goalscorer and although he only scored six for Aberdeen there was one absolute special strike that I still remember. It was a long-range effort which gave us a 1-0 extra-time victory over Hibs in the League Cup semi-final at Dens Park in December 1978 which was one of the hardest shot I have ever seen.

Gordon Strachan used to always say one of the reasons he did so well at Aberdeen was that Stuart was behind him to cover up his mistakes. Certainly Stuart and Gordon were close in many ways with the pair of them being room-mates as well as partners in the back of the bus card games where they regularly played against the other two card sharks at the club Alex McLeish and John McMaster.

He was a big presence in the dressing room and a born leader. He was also not scared to have his say during training, and maybe his time working in the Clyde shipyards as a teenager taught him how not to be shy.

He wasn't scared of taking on Sir Alex but did it in a clever way. One day the gaffer was giving him hell because of his poor crossing which he described as pathetic. Stuart disagreed and said he had been practising it a lot and thought he was pretty good at putting crosses into the box.

Looking around for someone to support his criticism the boss turned to his assistant Archie Knox and said: 'What do you think, Archie, his crossing is pathetic, isn't it?'

'Well Stuart's crossing has improved,' said Archie in what was a conciliatory reply for him.

'So, it's improved to pathetic?' said Stuart, quick as a flash. 'So how bad do you think it was to begin with if it has improved to pathetic?'

Even the gaffer had a laugh at Stuart's quick wit and his criticism of his crossing melted away then and there. Sir Alex used to describe Stuart as a Pied Piper figure because people followed him. He was absolutely right. He was the type of man who commanded respect and one that shared some of my most memorable times on a football pitch.

For that reason Stuart is my first choice as right back in my Dream Team. Stewart McKimmie, Willie Mitchell and Donald Colman all ran him close but on reflection there will never be a right back as good as Stuart.

5

CENTRE OF ATTENTION

Finding the right combination in central defence is vital if you want to have any success. Your centre half and sweeper must be almost telepathic and able to stay one step ahead of the opposition. They need to be able to establish a partnership as close as Morecambe and Wise and as in tune as Sonny and Cher.

Most times you need a big, brave centre half who is good in the air and doesn't mind taking a few broken noses for the team, coupled with a more refined sweeper who can read the danger before it happens. Through the years Aberdeen have many such players who made a special double act that hardly gave the opposition a kick.

When I first arrived at Aberdeen as a teenager from Glasgow I had no real interest in who was playing at centre half or sweeper because I was signed as a centre forward. It was only after reserve team trainer Teddy Scott changed my role and moved me into defence did I feel I needed to take a look.

What I found was a group of uncompromising bruisers, at least all the centrebacks were, who would win no beauty contests. Willie Young, George Murray, Tommy McMillan, Henning Boel, who had been changed from full-back to centre half, were all ahead of me in the pecking order.

It was Willie who had the number five jersey when I arrived at Pittodrie and he was the archetypal big, bruising centre half who took no prisoners. He was captain in my first full season at Pittodrie and I can tell you he was no shrinking violet. On and off the field he made his presence felt and he was a real tough guy.

The only time I saw him go a bit pale was when we were coming back from a world tour in the summer of 1974 after playing in places like Iran. We had had a stopover in Hong Kong where he had bought dozens of fake Rolex watches.

Going through customs he was taken away by a couple of security guys who thought he was trying to smuggle stolen goods back to Scotland. It took some diplomacy from Jimmy Bonthrone who was manager at the time to convince the Hong Kong Airport authorities they were all fakes and Willie was just taking them all back for pals and not to sell on the black market.

Now, it was an open secret that some top English clubs were trying to sign him, and maybe he knew what he was doing when he threw his jersey towards manager Jimmy Bonthrone after being substituted during a Premier League game against Dundee United in September 1975 which sped up him leaving the club. His actions were a big risk as only a few weeks earlier he had been one of the five Scotland players banned after a rumpus in a Copenhagen night club after a match against Denmark. He was sold to Spurs for £100,000 and then to Arsenal who he helped win the FA Cup through a famous last minute goal from Alan Sunderland.

Some of you may question why I have included him in my list of players who I considered for a central defender's berth in my Dream Team, considering his career at Aberdeen ended in such acrimonious circumstances.

I can only go on the player I knew and trained with and based on that he deserves consideration. Willie was a colossus for the team I played in and as a young defender he taught me a lot during his time at the club. It was probably his on the park attitude more than anything that rubbed off on me. Willie wanted to win at all costs and that was a similar philosophy to the one I had.

One man who I would argue is one of the unsung heroes of Aberdeen Football Club was Tommy McMillan, who was the centre half before Willie Young. He was the centre of defence in the

Aberdeen team that won the Scottish Cup final over Celtic in 1970 and for that alone has a special place in the history of the club.

He was signed by Eddie Turnbull who just got there in time as Tommy was about to emigrate to the sun in Australia. Bondi Beach in Sydney or the beach at Aberdeen? It appeared to have been no contest for Tommy.

He ditched his plans to go down under and started an Aberdeen career that was so successful that he was called up by the Scotland Under-23 team in 1966 for a match against Wales. He played in the Aberdeen team that lost the 1967 Scottish Cup final 2-0 to Celtic which made the 1970 win even sweeter for him.

Because Celtic were the holders of the European Cup it meant Aberdeen, as Scottish Cup runners-up, went into the Cup Winners' Cup where Tommy has the distinction of being one of the players who scored in Aberdeen's first competitive match abroad, which they won 10-0 against Icelandic amateurs KR Reykjavik on September 6, 1967.

Another centre half with a great attitude from days gone by was little Eddie Falloon who stood just five feet five inches tall. Can you imagine such a small man even being considered as a centre-back nowadays? Absolutely no chance. Falloon was a tough Northern Irishman from Belfast who signed during the 1927 close season as an inside forward. For the first few years he played in that position but in the early 1930s someone had the bright idea of playing him at centre half.

Now I would have loved to have found out who came up with the idea of playing a five-feet-five-inch man in the centre of defence or who suggested to the coach at the time, Pat Travers, that it made sense. To be fair it turned out to be a great shout as Falloon's timing in the air meant he managed to out jump much taller men.

With the number five on his back he went on to captain Northern Ireland and also lead Aberdeen in the losing Scottish Cup final of 1937 in the absence of regular captain Bob Fraser. He was transferred to Clyde for £700 a year later but during his ten years with Aberdeen showed that he was a real little big man for the club.

Playing in the central defence was a prime position for a player to be captain and one man from the same era who did just that was Frank Dunlop. He joined us during the 1936 close season and was originally an old fashioned right half, or right midfield, if you prefer. He was turned into a centre-back within the year and played alongside Falloon in the centre of defence in that losing 1937 Scottish Cup final team that I mentioned earlier and took the captaincy some time later.

Frank led the team to victories in the 1945/46 Southern League Cup final and the 1947 Scottish Cup final against Hibs before he upped sticks and emigrated to South Africa. What tickled me about Frank was that his other claim to fame was that he had one of the longest throw-ins in Scottish football. It was a weapon that he used to good affect, and could easily get the ball into the six yard box from a shy near the corner flag.

He was a well travelled man and in 1949 emigrated to what was then called Rhodesia, now Zimbabwe, where he coached their national team. He was still an avid Dons fan and had match reports from newspapers sent out to him at his home near Bulawayo so he could keep a check on their progress, despite the fact it took weeks for the papers to arrive. The pull of home was too great for Frank and he returned to Aberdeen in 1979 and I met the charming man before he died at the age of seventy-seven, in 1991.

There were lots of other great Aberdeen central defenders with fascinating back stories like Frank's in the first half of the last century, none more so than James Jackson. A football writer once described James as 'all grit and determination.' He certainly was that and shone in two, far-too-brief seasons at Pittodrie. He had joined in June 1923 for a club record fee of £2,000 from Motherwell. After plying his trade north of the border, he left Aberdeen to sign for Liverpool and gave the Reds eight years of quality service.

He established himself in the Liverpool side towards the end of the decade and only missed two out of 126 First Division games from August 1928 until May 1930 while captaining the side. He had three further seasons at Anfield before quitting the game.

What makes Jimmy that little bit different to other number fives who are supposed to be real hard men of the game is the fact that he left football to be ordained as a minister in the Presbyterian church in 1933. He had started his divinity studies at Aberdeen University and had continued them in Liverpool. Not surprisingly, because of his church connections, he was nicknamed 'The Parson' when he was at Pittodrie and the nickname stuck when he went to Anfield.

Before him Wilfred Low, a native Aberdonian, was another accomplished Aberdeen centre half who found more fame south of the border. He was born in 1884 and joined the club on his twentieth birthday. Although he was signed as a half-back an injury crisis at the club made him play centre half and he never looked back. He was transferred to Newcastle United in May 1909 in an exchange that brought Jimmy Soye to Pittodrie. At Newcastle he grew in stature with every game and was a vital part of their great cup sides prior to the First World War.

Jock Wyllie who was a no-nonsense defender from Hurlford in Ayrshire joined the club from Clyde in June 1910. He was supposedly the best header of a ball at the club and scored quite a few goals from corners and cross balls. He left to join Bradford in 1912 but never settled at Valley Parade and returned to Aberdeen in September 1913. A wise man, I say.

In his first season back he finished second top scorer despite playing centre half and was one of several Dons players who volunteered to serve during the First World War. Other notable players who did the same included Alex Wright who joined the 4th Gordons and Bobby Hannah who joined the 7th Gordons. They all returned but tragically great players of the day like outside left Charlie Neilson were killed in action along with John Mackay, an Aberdeen director who died on Flanders Fields.

There were other centre backs worthy of mention from roughly that era like Aberdeen University medical student Vic Milne who played for the first team on amateur forms in the final few weeks of the 1919/1920 season. Milne, a former Robert Gordon's College student, was the son of club chairman Baillie Milne and he was captain for a while in the absence of the injured Bert McLachlan before he was transferred to Aston Villa in the 1923 close-season. By that time Vic Milne had become Doctor Vic Milne and after he retired from playing he became the club doctor at Villa Park.

In the 1950s the main man at the heart of the Aberdeen defence was the great Alec Young who signed from Blantyre Vics at the start of the decade. His claim to fame was a sliding tackle that was perfectly timed and seemingly never failed to win the ball and put the man up in the air which not surprisingly made him a huge favourite with the Dons fans.

He was a member of the losing 1953 and 1954 Scottish Cup final sides and had the misfortune to score an own goal in the latter game. In the championship winning side of 1954/55 he was hugely influential and held together the defence on more than one occasion.

What also made me consider Alec for my Dream Team out of all the players from the past was his ability to come back from serious injury which showed the character of the man. During his seven years at Pittodrie he had to battle back from different career threatening injuries. In no particular order he had to have an emergency appendix operation which was a bigger deal back then than it is now. He also broke his ankle badly and for good measure needed three knee operations.

Alec captained the Scotland Junior international team when he played for Kilsyth Rangers but surprisingly in my opinion playing centre half in a top quality Aberdeen side didn't secure him full Scotland honours.

He never came close which I think is a travesty and I am sure that must have been the biggest regret of his time in football. He left Pittodrie in 1958 to be player-coach at Ross County where he played for six years before he finally hung up his boots at the age of thirty-nine.

Another one of our centre backs, George Kinnell, came from a great football family and was cousin of the legendary Jim Baxter.

Cowdenbeath-born Jim may have effortlessly glided through every match he played but George was a bit more belt and braces in his approach. He was versatile to say the least and played in all five defensive positions for Aberdeen and even popped up once in the forward line at the end of the 1962/63 season.

He was only with us for five seasons from 1959 but made a big impression during his short stay, being appointed captain for a short time before he was lured away to Stoke City in November 1963. Two years later he played with his cousin Jim at Sunderland. He even went on to play for Juventus. No, not the famous Italian side but the team in Australia.

When I first joined the club many talked fondly of the class of Jim Clunie, which isn't a name that many may know. Jim was always mentioned because he was a centre half who didn't just hoof it up the park. Long before it was fashionable, he tried to turn defence into attack by pinpoint passing and linking with his central midfield players. He was a Fifer who was part of the Aberdeen team that won the Scottish League Cup in 1955 with the win over St Mirren.

One man who also deserves a special mention is Willie Garner who, along with Arthur Graham, was the only ever-present in Ally MacLeod's team that won the 1976/77 Scottish League Cup when I was captain. He played in every minute of all eleven games in the competition – which was something I did not do – and he was a consistent performer.

Willie went to play for Celtic before returning as Sir Alex's assistant for a short time at the age of just twenty-nine. I must admit it was a bit of a shock because I had played with Willie and having him giving me orders at training was a bit weird. To be fair Willie was totally professional about the whole thing and kept his distance from the players he knew like myself once he was appointed as Sir Alex's number two. He certainly did me no favours and pushed me as hard as anyone in training before he left when Archie Knox took over.

One man who always impressed me – and even took my place in the Aberdeen team – was Brian Irvine. I was coming to the end of my career and had been struggling with the knee injury when Brian came on the scene. Despite having knee problems I still harboured some hope of playing in the 1990 Scottish Cup final against Celtic. The co-managers at the time Alex Smith and Jocky Scott broke my heart before the final by making it clear I wasn't fit enough to play and Brian would take my place.

It was hard to take at the time but Brian filled my shoes superbly. In fact he became an overnight hero when he scored the winning penalty in a thrilling shoot out that Aberdeen won 9-8 in front of 60,000 fans. It took great mental strength for Brian to take that penalty but he had that in abundance. I was cheering as loudly as I could when he scored and although I was not part of the squad I was delighted for Brian in particular.

He had started his career with Falkirk in 1983 and two years later joined us at Aberdeen when Sir Alex signed him. He was left on the bench to begin with and stepped in to fill Alex McLeish's number five or my number six jersey on ninety-seven occasions in his first four seasons.

When I retired in 1991 he became a regular. He played over 300 league matches, scoring forty goals, for Aberdeen before leaving in 1997 – two years after he was diagnosed with multiple sclerosis. An indication of the strength of character that Brian has came from the fact that just four months after he was diagnosed with MS he was back in action for us. He was a top-class, honest defender who was one of the most consistent players of the modern era and a huge asset to the club he graced for twelve years. He is a man who I have an incredible amount of respect for even though he did take my jersey! His strong Christian faith helped Brian through the tough days when he was first diagnosed with MS but he never complained and always had a smile on his face. A truly great man.

He had a good sense of humour and I remember Billy Stark reminding me that on a pre-season tour of Sweden in 1986, he convinced Brian that previously he was a trained hairdresser who had worked for Vidal Sassoon. Because Billy always had tidy hair Brian swallowed the story and it was only when Alex Ferguson, with a big smile on his face, came to check how Brian's haircut was going that the penny dropped. Suffice to say the end result was not of Vidal Sassoon quality.

An indication of Brian's integrity came when Alex McLeish, of whom you will read more later, tried to play his usual trick on newcomers to the squad. On Brian's first overnight stay before an away game Alex phoned his room and using an assumed voice claimed he was from a Glasgow newspaper looking for a quick interview.

He would ask his victim, in this case Brian, whether he thought suggestions that Alex McLeish and Willie Miller were over the hill were true. Some unsuspecting young players had actually agreed that the pair of us were past it but not Brian. He refused point blank to criticise either of us and slammed the phone down in disgust.

That incident sums him up completely. He didn't have a bad word to say about anybody and the two words that sum Brian up are commitment and honesty. He was first and foremost an Aberdeen supporter who gave his all to the club even after he was given the shock news he had MS. He was a model professional who did the club proud.

Derek Whyte is another player who I felt was a great servant to Aberdeen, although some of you will feel he is more associated with Celtic rather than us and may question me even mentioning him. True he played at Parkhead and also Middlesbrough before he came up the road in 1997 on a four-and-a-half-year contract but I felt Derek was a real leader and always a class act when he was Aberdeen captain. He joined the club during a turbulent time but he was part of the team that made and subsequently lost the Scottish Cup final to Rangers in the year 2000.

In his final season he helped us finish fourth in the SPL and get back into Europe which was a great way for him to bow out.

Out of all the central defenders who have played for the club since I retired the one that impressed me the most was Russell Anderson. Russell was a local boy who was a great servant to Aberdeen making more than 300 appearances during his eleven years with the club.

He left us at the age of twenty-eight in 2007 to join Sunderland in a £1m deal and I felt sorry for him when a string of injuries interrupted his chances of making an impact. On his full Sunderland debut, he damaged ankle ligaments and took three months to recover.

He returned to first time after a loan spell with Plymouth Argyle, then joined Burnley on a temporary basis, only to rupture his cruciate ligament in only his fifth game for the club. Sadly Russell, who went on to play on loan for Derby County, has never hit the heights he did with Aberdeen which is a tragedy.

I could always see the pride in Russell's eyes whenever he pulled on a red jersey. He grew up in the Mannofield area of Aberdeen and attended Aberdeen Grammar School. Since he made his first team debut in 1997 he has become a real fans favourite, and it was the ultimate honour for him to captain the side for four years.

Aberdeen granted him a testimonial match against Everton in 2006 to celebrate his ten years at the club and the fact that 12,000 turned out gave an indication of how well thought of by the fans Russell always was.

Even when he made his debut as an eighteen-year-old in January 1997 when Roy Aitken was manager he looked a pretty special player.

It is a sign of a good player that he keeps his place when the manager changes, and he did just that when Alex Miller, Paul Hegarty, Ebbe Skovdahl, Steven Paterson and Jimmy Calderwood all had various amounts of time in charge.

He played in the Aberdeen side that lost to Celtic in the Scottish League Cup final in 2000 and in the same season lost out to Rangers 4-0 in the Scottish Cup final, when striker Robbie Winters had to play in goals for some of the game after Jim Leighton picked up an injury. He was a real star for Aberdeen and who knows, one day, he may return to the club as a player. Stranger things have happened.

Over recent years nobody really personifies the spirit of Aberdeen than Zander Diamond who I was very disappointed to see leave the club. Big Zander is a real character who is larger than life both on and off the pitch. He is never shy of making his views known and I liked the big man.

He was always in the wars and I remember in his first match against Rangers at Ibrox back in 2003 when he was given a red card for fouling Shota Arveladze. He can't give anything less than 100 per cent and because of that he got his fair share of cards from refs.

He was a real unpolished Diamond, if you pardon the pun, but he was a real fans favourite because of his attitude to every tackle and to every game.

To be honest he had gone off the boil a bit before he left us but that does not take away all he achieved during his time at Pittodrie. He is the sort of central defender who wore his heart on his sleeve and I like that sort of player.

Zander didn't make the cut for my Dream Team but when you realise the two men who are my first choice central defenders you will understand why. In modern football my Dream Team pairing would be worth tens of millions of pounds to any top team. As a partnership I would say they would be the best in the world.

The first is a man I played alongside for many years for Aberdeen and Scotland and who took a few broken noses and hard knocks to keep strikers away from me and Jim Leighton. Alex McLeish, or 'Big Eck' as we all know him, was one of the greatest central defenders the Scottish game has ever produced.

Picking him for my Dream Team was probably the easiest choice of my outfield players. He is easily the best centre half that Aberdeen or for that matter Scotland has ever produced. He was fantastic in the air and could handle whatever was thrown at him. He put his head in where others feared to go, which is probably why I am so good looking nowadays and the big man has all the scars.

He is also my Dream Team captain as a stronger leader you could not find. I know I had the armband when we played together but at least he was close enough to me to learn a few things! Only joking Eck, honest.

Alex has what I would call an inner grit to him. For instance his decision to leave Birmingham City to join Aston Villa took guts. If anyone could deal with the fall-out from such a decision and even diffuse it a bit with some conciliatory words it is Alex. He always had great people skills, both as a player and a manager, and could get people on his side.

He has had a steely determination about him all the years that I have known him and he needed that to make it to the top and stay there for so long. As my Dream Team captain if we had any setbacks, which is unlikely with the side I have picked, he has the character to handle adverse situations and help the team come out the other side.

As you would expect Alex was a bit raw to begin with but became a much better player when he got older. When I first met him he was spotty-faced, gingery, thin and full of nervous energy. Now he is older and has hardly any ginger hair left, but he is still thin.

When we played together he would make the tackle, win the header and I would drop off and try and cover elsewhere. He never flinched once on the park in all the years we played together. Doug Rougvie, who I will come to later, was brave but more in a senseless kamikaze sort of way. Alex could see what was coming and although he still took the knocks he could read the danger ahead and he took the knocks to save certain goals, rather than for the sake of it.

His natural height advantage over most strikers, coupled with his superb timing and bravery, meant that when we played together I always ranked him as the best header of the ball from the long clearance anywhere in the world. He wasn't too great to begin with when it came to his directional headers away from goal from a set piece, but hard work made him better in that department than most other centre-backs in the game.

Like me he grew up in Glasgow and came to the club in 1976 when Ally MacLeod was manager but he was given his debut by Billy McNeill, albeit because Billy wanted to drop Willie Garner for celebrating too much one New Year before a big game. It was Alex

Ferguson that put Alex and me together in the centre of the Aberdeen defence on a regular basis.

People always think of big Eck as a tough, ruthless defender which he was, but he was also a clever player who had a sharp mind and a quick wit off the park. He trained as an accountant and he is one of those guys who would have been a success regardless of what career path he decided to follow.

We remain good friends to this day and roomed together with Aberdeen and Scotland despite the fact Alex claims I used to keep him awake all night with my snoring, as I see he has publicly claimed for the first time in the foreword to this book.

That was nothing compared to him banging doors as he used to go out on his midnight walks all over the hotel. Alex could never sit still and was always nipping into the room next door, regardless of the time, to see what was going on when I was trying to get my beauty sleep.

We hardly ever fell out despite living in each others pockets for so long and any small flare ups between us being on the pitch in the heat of the battle never, ever continued after the match.

The only time I think we nearly came to blows was against Dundee United, which Alex also mentions in his foreword. To summarise we blamed each other for not marking the correct striker. It wasn't exactly a Mohammed Ali against George Foreman type face-off and we burst out laughing when we looked at each other before a punch was thrown. What amazed us was rather than getting a bollocking from Sir Alex at half-time he praised us for being so committed.

Those of you with long memories will remember that Alex and I used to always do our pre-match warm-up sessions together in a corner of the pitch. We always worked as a pair passing the ball back to each other and helping each other with heading practise. In a way, and I have spoken to Alex about this, it became a bit of a superstition for both of us. We had to do it because we felt it was bad luck if we didn't.

On the pitch we had a natural understanding and it wasn't

something we had to work on too much. There was a football chemistry there and we seemed to be able to read each others minds on who to mark and when to move across the defence to cover for each other. The few times strikers broke past Alex they had run out of gas by the time they reached me because he would have been snapping at their heels and still trying to make life difficult for them.

Alex also used to come in handy for me at the coin toss. I had a terrible memory for names and sometimes I had to ask him the name of the opposing captain. It got such a regular occurrence that he even whispered in my ear when we played Celtic that I was about to shake hands with my old pal Danny McGrain. That was one of the few times I turned round to him and said: 'Yes, Alex, I know.'

We played around 500 games together for Aberdeen and more than forty times we formed the central defensive partnership for Scotland so we must have been doing something right.

On our day, and I'm not blowing our own trumpet here, we could handle any attackers who came our way, including top men like Mark Hughes, Ian Rush or Karl-Heinz Rummenigge. Like me, Alex wasn't the quickest but his mind was sharp which meant he always had half a yard on opponents.

As well as being partners in defence we were also partners in song – once that got Sir Alex furious. We were having a party at my house and decided for reasons best known to ourselves to serenade Sir Alex to sleep at two o'clock in the morning.

Alex introduced us down the phone as the Mike Sammes Singers, who were a British vocal group from the 1960s to the 1980s, and we gave Sir Alex a chorus of 'Delilah'. He was not happy. I knew he would give us a hellish time at training on the Monday morning for waking him up.

Now as you might realise by this point in the book, I was never the best trainer in the world and on that Monday morning I made some excuse about my car packing in and was late turning up. It was a good decision. When I did arrive Alex, my partner in the Mike Sammes Singers, was running round the hills at Seaton Park as a punishment which was hard enough to do at the best at times. What made it worse was that he had Sir Alex on his case nipping his head. I wasn't totally exempt from his anger and he had a wee go at me back in the changing room when he came back from training but he had let out most of his anger on big Eck and I got off relatively easily.

Alex played 696 games during his seventeen years at Pittodrie and scored some vital goals along the way. The one I keep hearing about to this day was his curling shot into the corner of the net against Rangers in the 1982 Scottish Cup final. To be honest if it had been scored by a Brazilian the world would have been talking about his great strike. But as a few of my mates said at the time not many Brazilian's have plukes and ginger hair so there was no mistaking that the goal had been scored by a Scotsman.

His goal cancelled out a John MacDonald goal for Rangers and took the game into extra-time during which we ran the show and won 4-1. Alex was so full of himself after his great goal I kept winding him up and said it was a hit and hope lucky strike. Then he reminded me that three days beforehand during a training session at Cruden Bay he had hit a similar free-kick into the net. History had repeated itself and nobody was more pleased than Alex who claimed he had planned to curl the winner into the corner all along. Aye right!

To give the big man his due he also scored a vital goal in our European Cup Winners' Cup second leg quarter-final against Bayern Munich in 1983 to make the score 2-2 which set things up for a thrilling finish to the match in which John Hewitt scored the winner.

For all his laid-back, fun approach to life away from football Alex was a man who never wanted to let his team down. He even played through the pain barrier in our famous European Cup Winners' Cup final win over Real Madrid.

We kept it quiet at the time but the big daftie hurt his back trying to move heavy paving stones at his home. Even the workmen he had employed to help him said it would take both of them to lift one, but despite that one day before they arrived Alex tried to move some himself with disastrous results.

He badly injured his back and had to get extensive treatment on it before we left to fly to Gothenburg. Our physio Roland Arnott had to work overtime to make sure the pain was bearable and the club made sure Alex got the best seat on the plane with plenty of leg room for the flight.

When we got there I was sharing with him and he turned our bedroom into a scene from Casualty. There were rubs and all sorts all over the floor. Alex was never the tidiest at the best of times but this time he really took the biscuit.

On top of that he decided he couldn't sleep in his bed even after trying to put a wooden board under the mattress to make it harder. In the end he spent the two nights before the game sleeping on the bare floor of our hotel room with a duvet cover over him and me doing my best not to step on top of him if I needed the loo during the night.

Because I made it clear I would not be picking myself in my Dream Team the man who would partner Alex in the centre of defence is Martin Buchan, who was one of the classiest players to ever grace Pittodrie.

Martin will always have a place in the history books as the only player to captain both Scottish and English FA Cup winning sides. Every Dons fan will know about how he lifted the trophy after the famous win over Celtic in 1970 and seven years later he lifted the English FA Cup with Manchester United after they beat Liverpool 2-1. He was also in the Manchester United side that lost one of the greatest finals in FA Cup history 3-2 when a late Alan Sunderland goal won Arsenal the trophy.

Like Alex McLeish he was a real brainbox and the Buchan/McLeish central defensive partnership would be good enough to keep out attackers and also win a few rounds of Mastermind into the bargain.

Although he left school at seventeen just three days into his sixth year, he already had the grades to get into Aberdeen University but

The proudest moment of my football career was lifting the European Cup Winners' Cup with Aberdeen.

Stuart Kennedy was a magnificent all-round defender for Aberdeen and Scotland and the main reason I never had to worry about the opposition left winger.

You will never find a safer pair of hands than Jim Leighton's. He is the most consistent goalkeeper Aberdeen has ever had.

Not many players got the better of big Alex McLeish. Brave and strong with a great football brain, he was always half a yard ahead of the opposition.

Big Eck and I were close as players but not usually this close!

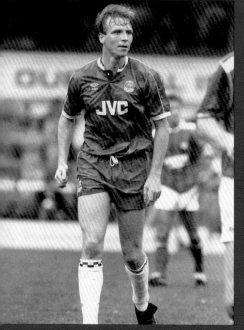

John McMaster was one of the most under-rated players of his generation.

You couldn't get a more class act than Martin Buchan who captained Aberdeen to the famous 1970 Scottish Cup final win over Celtic.

On his day Gordon Strachan was one of the greatest midfield players in the world.

Jim Bett was never flustered and stamped his authority on matches.

Being part of a successful Aberdeen team meant that players like Gordon Strachan and I were regularly called up for Scotland duty.

Sir Alex Ferguson used to say if Peter Weir played well then Aberdeen played well. He was absolutely right.

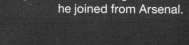

Way back I described Joe
Harper as being as important to
Aberdeen as North Sea oil and I
stand by every word.

'Champagne' Charlie Nicholas
gave the club a huge lift when
he joined from Arsenal.

You won't find a deadlier finisher than
Mark McGhee who could always be relied
on to score vital goals.

There is no question in my mind that Sir Alex Ferguson is the greatest manager of all time.

Dick Donald was a great club chairman who fully supported Sir Alex during his time at Pittodrie.

The heart and soul of the club was always Teddy Scott (right) who is pictured presenting a crystal decanter to Alec Young to celebrate his induction into the Aberdeen Hall of Fame.

As an assistant manager there can be no better than Archie Knox who was a great support to Sir Alex Ferguson and Craig Brown.

Duncan Shearer was one of the club's most prolific strikers and came back to Pittodrie as assistant manager under Steve Paterson.

Stewart McKimmie was a fabulous Aberdeen captain who was one of the best defenders the club ever had.

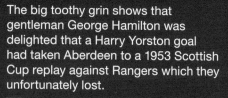

Bobby Clark's dream was to win the Scottish League championship with Aberdeen and you can see the pride in his eyes as he holds the trophy aloft after he helped us secure it in 1980.

The big toothy grin shows that gentleman George Hamilton was delighted that a Harry Yorston goal had taken Aberdeen to a 1953 Scottish Cup replay against Rangers which they unfortunately lost.

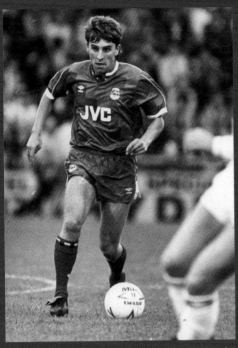

They may have called John Hewitt supersub after his winning goal in the European Cup Winners' Cup final over Real Madrid but there was a lot more to his game than that.

The fact that Steve Archibald scored goals at Tottenham Hotspur and Barcelona after he left Aberdeen shows how talented he was.

Big Frank McDougall was absolutely lethal in front of goal and it was an absolute tragedy that injury cut short his career.

I have huge respect for Sir Alex Ferguson. Even now I could never call him Fergie as that sounds disrespectful. He will always be boss, gaffer or Sir Alex to me!

Flanked by Eric Black and John Hewitt, I get my hands on the European Cup Winners' Cup once again at a gala dinner in Aberdeen in 2008.

Out of all the tributes I got from the fans through the years the picture of me looking like Che Guevara is the one that made me smile the most.

he chose football instead and signed for Aberdeen from the Banks O'Dee in 1965. He had to wait less than a year to make his debut which came in a 1-1 away draw against Dunfermline at East End Park on October 8, 1966.

Under the watchful eye of Eddie Turnbull he turned into a top-class sweeper who could read a game superbly well. Martin was a cool customer under pressure and I remember watching him as a young apprentice and marvelling at how he organised his defence.

Martin came from good football stock with his dad Martin senior also playing for Aberdeen at inside forward in the late 1930s, before going on to play for Buckie Thistle for twelve years, and his brother George also played for Aberdeen.

During his playing days Martin was known as Elvis because whenever Aberdeen travelled to away games he took his guitar. He was also quick-witted and according to Gordon Strachan, who was credited with first using the jibe, the first person to actually answer a reporter's request for a quick word with the one word answer 'velocity'.

Because of his supreme confidence he was given the captaincy a month short of his twenty-first birthday in February 1970 and just three months later became the youngest ever captain of a Scottish Cup winning team. He won the first of thirty-four Scotland caps when he was at Pittodrie against Belgium and finished in a winning team after John O'Hare of Derby County scored the only goal of the game. He went on to play for Scotland in both the 1974 and 1978 World Cup finals.

Martin had six seasons at Pittodrie during which time he played 192 times and scored eleven goals but those statistics only tell part of the story of his influence on the club. He remains one of the greatest defenders in Aberdeen history and a man who, when I first joined the club, people talked about in reverential tones.

Martin and I may have played in the same position but we were very different characters. Martin was quick with his responses while I was much more measured or quieter if you like. Eddie Turnbull used to say Martin's problem was that his brains were all in his head.

I remember Stuart Kennedy coming back from the 1978 World Cup and telling me a great story about Martin who had been asked to stay in one sub-standard hotel room once too often by the SFA. He turned to Stuart and said: 'Stuart, why don't we leave our room doors open and hope someone will break in and decorate the place.'

Like all great defenders Martin was an organiser and a good talker. He was a man who called the shots and nobody was allowed to cross him. Aberdeen were well known in his day for playing a high and square line in defence and shouting for offside a lot. See, it wasn't just me who used to do that.

It was Martin's responsibility to push the other defenders up or pull them back. He kept it simple and made sure the back division moved as a unit. He did it superbly well and I learned a lot from watching him in action. So if I tried to play offside a bit too much for your liking when I was at Aberdeen, blame Martin. I learned my trade watching the master.

Ironically a combination of an injury to Henning Boel and Martin's move to Manchester United gave me my big chance in the first team.

Jimmy Bonthrone had bought Eddie Thomson from Hearts to replace him but it never worked out and he ended up playing in midfield and yours truly took over from Martin. I had big shoes to fill and maybe knowing that pushed me on even more to prove myself in my early days at the club.

Manchester United manager Frank O'Farrell paid £125,000 for Martin and in turn he also had big shoes to fill when he became captain at Old Trafford following the retirement of Bobby Charlton, but he did so with aplomb and good grace. After leaving United, Martin had a brief spell as a player with Oldham Athletic and an equally brief time in management with Burnley in 1985.

As I said earlier I have Sir Alex Ferguson to thank for helping my career to flourish and Martin feels the same about Eddie Turnbull. At Eddie's funeral in May 2011, he told mourners in an eloquent speech how his faith in him as a player shaped his career and the rest of his life during an address at his memorial service. Martin Buchan will never forget Eddie Turnbull. For what he did for Aberdeen Football Club I like to think every fan will always remember the class of Martin Buchan and it is a privilege to name him in my Dream Team.

6

BY THE LEFT

The left back position caused a lot of problems to Aberdeen managers, including Sir Alex Ferguson, through the years. I don't want anybody to take this the wrong way, but although there have been many reliable players that have worn the number three jersey there weren't too many good enough to be considered for my Dream Team.

Even in our very best Aberdeen side the left back position caused me so much concern that I tended to overcompensate and play on the left side of defence to provide cover in that area allowing Alex McLeish to drift right when required.

The right back position with Stuart Kennedy there looked after itself but on the other side of the pitch we struggled a bit. Obviously everything is relative because we still won major honours despite the fact a lot of teams targeted us down our right flank.

My Dream Team left back choice may surprise many of you who associate him with another position but he is far and away the outstanding candidate in my eyes.

Before I get round to naming him can I pay tribute to the other players who did enter my thoughts which include a true Aberdeen cult hero and a man who was an exciting player to watch despite the fact he left us to join Rangers!

One man who I know for a fact had a great attitude to the game and was a top-class player into the bargain was Jim Hermiston as he was at the club during my early years at Pittodrie. Teddy Scott told me many times that the best left back he had worked with during Eddie Turnbull's time in charge was Jim.

He left a big impression on many people, none more so it seems than BBC Sports broadcaster Richard Gordon who has named him at left back in his Aberdeen Dream Team later in the book.

To be honest I can understand why he gets the nod from Richard. I trained alongside Jim for most of the 1972/73 season and he was an impressive character. He had a real physical presence about him and was a tough tackling, no-nonsense defender.

He was most definitely not one of those left backs who was scared to cross the half-way line and more often than not I would see Jim linking up with the midfielders.

Jim was signed by Eddie Turnbull from Bonnyrigg Rose in 1965 and made his debut in a 2-0 win over Ayr United the following year. Remember I said the left back position caused lots of Aberdeen managers all sorts of problems? An indication of that comes from the fact that Jim played up until the start of the 1969/70 season at right back before Eddie moved him across to fill in at left back to see him through an injury crisis. Jim made such a big impact that he played there in the Aberdeen team that gained immortality by winning the Scottish Cup in 1970.

He kept growing in stature and went on to captain the side under Eddie before Martin Buchan came on the scene. Jim was playing at left back when I made my debut against Morton in April 1973 and was great to play alongside.

It was a big blow to Jim not to make the Scotland 1974 World Cup squad, especially with his ability to play either side of the defence, and I could see that affected him and made him a bit disillusioned with the game. After a proposed transfer to Chelsea, which may have revitalised him, broke down he retired from the game at the age of just twenty-seven to join Grampian Police in 1975. In 270 appearances for Aberdeen he managed to score sixteeen times which is a decent return for a full back who could also play in midfield when required. There is a story that when we won the

Scottish League Cup in November 1976 Jim was one of the officers who was walking ahead of the bus as it went down Union Street. I must confess I didn't see him but it must have been a bit of a weird feeling for him if that were the case, and maybe Jim liked to blend into the background on that occasion.

He emigrated to Australia in 1977 where he resumed his football career which he combined with his time in the Queensland police force. He played football for Grange Thistle and the Brisbane Lions and became such a respected football figure that he had a children's coaching manual published under his name. He was so highly thought of that the Australian FA tried to pave the way for him to play for their national side, but the fact he played forty-five minutes for the Scotland Under-23 team in 1969 killed his dream of turning out for his adopted country.

He remained a highly respected police officer to the extent that in 1999 he was presented with a bravery award after intervening in a bank robbery while off duty.

Another full back from yesteryear that caught my eye was Don Emery, a man who reputedly had one of the hardest shots ever seen at Pittodrie. The Welshman, like Jim Hermiston, could play at right back or left back and because we have an embarrassment of riches at number two I have moved him across to consider him at the other side of the park.

Don only played at Aberdeen because he fell in love and married local girl, Maude Cheyne, when he was serving in the army down south and she was working near his barracks. Although he started his career at Swindon he came north in 1948 as Maude was homesick.

Believe it or not but newspapers of his time claim that Don hit a free-kick against Morton from thirty-five yards out that hit the back of the net with such power it rebounded without bouncing to the eighteen-yard line. Don clearly didn't know his own strength as Aberdeen goalkeeper Fred Martin maintains he was left with a badly bent finger for the rest of his life after Don hammered a shot towards him in training. Don was supposedly wearing training shoes at the time. There is even a story, unconfirmed, that a Celtic goalkeeper refused to face an Emery penalty and another that he split the Partick Thistle crossbar in two.

What I love about Don's approach to penalties was the fact that it was so straight forward. If Aberdeen got a spot-kick one of the players, usually Harry Yorston, put it on the spot for him. Don lumbered up from defence when he was ready and ran in a straight line and didn't stop for a second to work out where he was going to place the ball.

A bit like Forrest Gump in the Hollywood movie of the same name he just kept running and running. When he reached the ball he just belted it hard, mostly into the net. It was a simple technique that worked as penalties made up the vast majority of the twenty-five goals he scored in eighty-nine appearances for the club.

That is a pretty good run for a full-back who stood just five feet eight inches tall and was well over thirteen stone. He wasn't fast but he was effective as a defender and as a dead ball expert he was one of the best ever. Don moved to East Fife where he won the Scottish League Cup in the same side as future Aberdeen manager Jimmy Bonthrone but he never forgot the club where he made his name. When he retired he became a very successful businessman who drove a big Mercedes with part of the registration plate reading DON. Depending on what mood he was in he would tell people he had bought it because that was his name but others he would tell it was his tribute to Aberdeen Football Club. I like the second explanation best.

Way back before the First Word War there were other fascinating characters who played at left back like Charlie 'Oor ba' McGill who played from 1931 to 1938 and earned his nickname because he was very territorial. Any ball that went out on the left side he had to take the throw-ins or likewise any free-kicks on that side of the pitch. I'm not entirely sure I could have handled that sort of attitude too well if I was playing alongside him.

Kevin McNaughton was a player who was at Aberdeen all too briefly and I felt he was one of our top young players when Jimmy

Calderwood was in charge. He was given a chance in the first team by Ebbe Skovdahl in the year 2000 as an eighteen-year-old. In only his second season he was named Scotland's Young Player of the Year and the award was merited.

I notice Chris Cusiter, the Scotland rugby star, has named him in his Aberdeen Dream Team and I can see why the younger generation would have enjoyed watching Kevin play.

He was an incredibly exciting player who sadly we lost to Cardiff City where he became an important part of their squad and every time I see him play I am still impressed.

As I said earlier the left back position caused Sir Alex lots of headaches but to be fair to him he bought well in that position. The two men he brought to Pittodrie before he went to Manchester United turned out to be real finds.

Tommy McQueen was signed by the gaffer in 1984 from Clyde after Doug Rougvie (more of big Doug later) signed for Chelsea and started all but three of the thirty-six Premier Division games in his first season.

He was in the team that won the 1986 Scottish Cup final by beating Hearts 3-0, but a leg break three months into the following season was a major setback for him. When he returned to action Sir Alex had gone to Old Trafford and Ian Porterfield had started to regularly play another Sir Alex signing at left back in his place.

The man in question, David Robertson, did leave us to join Rangers in the end but nobody's perfect! He was one of the best teenage players in Britain when he made his breakthrough at the age of just seventeen at the start of the 1986/87 season when Tommy McQueen was injured.

I always felt pretty comfortable playing alongside David despite his lack of experience. He was lightning fast, and the way he bombed up and down the wing reminded me of Stuart Kennedy who did the same with incredible regularity on the right flank.

David was in the 1990 team that won the Scottish League Cup by beating Rangers 2-1 and was also in the side that famously beat Celtic 9-8 in the penalty shoot-out that decided the Scottish Cup final that same season. A year later he was part of the team that ran Rangers close in the league with only a 2-0 last day of the season defeat to them at Ibrox costing us the title.

Unfortunately David left at the age of just twenty-two to go to Rangers for £970,000 in 1991, which was a huge blow to the club but in those short few years he did enough to convince me he was one of the most talented left backs to play at Pittodrie. I was surprised he didn't win more than the three Scotland caps he picked up and it was a shame for him that injury cut short his career with Leeds United who he joined after leaving Rangers.

Commitment is something you need in football so can I give an honourable mention in my Dream Team discussions to Billy Smith. No, he was never a household name at Pittodrie but I take my hat off to him for breaking off his wedding celebrations to play for the Dons.

On August 12, 1953 he was married in Garthdee Church and then jumped in a cab in his morning suit and top hat to play left back against Airdrie in the Scottish League Cup. Maybe his bride didn't see it this way at the time but the fact they won 2-0 made him interrupting the proceedings worthwhile in my view. At the end of the game Billy jumped in the bath, slicked back his hair, stuck his morning suit back on and was in time for the start of his own wedding reception in the Palace Restaurant.

But the story does not end there. His bride got a one night honeymoon in the Highlands before he was back for the Wednesday night away League Cup tie against East Fife that Aberdeen lost 2-0.

Billy was a vital player for Aberdeen at the time and one of the most versatile players around in the early 1950s. As well as playing regularly at left back he also turned out at centre half, inside-right and twice took the place of injured goalkeeper Fred Martin during matches. He was left back in the League championship winning side of 1954/55 when he played twenty-five out of the thirty league games but two broken legs in quick succession – the first against Clyde in the Scottish Cup semi-final of 1955 – unfortunately was the beginning of the end of his career at Aberdeen.

Like Billy, Doug Rougvie was a hugely charismatic character and I would argue Aberdeen's biggest ever cult hero. I retain a lot of affection for Doug who as a player would have laid his life on the line for his beloved Aberdeen Football Club. For such a big, physical tough guy he was a real gentle giant off the field. Don't get me wrong, if he was riled and got angry he was ferocious, but overall he managed to vent his anger only on the opposition.

The only time Doug was found wanting as a player was when he was trying to do things on the football field he was not capable of carrying out. He was a competent player but trying to dribble from deep in his own half did nothing for my blood pressure.

Doug was one of the bravest, craziest defenders I ever played alongside and one of my first memories of him showed how fearless and mad he was at times. At a training camp at Gordonstoun School in the Highlands we were larking about in the swimming pool one day when Doug saw a kayak in one of the poolside cupboards.

He had never been in one in his life but got it into his head that he fancied trying to do an Eskimo roll. Now remember we were at a school so this was a kid's kayak, which was why it was such a tight fit for Doug who stood well over six foot two inches tall. He squeezed in and managed to do a few strokes with his paddle before upturning the kayak, losing his balance and plunging under the water.

Not surprisingly he struggled to get back up to the surface. First we saw his head and shoulders pop up for a few seconds before he went under again. It soon became evident that Doug was not coming up at all and needed rescued, otherwise he would drown as he could not physically get out of the kayak as it was such a tight fit.

Four or five of us joined the rescue party into the pool to get him out and let me tell you it was not easy. We just about managed to get the big lump upright in his kayak which we then pulled to the side of the pool before yanking him out.

When we got him back to dry land he was really short of breath as his lungs had filled up with water. We were all damn sure we weren't going to give the big man the kiss of life so we slapped him on the back instead. We seemed more shaken than him after his escapade. He simply got up off the poolside floor, thanked us politely, and walked away for a shower. It was as if nothing had happened.

It was the same on the pitch. He never let anything bother him at all. Even with opposition fans baying for his blood he would simply smile. He was a man who knew how to wind them up big-time, which he did superbly every time we played Celtic in Glasgow. At Parkhead all of us with a bit of sanity would all do our warm-ups in front of the Aberdeen fans. Apart from Doug of course.

He would be sprinting up and down directly in front of the old north stand which was known as The Jungle and which was home to some of the most passionate Celtic fans who would give him dog's abuse as he did his sprints and stretching under their noses. Being left back meant that when the match kicked off there was no escape for he was right next to the Celtic support on either wing, as the Aberdeen fans were behind the goal. The abuse aimed primarily against him continued – especially if we were winning – but it did not bother Doug. I had seen some left backs crumble through the pressure of playing in front of The Jungle but that never happened to him. The more abuse they shouted at him the more he raised his game.

By his own admission he was not the most skilful footballer but in terms of commitment remains one of the best and most passionate to have played for the club. I always had an affinity with big Doug partly because I was responsible for him having to play left back, or sometimes right back, rather than his favoured central defensive role.

He joined us from Dunfermline Athletic in 1972 as a central defender but couldn't get a game because there were a lot of guys in front of him like me. He was farmed out to local Highland League side Keith to get more experience before he made his debut as a midfielder against Celtic on August 9, 1975 when Ally McLeod was manager. He still had plans to play centre half but with Alex

McLeish and myself around it was only when Sir Alex took over and moved him to left back did he get a regular run in the team, starting in the 1979/80 season which was when we won the league. He did play centre half alongside me in one game when Alex McLeish was injured in a 1-1 home draw against Partick Thistle but mostly he played left back.

Being a regular helped Doug's confidence and he started to score some vital goals for us. He also showed his ability to move across the backline at ease at crucial times.

For instance, when we were 2-1 down in the famous European Cup Winners' Cup quarter-final against Bayern Munich in 1982/83 season he was moved during the game from left back to right back in a tactical switch by Sir Alex.

Doug was known as the Ballingry Bat because he came from Ballingry in Fife and looked like a giant bat with his arms and legs outstretched when he used to hit the deck after a tackle. For a while we also called him Dougie Rummenigge after we played Bayern Munich in the European Cup Winners' Cup tie that I mentioned earlier. It was a wholly ironic name as Rummenigge was soft on his feet, had a light touch and could glide past players, which with the best will in the world Doug never could.

Although he was a real tough guy on the pitch in terms of tackling he had broad enough shoulders to take personal criticism. On the times when I had to give him a good blast for losing concentration he would simply say, 'Yes, sir,' and never argue back.

He was also a strong enough character to take being the brunt of a few jokes as well. I remember at the height of Aberdeen's fame some of us did adverts for cars and hotels. What did Doug endorse? Cream-cakes. Yup, cream-cakes from a local bakery. Imagine a diet-conscious player trying to get away with that nowadays? He got a lot of leg-pulling about the advertisements that ran on local radio when he confessed to the listeners: 'Yes, it is true I have a weakness and it's for cream-cakes.'

We used to wind him up a few days before games and tell him the easiest way for the opposition winger to get the better of him would be to carry a tray of cream-cakes onto the pitch as he would find them irresistible and would put him off his game.

Doug also had the worst singing voice I have ever heard, and that is something coming from someone as tone deaf as me. As part of our European Cup Winners' Cup campaign we recorded a song called 'The European Song' which wasn't the best. It was recorded at North Sound studios in the Kingsgate in Aberdeen and to be honest only Alex McLeish from memory had anything resembling a singing voice.

Doug was at a mike with his close pal Andy Watson for the recording session and the minute Doug tried to sing Andy fell about in tears of laughter. He told me later Doug sounded like a demented walrus.

As a gentle giant he never knew his own strength and Alex McLeish reminded me of a hilarious encounter with big Doug during a holiday in Majorca which earned him the nickname Sheriff Rougvie. He was a big fan of Westerns and lived out his cowboy fantasies by hiring a horse, sticking on a cowboy hat and taking off into the Majorcan sunset.

Only the horse didn't want to move with such a big hulk on his back which meant Doug had to give him a friendly slap on the head. Now for Doug a friendly slap on the head must have felt like being punched hard for the poor horse.

For the first few times the horse was fine but not surprisingly got sick of Doug's 'friendly slap' and tried to bite his hand every time he went near its head and even tried to buck Doug off his back. The horse had the last laugh and would not break into a trot which meant Doug had to walk him back to the hotel stables. It wasn't exactly the John Wayne stuff that Doug had in mind but everyone had a laugh at his attempts to be a cowboy.

Also I remember when Jimmy Bonthrone was manager back in 1974 he decided to take us on a pre-season tour to far off places like Iran and New Caledonia, which is a small island in the south-west Pacific.

Doug always loved his British food and clearly thought to himself he would starve in such places, so turned up at Aberdeen Airport with a separate suitcase full of cornflakes, tomato sauce and rashers of bacon. Not surprisingly the big man wasn't allowed to take his food stash out of the country.

To me Doug deserved all the great support he got from the Aberdeen fans through the years as he was a really endearing character. I still remember the sound of 'Rooogveee! Rooogvee!' echoing round Pittodrie whenever he touched the ball.

Because big Doug was so harum-scarum he sometimes was on the end of a blast from Sir Alex. One day the gaffer blew his top when Doug turned up at training on a motorbike he had bought with the bonus money he got for helping us win the 1980 Scottish Premier League. Sir Alex rated Doug highly and didn't want his left back falling off his motorbike so he was ordered in no uncertain terms never to get on it again until he left Aberdeen Football Club. To be fair to Doug, I don't think he ever did, at least that is what Sir Alex was led to believe.

But the sting in the tail was that Doug decided to buy a pushbike instead rather than a motorbike to keep Sir Alex happy. And what happened? A few years later he got knocked off it by a lorry and required hospital treatment only two days before the 1984 Scottish Cup final against Celtic, although thankfully he was not seriously injured and was fit enough to play and celebrate our 2-1 win. That could have only happened to Doug.

One of the last things I remember about Doug before he left the club was when one of his false teeth fell out of his mouth and into the crowd below as he was on the open-top bus after our Scottish Cup final win over Celtic in 1984. The bus had to stop as Doug shouted down to the fans to look for his false tooth. Luckily nobody stood on it and I remember someone throwing it back up to him and us all giving him room to pick it up off the floor and stick it back in his mouth. Charming.

Doug was no stranger to lengthy bans which interrupted his Aberdeen career but he was never dirty, just occasionally he mistimed tackles like the rest of us all did. But being such a big man who could be very clumsy at times his challenges usually looked worse than they were. He was also sometimes wronged against, the biggest example of that coming in the Scottish League Cup final of 1979.

To this day I don't believe he deserved to be red-carded following a penalty box incident involving Derek Johnstone, who Doug said had dived and conned the referee. The big man became the first player to be ever sent off in the final of the League Cup and that was an ordering off that was very wrong. To make matters worse we lost 2-1.

When Stuart Kennedy was forced to retire after our European Cup Winners' Cup win it showed the versatility of Doug that he managed to move across and fill in at right back for a while before he left us to join Chelsea for £150,000 on the recommendation of former Aberdeen player Ian McNeill who was the assistant manager at Stamford Bridge. Not having him around the club was hard to take for us all because he was such an influential and fun figure who brought a smile to the Aberdeen dressing room.

He was part of a high profile Chelsea side that included the likes of Kerry Dixon, David Speedie and Pat Nevin who were all incredibly skilful players. He made his debut for the club in the opening game of the season against Arsenal at Highbury and I remember he put Viv Anderson up in the air within the first few minutes with a ferocious tackle. He hasn't lost it, I thought to myself, as I watched the tackle replayed in slow motion on Match of the Day.

Although he moved to Chelsea it was clear that Doug cared passionately about Aberdeen Football Club. He was maybe not the best footballer but a great servant of the club and a man I felt privileged to play alongside.

Overall he spent nine good seasons at Aberdeen which was one more than Ally Shewan who was another left back who I considered for my Dream Team. Ally had a remarkable playing record that anyone would have been proud of. He signed for the Dons from junior club Formartine in 1960 and spent a couple of seasons in the reserves but then made the left back position his own. From October 19, 1963 until August 30, 1969 he did not miss a single league game and in doing so beat Willie Cooper's post war record of 162 straight league appearances.

I have to take my hat off to Ally for playing so many games in a row. I know from experience how hard it is to escape injury or loss of form but Ally appeared to have overcome both obstacles. He was a left back who tackled hard and who could be relied upon by the rest of the defence not to make many mistakes. He is a member of the Aberdeen Hall of Fame and thoroughly deserves his place in that august body.

Now let me turn my attention to the man I have chosen as my left back in my Aberdeen Dream Team. Some of you may know John McMaster as a left midfield player but I knew him also as a left back and that is where I want to play him.

He was an absolutely superb left back and also an equally talented midfield player, so if any of my Dream Team midfield men got injured he would step forward to fill their shoes and I know I could rely on him to do a great job.

John beats the likes of David Robertson, Doug Rougvie and Jim Hermiston to the Dream Team left back spot due to his superb use of the ball. He hardly ever wasted a pass and could land a football on a sixpence. During training his pinpoint accuracy was incredible to watch. Even under pressure he kept up the same level of consistency when it came to his passing. For me John had the sweetest left foot in the business apart from maybe Davie Cooper.

Although I said I always worried about the left back spot at Aberdeen I did a lot less, and sometimes not at all, when John was playing there which he did a lot from 1982 to 1984 and also in the European Cup Winners' Cup final.

John was a Greenock boy who joined us in April 1972, the same month I had made my debut against his hometown club Morton at Cappielow. John paid his dues before he broke through to the first team and had three seasons in the reserves before he made his debut also against Morton when he came on as a substitute in an easy 3-0 win on April 19, 1975, a result that would not have pleased his local relatives. Ally MacLeod gave him a run on the left side of midfield to begin with, and occasionally at left back and from that moment on John was a vital member of the Aberdeen first team squad.

Billy McNeill, who took over from Ally, also rated him highly as a player when he was manager and gave him regular games. Although they had faith in him it was when Alex Ferguson took over that John McMaster really flourished in Aberdeen colours.

He was an important player for us all through Sir Alex's time in charge and although he played mostly in midfield in the 1979/80 season when we won the Scottish League championship he was also used at left back in the coming seasons.

As well as being a great passer of the ball some of his goals from well outside the box were more than a match for anything Roberto Carlos scored from left back for Brazil. Granted John wasn't the fastest player on earth but he was one of the most intelligent and that allowed him to read the game better than most players.

He also showed great resilience after picking up two horrific injuries that lesser players would have struggled to come back from. First Willie Johnston of Rangers stood on his neck during a League Cup tie at Ibrox in September 1980, and although people thought our physio Roland Arnott had to give him the kiss of life that wasn't the case. Roland had the presence of mind to rush onto the park without asking the referee as John had swallowed his tongue and needed it released.

John got a huge scare over that incident but recovered enough to play for us against Liverpool at Pittodrie in the first leg of a European Cup tie a month later. Now I don't know what John had done in a previous life to get so much bad treatment but against Liverpool he was in the wars again. He picked up the ball in our own half and beat two men before Ray Kennedy went over the ball and caught him on the knee in one of the worst tackles I have seen in my life. Kennedy wasn't even booked for his actions which was ridiculous.

There were worries that John may never walk again and he

needed an immediate knee operation. Doctors recommended he should never play again but thankfully John was never good at taking advice. Although he was out of the game for a whole season he was such a dedicated player it didn't surprise me when he returned to action two games into the 1981/82 season when he came off the bench against Celtic at Pittodrie.

When he did make his comeback Sir Alex told John, who as I said was never the quickest but was versatile, he should drop back from midfield into the left back position on a permanent basis. From then on in he was our left back most of the time, sometimes alternating with Doug Rougvie who could also play on the right.

There are certain little incidents that John will always be remembered for by the fans. For instance who can forget his Laurel and Hardy act with Gordon Strachan in the quarter-final win over Bayern Munich at Pittodrie the year we won the European Cup Winners' Cup.

He had come on as a second half substitute, and with us 2-1 down confused the Bayern defence with his antics at a free-kick with Gordon on the edge of their area. The pair of them bumped into each giving the impression they had no idea what they were doing which most definitely was not the case as they had practised their bumbling routine in training time and time again.

After running into each other Gordon turned swiftly round to put in a cross that Alex McLeish scored from and soon after that John Hewitt scored the winner. John started seven out of eleven of our European Cup Winners' Cup games that year and also played left back when we won the Super Cup against Hamburg. The fact that nearly 17,000 fans packed Pittodrie for his testimonial match against a select put together by Billy McNeill on December 16, 1985 showed the affection in which he was held.

As a person John was a real diamond. He was a really friendly guy and in the dressing room played the role of the straight man to his big mate Stuart Kennedy's joker. The pair of them were always winding each other up and were a great laugh together.

John liked to think he was a real snappy dresser and tried his best to be in vogue with his choice of clothes. His attempts at times were hilarious and invariably he was just ahead or just behind the fashion of the day. I remember one time he walked in with a pair of white shoes on with his dark suit and looked like he had just walked off an old Hollywood movie set. 'When did you buy the pair of bobsleigh's you've got on your feet?' asked Stuart in a flash when he saw John's huge white shoes which had all of us falling about laughing.

John went by the nickname of 'Spammer' which stemmed from the chat we had on the team bus going to a game against Morton at Cappielow near to where he grew up. As we drove past his former home he let slip that the area he used to live in went by the nickname of Spam Valley. According to him that was not because they were all posh but because the tinned meat which the Americans used to ship to Scotland as part of their aid programme during the Second World War was brought ashore at Greenock.

Because of that there was lots of tins in the local shops and it became part of the staple diet of Greenock, or at least the part of the town that John grew up in. Spam and chips, spam and beans, John knew all about what was the best food to eat with spam.

I always felt he was one of the most under-rated players in Scottish football ever. He never was selected for Scotland despite the fact I always felt he was international class. In fact out of any player I played with or against John was the one who I felt was hardest done by at international level.

The last word on the talent of John has to go to Sir Alex. I remember talking to him a few years ago and he described John as a genius who stroked the ball around with the smoothness of an artist's brush. I couldn't put it any better myself. John McMaster is the artistic left back in my Dream Team.

7

MIDFIELD MAESTROS

Selecting the men to play in the engine room of my Dream Team gave me more trouble than any other position. The problem was that we have had more than our fair share of great players in midfield through the years.

I am happy to debate the issue but am comfortable that the three I have chosen have a good balance about them and could run a game against any team from any era.

By the way, I realise that some players from the past played left or right half and some inside right or inside left. I have done my best to work out who did what and for my own benefit have deemed all of them under the modern term of midfield players.

Casting my eyes over the players from the past showed me there were many who graced Aberdeen who should never be forgotten because of their undoubted talent. Hopefully my mentioning them in this book brings them to the attention of a new generation.

Let me tell you it took lots of late nights and many cups of coffee before I came to my final decision on who to pick as my middle three. And yes I have gone with a three, rather than a four, or a two, for reasons I will outline later.

It was such a tough decision that the men who didn't make my line-up I am going to go through mostly in alphabetical order to explain just why they deserved consideration in the first place. There were so many of them it showed me that this is the one area of the park where the club has always been blessed with major talent.

Although it was a tough decision I am pretty confident that most fans will agree with my midfield choices, although one of them you might think should be playing further up the park. I accept there will be a few of you who will be wondering what I put in my coffee when I was making my decision when you hear my selections because I maybe missed out your favourite.

Aberdeen always had players a bit ahead of their time, and I believe the man I am going to start with could have slotted into any modern day team. Jack Allister comes from the Scottish League and League Cup winning team of 1955 and played on the right side of the park.

He was essentially a defensive midfielder a bit in the mould of Michael Essien of Chelsea and Ghana if you are looking for modern day comparisons. He started his career at Tranent Juniors in East Lothian and joined us from Chelsea for £6,000 in 1952, which was a fair sum back then. He was a tough half-back who played twenty-one out of the thirty League games in the championship winning season.

He was the sort of player who was able to win the ball and protect whoever the big centre half was at the time. Invariably it would be big Alec Young, not that he needed much protecting. Jack was a ferocious tackler and although hampered by injury he had five good seasons with us before he left for Chesterfield in 1958. He played 117 times for Aberdeen scoring twenty-four goals in the process. I met one of his daughters years later as she married Ian Porterfield who was Aberdeen's manager at the time, and she told me some great stories about her dad.

The next man I want to mention, or in this case pay my own tribute to, is Chris Anderson for what he did for Aberdeen both on and off the park. He was a true fan who grew up in the shadow of Pittodrie. He used to tell me about all the great players of the 1930s he was brought up watching like Matt Armstrong and Willie Mills and was steeped in the history of the club.

He was a Scottish Schoolboy internationalist and joined from Mugiemoss in 1943 when he was eighteen. Chris made his debut in 1948 when the club was struggling in the league and within two years he had tied down a starting place at right half and had become a hugely influential player. He seemed to save his best for big matches and the one that many fans talked about at the time was his performance against Celtic in a Scottish Cup tie on February 25, 1950. He scored the only goal that day in what was Aberdeen's first Scottish Cup win at Parkhead in front of 65,000 angry Celtic fans.

Chris clocked up seventy-one appearances over his five years in the first team but by the end of the 1952/53 season he had fallen down the pecking order to the extent Dave Halliday transferred him to Arbroath, but that wasn't end of his connections with Aberdeen.

What made Chris a real Pittodrie legend is the amount of time and effort he gave to the club when he came back first as a director in 1967 and then as vice-chairman during the glory days when, along-side Chairman Dick Donald, he helped turn Aberdeen into a world class side. He also had the good of Scottish football in general at heart and was one of the men who pushed ahead plans for the first ever Scottish Premier League.

He instinctively knew what the club needed and when Jimmy Bonthrone resigned as manager it was Dick Donald and Chris who made the first overtures to Ally MacLeod, who was one of the rising stars of Scottish management at the time, to come to Pittodrie. It was a controversial appointment but Ally's image gave the whole club a lift.

I had the pleasure of knowing Chris for many years and nobody had a bigger smile on his face than him when we won the European Cup Winners' Cup in 1983. I can still see the pride in his face to this day as he triumphantly walked around the team hotel in Gothenburg with the trophy. I remember him too as a bit of a football visionary as he predicted television would take a major hold over football.

Tragically Chris knew when we won the Scottish League Cup in 1985 that he was in the later stages of motor neurone disease which came as a shock to us all. I remember the gaffer being especially shaken and deeply saddened when he heard the news. Chris could only watch on television when we won the Scottish Cup final 3-0 against Hearts on May 10, 1986, and I like to think that win gladdened his heart in his final few days. Chris sadly died on May 27, 1986 and is missed by us all. His good friend, journalist and broadcaster Jack Webster, described him as 'the fair face of sport, an intelligent, articulate spokesman and the brain behind so much of the change, not only at Pittodrie but throughout football'. That was a fitting tribute to a great man who will always be remembered as part of the Aberdeen success story, first as a player and then as an administrator.

Another remarkable man was Archie Baird who signed for Aberdeen from Strathclyde Juniors in 1938. He was a clever man and a trainee architect in Glasgow before he signed for Aberdeen. As a precaution he kept up his studies with an Aberdeen firm which was just as well as the outbreak of the Second World War denied him the chance to play first team football.

In 1940 Archie had packed away his boots and joined the medical corps of the Eighth Army who were in involved in the North Africa campaign. He was captured by the Germans as he bravely manned a field ambulance near the front line at Tobruk but escaped from the prisoner of war camp in Rimini, Italy where they had taken him.

In an incredible wartime adventure he was taken in by an Italian farming family who hid him whenever German soldiers came calling and he repaid them by working hard in their fields. It was only once the British forces liberated Italy in 1943 did he feel it was safe enough to make himself known.

He returned to Scotland where he made his belated professional debut in the Southern League in the 1945/46 season when he played fourteen times and helped Aberdeen win the Southern League Cup when they beat Rangers in the final. He also played a major role in the 1947 Scottish Cup win over Hibernian.

Unfortunately for Archie he never reached his full potential due to a series of bad injuries including a broken leg and three cartilage operations. Despite such setbacks during his six years at Pittodrie he still managed to play 104 times and scored thirty-seven from the inside left position.

One player I had close associations with was Doug Bell, and I make no apologies for considering him for my Dream Team due to the fact he played a major role in the Aberdeen team that I played in. To be honest I always thought Doug was a bit of an unsung hero, although I accept he hasn't been the only one through the years.

Yes, I know he struggled to hold down a regular place in our midfield at times but who wouldn't as it was so strong. Dougie was a selfless player who, remember, was also unlucky with injury which did not help his cause.

He helped us win the Scottish League title in 1980 and came off the bench when we destroyed Rangers 4-1 after extra-time in the final of the 1982 Scottish Cup. But the following year injury kept him out of our second Scottish Cup final in a row when we beat Rangers again which was a real shame for him.

We all felt even worse for him when, after starting eight out of our eleven European Cup Winners' Cup ties, he missed the final against Real Madrid in Gothenburg through injury. What made it worse for him, and the rest of us for that matter, was the fact that it was partly down to Doug that we made it to the final in the first place.

To start with he scored the only goal in the second round second leg away match against Lech Poznan in Poland which helped us qualify for the next round on a 3-0 aggregate, which wasn't as easy as the scoreline suggests as they were a tough team to break down.

Although everyone remembers how we beat the mighty Bayern Munich at Pittodrie in the second leg of the quarter-final what should not be forgotten is our terrific performance in the first leg in the Olympic Stadium in Munich. Bayern were desperate to get at least one goal and laid siege to Jim Leighton's goal late on.

What saved us was Dougie's ability to get the ball and take it on one of his mazy runs that took the sting out of things and left the Germans incredibly frustrated. They simply could not get the ball off him that night and at times I thought he had stuck it to his boot with glue as it never left his foor for minutes on end.

In the semi-final first leg against Waterschei at Pittodrie it was Doug's run and pass within the first two minutes that led to the opening goal from Eric Black which opened the floodgates. Neil Simpson got another one soon after and a great run by Doug midway through the second half gave Mark McGhee the easiest opportunity to make it three. With Doug pulling the strings for us Peter Weir scored before Waterschei got a consolation before Mark scored again to make it 5-1. Sadly for Doug he picked up a knee injury in a league match just before the second leg and Sir Alex decided not to risk him in a game we lost 1-0.

Unfortunately his knee problem turned out to be more serious than first thought and although Sir Alex arranged a behind closed doors against Hibs two weeks before the European Cup Winners' Cup final to check his fitness he knew he would never be fit enough to play.

Doug put a brave face on things and was part of the travelling party and gave us great encouragement in the run up to the game. It must have been heartbreaking for him to miss out and I could understand how he did not really feel part of things after the win. He had every right to as he had done so much to get us to Gothenburg in the first place, but not to play in the final against Real Madrid put an understandable damper on things for him.

I was pleased for Doug that he got over that disappointment and was part of our team that won the European Super Cup by beating Hamburg over two legs. I was also happy that he made the team that won the 1983/84 League title and also the one that won the Scottish Cup by beating Celtic that same season.

While Doug's time at Pittodrie was hit by injury, one fascinating man from a different era didn't reach his peak with us for self-inflicted reasons. Jimmy Black may have left Aberdeen under a cloud but he was a great player who many felt was one of the best midfield men in Scotland when he played in the late 1920s and early 1930s. He was born in Midlothian and played for his local junior team Newtongrange Star which was a great junior outfit even way back then.

He spent three years at Cowdenbeath before moving to the USA in 1926 to join Springfield FC but within six months of him arriving the club had gone bust. His registration was moved allegedly without his knowledge to Providence FC who he refused to play for.

Stuck for where to go next and unable to play anymore in the States he managed to make it known back in Scotland he was available again, and when Aberdeen helped him pay his plane fare home he signed up early in 1927.

The drama wasn't over yet for Jimmy as the United States Football Association banned him from playing at Pittodrie as they claimed he was still signed to Providence, despite the fact he hadn't played a game for them.

It wasn't until December 1927, halfway through the Scottish league season, that the contract wrangle was resolved and Jimmy was given permission to play. He quickly became one of the greatest right-halves in the history of the club and played for the Scottish league team in 1931.

You would think after being at the centre of a row between the States and Scotland over his registration he would have kept his nose clean but just as his career was peaking it came to an abrupt halt. Unfortunately Jimmy was implicated in the betting scandal I mentioned earlier called 'The Great Mystery', when five Aberdeen players allegedly put money illegally on the outcome of games.

Although names were never mentioned a whispering campaign suggested he was one of the men involved and that incident brought the curtain down on Jimmy's career. He never played football again and tragically died suddenly on April 13, 1933 at the age of just thirty-three in Edinburgh's Royal Infirmary. A sad early end to an undoubted talent.

Robert Connor may not have got the pulse racing like Jimmy Black but he was a man I played with and also managed who had a great left foot. He played on the left side of midfield and was part of the team that lost 2-0 to Rangers at Ibrox when we lost out on the

1990/91 League title. Although he wasn't at his best that day he was a hugely consistent performer at Pittodrie.

He had been signed by Sir Alex just before he left for Manchester United from Dundee for £275,000 with Ian Angus, who was another very good midfield player, going to Tayside as a makeweight. Bobby gave his best to the cause over eight years at Pittodrie before I released him when I was manager after his appearances had been reduced greatly, partly because of a nagging achilles injury.

Next up is a man I still know well and always makes me smile, Neale 'Tattie' Cooper, a central midfield maestro, had ridiculous blonde curly hair when I first knew him. He may be as bald as me nowadays but his sense of fun is thankfully still intact.

Neale was a local boy who joined the club from Hazlehead Academy after his primary school janitor Ernie Youngson recommended him to our reserve team trainer Teddy Scott. Neale was a real child prodigy and because he was built like a tank and could look after himself out on the pitch he turned out for the reserves at the age of just fourteen when Billy McNeill was manager. I felt a bit sorry for Neale in the early days as he had come to us as the Scotland youth team first choice sweeper but quickly found I wasn't going to give up my place very easily!

Although he knew my good self was blocking his path to the first team it didn't make him throw his toys out of the pram in frustration. Sir Alex rated Neale so highly as a footballer that he nurtured his talent and decided to make him a regular in our midfield.

Tattie who had been born in Darjeeling in India when his Aberdonian parents were working over there for a tea-making company, had the reputation as a hard man and I can't argue with that. Watching some of his bone-crunching tackles up close, even in training, sent shivers down my spine but there was a lot more to his game than that.

He was quick-thinking and many a time provided the killer pass required to split defences. I used to hear the chant 'Godzilla get him' from the fans whenever he went into a tackle and invariably he did get the ball and yes, sometimes the man as well.

The incident that sums up Tattie for me came in the 1982 Scottish Cup final when we were 3-1 up against Rangers and cruising to victory. Rangers' goalkeeper Jim Stewart made a hash of a kick-out that hit Tattie on the chest and went spinning towards his own goal. With the Rangers goalie stranded it left our man with an open goal.

Some players may have calmly rolled the ball into the empty just to make sure but remember this was our Tattie who never did things by halves. He slammed the ball home from a few feet out and for good measure did a forward role in celebration.

I remember taking the mickey out of him in the dressing room afterwards by saying I wondered how wild his celebrations would be if he ever scored a half-decent goal. He just smiled and told me at least he could score goals, which was something I hardly ever did. Touché, Tattie, touché.

He was a mainstay in our midfield for five seasons and he was an incredible worker in the middle of the park. He won the European Cup Winners' Cup, the Super Cup, two Premier Leagues, four Scottish Cups and one League Cup before he left us in 1986 to join Aston Villa.

You have to remember he was just nineteen when he won the European Cup Winners' Cup. Imagine picking up such an honour at such a young age. I certainly remember he celebrated our win over in Gothenburg like a teenager by going out to get plastered. Most of the guys went back to the hotel for a celebration but Tattie and the younger guys like Bryan Gunn went into town afterwards to meet up with the Aberdeen fans in Gothenburg and were never seen again.

To be fair I think Tattie was originally going to meet his family at the Europa Hotel in town but I believe one thing led to another, as it was always going to. I remember him telling me when he walked into the Europa Hotel he saw his mum and sister at the far corner of the bar. Rather than having to fight his way through, the Aberdeen fans simply lifted him over their heads in a form of crowd-surfing you sometimes get at rock concerts. Suffice to say it was a miracle that Tattie and Bryan made the flight home to Aberdeen after their night out.

Another player who impressed me in my early days as a teenager visiting Pittodrie during my summer holidays was Tommy Craig who played on the left side of midfield. He is the man who Bobby Calder, the Aberdeen chief scout who signed me up, always thought of as one of his best ever finds and one of Scotland's most under-rated left sided players.

He joined Aberdeen from Drumchapel Amateurs in 1966 and although he only had two seasons with us showed in that time his quality. Eddie Turnbull did not want to lose him but in May 1969 when Sheffield Wednesday came in with a £100,000 bid for his services he had no choice but to let him go. The fact that Tommy was the first Scottish player to join an English side for a six figure fee tells its own story as to how good he must have been at Aberdeen.

Following that transfer Tommy spent most of his time south of the border with Newcastle, Aston Villa and Carlisle among his many clubs. I actually played against him in the 1984/85 season which was his last year at Hibs. We were flying then and although Tommy will hate to be reminded we won 4-1, 3-0, 2-0 and 5-0 that season, which was our highest aggregate score in the top flight against any other side.

Classy is the only word to describe Stewart Davidson, whose picture I noticed in early Aberdeen team pictures from the 1900s which show him to have movie-star looks. He signed from a local club with the rather interesting name of Shamrock at just sixteeen, and started as a right winger way back in 1905. He moved back to play right half and by all accounts could run games from that position, hence the decision of the fans to nickname him 'brainy Davy'.

Stewart moved to Middlesbrough just before the outbreak of the First World War and returned to the Teeside club at the end of hostilities. He had a long career there and came back to Aberdeen in 1923 to play for another two seasons. What also interested me about Stewart is that he was appointed Chelsea assistant manager in 1939 and held that job for nineteen years until he retired in 1957. That was quite a shift as a coach at one club, even back then.

Many senior Aberdeen figures I respect suggested to me that Archie Glen deserved inclusion in my Dream Team and certainly he merited my attention at the very least. John Hewitt may always be remembered as the man who scored the winning goal in the European Cup Winners' Cup final but Archie has an equal claim to fame. The left half scored the goal that clinched our first ever Scottish League championship in 1955 after an agonising fifty-two-year wait to get our hands on the trophy. The championship winning goal, which I have mentioned in other parts of the book because it was so significant, came against Clyde at Shawfield on April 9, 1955 and it was the strike that gave Aberdeen the 1-0 win required to help pip Celtic to the title.

It tells a lot about the mentality of the man that he volunteered to take the spot kick in the thirteenth minute despite the fact he had missed one a few weeks earlier in the season. He went on to become club captain in 1956 and was a man who led by example and who never questioned the decision of the referee. Some would say he differed greatly to me in that department but I couldn't possibly comment.

Archie was known as a tough tackler but what I found remarkable about him was that he was never booked in 269 appearances. Again that was very different to me.

He had joined us from Annbank United in Ayrshire and was another bright bloke like many of our players in the 1950s seemed to be. He had a degree in Chemistry from Aberdeen University and was dedicated to football despite his strong academic background.

Even during his year of National Service in 1951 he played in a British Army team that included the legendary Welshman John Charles and Manchester United's top talent Tommy Taylor, who was tragically killed in the Munich air disaster of 1958. Our Archie didn't look out of place among such distinguished company.

At the start of the 1959/60 season he was established as the Aberdeen captain but fourteen seconds into the eighth game of the league campaign against Kilmarnock he was the victim of a crunching tackle by Willie Toner that put him out of the game for nearly five months. He came back for six of the last seven games of the season but never fully recovered and at the age of just thirty-one had to retire. Once a Don, always a Don, he kept close contact with the club as he forged himself a successful business career as managing director of a local Aberdeen paint firm.

Brian Grant may have never hit the heights of say an Archie Glen but he spent twelve years in total at Pittodrie and was a consistent performer. He was in the sides that won the 1990 Scottish Cup and the Scottish League Cup in 1989 and 1995 so he picked up a lot of silverware along the way. He was another Sir Alex signing back in 1984 but it wasn't until Alex Smith and Jocky Scott took over from Ian Porterfield in the hot seat did his fortunes change. He played a lot in the centre of midfield with Jim Bett, more of whom later, and it was a perfect partnership. Brian was a solid player who proved an anchor in midfield which allowed Jim the freedom to roam around at will.

He was part of my team that finished runners-up in all three domestic competitions in my first year as manager, and overall made 329 appearances for the club and I was always impressed with him when we worked together. He was given a testimonial against Everton in August 1996 when nearly 10,000 people turned out to sing his praises.

A rather more flamboyant player than Brian who caught my eye was Alex Halkett. The man they called 'Ecky' played at Pittodrie for four years from 1904 just after the club was founded and was a former captain.

What made him stand out from the crowd was the fact that in the days before numbered jerseys he was always easily identified due to his socks which had his initials 'AK' on them. 'AK' was a man the fans loved and I'm thinking to myself what a great idea it was to put his initials on his socks. I'm surprised in these days of merchandising that not more players have followed his lead.

Another player from the past who fascinated me was Frank Hill who was from Forfar originally and was given the name 'Tiger' because of his ferocious tackling. He joined us in 1928 and was capped three times by Scotland in 1930 and 1931 but was one of the players implicated in the betting scandal at the club called 'The Great Mystery' and left soon after. The reason I mention Frank is that he was a player who went on to have a great football career after four years and 106 games at Pittodrie.

He joined the great Arsenal side of the time straight from Aberdeen and played a big part in securing their three straight English League titles starting in the 1932/33 season. He also went on to captain Blackpool to runners-up spot in the First Division.

During the Second World War Frank served in the Royal Air Force in India and when he returned to Britain picked up his playing career at Crewe Alexandra at the age of forty-two where he was also first team coach. He went on to become manager of Burnley and Preston North End which was good enough but it is his third managerial posting that caught my eye.

In January 1957 he went to coach the Iraqi military team. He was there for a year before returning to take over at Notts County who he led to promotion from the Third Division in the 1959/60 season before he rounded off his managerial career at Charlton Athletic.

Clearly Frank was a man who liked a bit of adventure and he moved his family to California in 1967 where he owned the Piccadilly Circus Fish'n Chips shop. He didn't give up football altogether and coached local sides over there before starting a love affair with baseball to the extent he became a referee in his adopted sport. Seems quite a guy.

Local boys Henry and Wilfred Low graced the jersey from 1904 until 1907 with Henry joining the club from Orion, following the amalgamation with local sides Victoria United and Aberdeen to form the one club in 1903. He was a first pick for four seasons. He was more versatile than his brother and although he was a half-back he also played occasionally up front. Transferred to Sunderland in May 1907 he was a member of their team that lost the English FA

Cup final to Aston Villa in 1913. He died young, at the age of only thirty-eight, in September 1920.

His brother Wilfred could play right or left half and was reputedly the better of the two players. He played 107 times over five seasons at Pittodrie before being transferred to Newcastle United in May 1909 in a deal that brought Jimmy Soye to Pittodrie, before his death in a road accident in April 1933.

Paul Mason currently runs The Gables Hotel in Southport and if any Dons fans are passing, book in and thank him for helping us to one of our most important results in the history of the club back in 1989. We had lost twice in a row to Rangers in the Scottish League Cup and nobody, especially me, wanted them to get the hat-trick.

Graeme Souness was in charge at Ibrox at the time and they had some highly paid stars on their books but they were all overshadowed by Paul's display. He put us ahead in twenty minutes and although Mark Walters scored a controversial equaliser from the penalty spot it was Paul who got the winner from a Charlie Nicholas flick-on in extra-time when he shot through a ruck of players to score. It was an important result as the balance of power in Scottish football had turned towards the Old Firm and this had been our chance to show that at the very least we were still a force to be reckoned with in Scottish football. Paul was a great servant and was in the 1993 team when I was manager that lost the Scottish Cup to Rangers.

In his five years at the club he was a vital cog in the Aberdeen machine. He was a clever player who had learned his trade in Holland with Gronigen. In fact Alex Smith was across in the Netherlands watching Theo Snelders at Twente Enschede in action when he noticed Paul in the opposition ranks and promptly signed him as well.

One man who left Pittodrie just as I arrived was Steve Murray, who had four good seasons at the club up until the end of the 1972/73 season. I always felt sorry for Stevie because he had been signed from Dundee in March 1970 by Eddie Turnbull and went straight into the team because he was such a class act.

The reason I feel sorry for him was because he had played for the Dens Park club in an early round of the Scottish Cup and was ineligible to play for Aberdeen in the famous Scottish Cup final win over Celtic on April 11, 1970. He was captain of the club for a while after Martin Buchan left for Manchester United, but Steve was also soon on his way out of Pittodrie to join Celtic in May 1973.

I hadn't seen the last of Steve because after receiving acupuncture treatment to the toe injury that had put him out of the game after two years at Parkhead he attempted to return to the pro ranks and briefly made a comeback as a player for Dundee United. I played against him in the Scottish League Cup final of 1979 but unfortunately he had the last laugh against his old club as we lost. It was apt that when Stevie finally retired from football after a spell on the coaching staff at Tannadice he became a sought-after artist and cartoonist as he could always do artistic things with the ball.

Jocky Scott came into my thoughts as a candidate for my Dream Team due to his work for Aberdeen as both a player and a coach. He was a local boy who went to Aberdeen Grammar School before signing on as an apprentice at Chelsea. He moved from there to Dundee before joining us. When he signed at Pittodrie he was following the family tradition as his dad Willie had played for Aberdeen in the 1930s. He scored a hat-trick in the famous 5-1 semi-final win over Rangers in the Scottish League Cup in 1976 and was part of the side that made it an Old Firm double by beating Celtic in the final.

Jocky played for, managed and coached more clubs than he probably cares to remember, but his role alongside Alex Smith as co-manager at Aberdeen in the late 1980s and early 1990s cannot be underestimated.

Alex was the front man who did all the press conferences but Jocky was the power behind the throne. He took most of the training and was a real hard task master. It is an honour to play for and then go on to coach Aberdeen and that privilege is something Jocky, like myself, realises and will always be proud of. His football knowledge is second to none and I am sure there will be a role in football for him as long as he wants one.

Although Scott Severin never won anything during his time at Pittodrie I always felt he was a very good captain and did his best for the club either in the centre or on the right side of midfield. He took over the armband after Russell Anderson moved to Sunderland in 1997 and was a player I know Jimmy Calderwood, who was manager at the time, rated very highly. He was worthy of a mention as although Scott didn't bring success to Aberdeen he was a great professional who gave his all when he was at Pittodrie.

He was similar in outlook to a man I thought long and hard about possibly including in my starting line-up. Neil Simpson may have been born in London but that was an accident of birth; he was brought up in Newmachar and lived the dream of playing for his local team. He signed from Middlefield Wasps on a schoolboy form and first came to the fore when he took full advantage of injuries to John McMaster and Gordon Strachan midway through the 1980/81 season to pin down a place in the heart of the midfield.

He was always known as a ferocious tackler but I prefer to call him Aberdeen's finest ball-winner. There was much more to Simmie's game than just crunching tackles. He was a real class act who was a vital piece in the centre of midfield alongside Neale Cooper when Sir Alex was in charge.

Unfortunately for Simmie the one incident that non-Aberdeen fans remember him for was a tackle on Ian Durrant of Rangers that put Durrant out of the game for a considerable length of time. I didn't defend the tackle then and I am not going to defend it now. I remember speaking to Neil about it at the time and if he had his time again he would never have made the challenge.

In his defence he never went over the top on purpose, it was just not his way. What kept the backlash over the challenge going for much longer than it ever should have was the fact that referee Louis Thow didn't send Simmie off and only booked him. If he had seen a red rather than yellow card then I really do think that would have been the end of things and we could have all moved on.

As it turned out there was a sense of injustice among Rangers fans surrounding the fact Ian was out for a long time and Simmie had walked away with just a yellow card. Now as I said earlier I am not going to defend the challenge. Simmie knew it was a bad one. What I will always defend is Simmie's exemplary character as a man and a player.

What I could not stand was the witch-hunt he had to endure after the incident, and he remained strong throughout. The tackle did not deserve to be brought up time and time again in the media whenever Rangers played Aberdeen for years and years. Thankfully the memories have faded and for me the fact Neil went on to be a respected youth coach and head our academy at Pittodrie should be part of his legacy, not the fallout from an ill-advised tackle made years ago.

He was an absolutely magnificent player for Aberdeen and was part of the spine of our European Cup Winners' Cup team that started with Jim Leighton, through myself, then Simmie up to Mark McGhee. He was a real class act which was shown by the fact he was a former Scotland Under-21 captain, and was picked by Jock Stein to play at that level. What made Simmie stand out from the crowd was his ability to score important goals from the middle of the park and during his time at Pittodrie he played 331 times and scored thirty-one goals, most of them, if I remember correctly, pretty special.

He really was one of the boys and I remember he was on the receiving end of a great wind-up when we were on a training camp at Gordonstoun when Sir Alex was in charge. The private school was a great pre-season training venue but the worst thing about the place was the midges. They were everywhere and even at night some used to get into our dormitory.

Simmie decided to buy himself a pair of the most horrific 'dad' pyjamas you could imagine which didn't go down well with all of us young, trendy dudes. The morning after he had turned up in his old man's pyjamas a few of the boys nicked them from behind his pillow and the next thing he knew they were hanging from the flagpole of the Gordonstoun dormitory.

He was also one of the biggest eaters I have ever met. When it came to eating he could not be beaten. I had no idea why he was wasn't twice the size he was. He was also quick-witted which showed itself in a quiz we held once before a game. The question was which three footballers have surnames which are also the name of countries? We got Joe Jordan and Alan Brazil but could not get the third, although Simmie's answer of Jock Liechten'stein'had us all in gales of laughter.

Another local lad who made the grade with us was Dave Smith. He may be remembered more for being a member of the Rangers team that won the European Cup Winners' Cup in 1972 but he had five great seasons at Aberdeen before that. Dave was a wing half who had a great football brain and stood out in an Aberdeen team in the early 1960s that never really hit the heights despite his best efforts.

Like Dave, another one of the men who I never thought received all the credit he deserved during his time at Aberdeen was Billy Stark who was a silent assassin type. Just when you thought he was having a quiet game he would pop up and do something amazing. He was a midfield man who could get forward and ghost into positions to score.

He scored one of the three goals in the Scottish League Cup final win over Hibs in 1985 which was Sir Alex's first success in the tournament. In the Scottish Cup final of the same season he came off the bench to score in the 3-0 win over Hearts.

Sir Alex was a huge fan of Billy's and that should tell you all you need to know about his talent. He twice tried to sign him from St Mirren before it was third time lucky as he got his man with a £75,000 bid in the summer of 1983. When we won the league for the second time in a row in the 1984/85 season he was simply magnificent for us. Wearing the number four shirt he played in all but six of our matches as we ran away with the title with ease.

I was not surprised in the slightest when Billy went into management as he was a great thinker about the game. He was a man who had great success at Celtic during his playing career and did great things with the Scotland Under-21 team as coach, but his time at Pittodrie should not be forgotten.

Like Billy, there was George Thomson who was also a cultured player, who joined Aberdeen in 1932 from junior side St Rochs. He had a great engine on him and his displays at left half were vitally important to an Aberdeen side that did well to finish third in the 1936/37 season and narrowly lost 2-1 to Celtic in the Scottish Cup final the following year.

Some players had their Pittodrie careers cut short because of either the First or Second World War with George Taylor being a prime example. He was originally a centre forward who was converted into a left half and signed for us from local junior side Hall Russell's in 1937. He was just starting to make his mark when war broke out and although he kept playing for the club in friendly matches during the hostilities, it wasn't until after the conflict was over that he became a major star.

He earned himself a place in the Aberdeen history books by scoring a last-minute winner in the 3-2 win over Rangers in the 1945/46 Southern League Cup final. He was also the only native Aberdonian in the Dons' 1947 Scottish Cup winning side, and in the 1947/48 season became captain before his form attracted clubs from down south with Plymouth Argyle winning the bidding war for his services.

Another medal winning Don was Bobby Wishart who was a product of the rugby-playing George Heriot's school in Edinburgh and who signed from Merchiston Thistle. Bobby, who played left half and also inside left, spent seven years at Pittodrie, and although he had a slow start he won the inside-left berth from Joe O'Neil and went on to become a vital part of the Dons title triumph in the 1954/55 season providing the opportunities for Harry Yorston and Paddy Buckley.

He was also part of the Scottish League Cup winning side the following season but missed out on a domestic treble after St Mirren beat his team in the 1959 Scottish Cup final.

He moved to Dundee in 1961, winning a second championship medal there in 1962 and keeping Craig Brown, yes Aberdeen manager Craig Brown, out of the team. He ended his career with Airdrie and Raith, and while still playing was taken under the wing of then Hearts chairman Bill Lindsay, who he succeeded as secretary of the National Farming Union Scotland.

Another man who caught my eye was Alex Wright, who was a six foot tall, right half who made his breakthrough at the outbreak of the First World War. Bad timing or what. After active service he returned to the club in 1919 at the resumption of peace time football.

Clearly the players way back then had an equally biting sense of humour as they do nowadays as guess what they called Alex, who was known as one of the toughest, hardest tackling, uncompromising men in Scottish football?

'Skill' was the nickname, given to him with more than a little sense of irony I suspect. No doubt that would have made the players he put up in the air with his tackling during games laugh a little when his team mates would shout, 'Great tackle, Skill.' Alex's mixture of stamina-sapping box to box play and tough tackling made him a sought after property and he was transferred to Hearts for a club record fee of £2,500 on May 23, 1922.

There are others who I considered but after a lot of thought, let me come to the first player who makes my Dream Team. He will be playing on the right side of a three man midfield and he will be my vice-captain. Gordon Strachan is one of the most exciting playmakers Scotland has ever produced. He could have joined Manchester United straight from school in Edinburgh but wanted to mature at home, so he first joined Dundee at the age of nineteen where he became captain.

I played against him a few times before he moved to Aberdeen in 1977 and he was always a real handful. He would really get on your nerves with his runs into the box which you could never predict.

He made an immediate impact at Pittodrie and was a main man

during our glory years. Wee Gordon had great individual skill and extraordinary vision and played a huge part in bringing the League Championship to Aberdeen in 1980. He also made his mark on the world stage with some great performances for Scotland at the World Cup in Spain in 1982.

Gordon and I shared some great experiences and he was the man I nearly fell out with the night before the European Cup Winners' Cup final as I explained in the chapter on managers, when Sir Alex arranged a pre-match quiz that ended in a draw and had to be settled with a controversial tie-break question.

During the European Cup Winners' Cup final itself the wee man was magnificent and put in a great shift as usual. It was great to see him with the cup at the end as he had worked his socks off to help us to victory.

After the match the pair of us were the two Aberdeen players chosen for the routine dope tests and ordinarily would have drank lots of water to assist with the urine sample. This time round we were adamant we would not be sticking to water and opened a couple of bottle of beers to help our flow. We were in the same room as the Real Madrid players who were being tested and one of them, Johnny Metgod the great Dutch midfielder, was trying to pee.

I didn't understand Dutch but Johnny had a good command of English and was going red in the face and getting more and more angry as he kept complaining to us that Mark McGhee had elbowed him in the face during the game. Gordon and I had a good laugh at his expense and toasted Mark with a beer for getting on Metgod's nerves so much.

Gordon made the right midfield position his own during his time at Pittodrie although he could sometimes pop up on the left as well. Some people, who clearly didn't understand Gordon's role at Aberdeen, used to pigeon-hole him as a winger which was ridiculous. Jimmy Johnstone was a winger. Gordon Strachan most definitely wasn't. Yes he could get to the line and put in some fine crosses but there was a lot more to his game than that. He was a box-to-box player who could win a tackle on the edge of his own area and then be in the penalty box at the other end to score. Gordon was a real team player whose game revolved round playing quick one-twos and was more like an old fashioned wing half going on a wing forward than anything else.

I always enjoyed Gordon's company and his cheeky-chappy approach to life made it impossible for me to get angry with him for long. Apart from nearly falling out with him at the quiz I told you about earlier, I did come close again when we were sharing a room and I could not understand why my toothbrush was damp and had toothpaste stuck between the bristles whenever I went to use it. One night I came back a bit earlier than expected to find Gordon brushing his teeth with my toothbrush. Not bothered at all he claimed he didn't have space in his toilet bag for a toothbrush of his own and thought I wouldn't mind him using mine.

I liked his laid-back attitude to some aspects of life and his big smile as he brushed his teeth with my brush made me realise there was no point me losing the rag with my wee pal. I told him to keep the toothbrush we had been sharing without my knowledge and I went out and bought myself a new one that I kept well out of his way.

I'm just thinking that it was amazing Gordon even had a toilet bag at all on that trip. In his early days he was totally disorganised. No toilet bag, no shampoo and definitely nothing to tame his wayward perm that he was so proud of. Shamefully we all had perms in those days but you needed those big long combs to look after them.

Gordon didn't ever bother using one of these huge combs to look after his hair so when he came to training in the morning the side he had been lying on during the night was flat as a pancake and the other half of his hair was really frizzy and sticking out. He looked hilarious but didn't seem to care.

He may not have looked after his perm but he did look after his body. I was not surprised that Gordon played for so long at the top level as he looked after himself better than anyone. While he did not have much of a physical presence he was incredibly skilful. He was like the orchestra conductor in our midfield. With his football brain he did not need to be quick. All I had to do as a defender was to get the ball to his feet and he would do the rest. He had great vision.

Watching him and Stuart Kennedy in action was something else. It was quite funny at times because Gordon was never going to bomb up the wing and make the byline very often. He was going to beat his opponent by wrong footing them or drifting inside where he would link up with the strikers. Whenever he got the ball he would invariably stop it and look up. He would take a wee touch and if there was nothing on he would move inside, try and play the pass.

Usually when he was doing all this Stuart was going past him like an express train up the wing from his full-back position to give him an option up the line shouting at him all the time to give him the ball. Having that option meant Gordon could either role the ball to Stuart or play it up to a striker. If one striker dropped off, say Eric Black, and came deep, Gordon would bypass him, dink it over the top to the second striker, maybe Mark McGhee, then both Eric and Gordon would then make gut-busting runs to support him. It was the way we attacked at times. We came in waves.

Gordon always managed to give himself time to find space because his close control was magnificent which bought him a few vital seconds on the opposition. If you were a defender going into a guy like that who can control the ball instantly and keep it tight you know you have problems. On top of that talent because Gordon could see the killer pass faster than others he probably had more goal assists than any one midfielder I ever played with.

With such a talent on the books as Gordon it was obvious that other teams were looking to take him away. That is where it understandably became fraught for Sir Alex as he wanted to keep his best players. Remember Doug Rougvie went to Chelsea and Gordon's big mate Mark McGhee to Hamburg around the same time that Gordon was thinking of leaving.

Because Gordon was a touch player who took risks, sometimes what he was trying didn't come off which didn't help his relationship at times with Sir Alex. Everyone knows Sir Alex was a fiery personality and Gordon a skilful player and sometimes he would try the hard pass and the gaffer would give him a roasting for giving the ball away. By the same token despite the fact there may have been a bit of tension between them deep down there was a mutual respect in the football sense.

One of the reasons Gordon is in my Dream Team is his fantastic attitude to the game and how it would rub off on others. He would never give up, would chase lost causes and always provide the spark required to unlock defences. He could bring his team mates into matches and set up chances for them. He always set a magnificent example to younger professionals and was the one man I would tell youngsters to look at and learn from.

He is a man who really played on instinct and in my book it was in the middle of the 1983/84 season when he played fourteen incredible games in a row that he was at his best. He scored his 100th goal for Aberdeen that season and at that time in my opinion was one of the greatest midfield players in the world.

To complement Gordon I wanted a man who can dictate play and provide a link between my three man midfield, our defence and our Dream Team strikers. Either Neil Simpson or maybe Neale Cooper could have fulfilled that role because both were workers who got up and down the park. Neil Simpson came closer to making my Dream Team that Neale Cooper simply because he was a better passer of the ball and could release his front men a lot better.

But I was looking for a man who could get up and down the park, spray passes all over the place, feel comfortable using his left or right foot and who could also come back and pick the ball off the defence to start moves. Sounds like Superman? No, just Jim Bett.

If you have your two other midfield men on the right and left man-marked you need a guy in the centre you could give the ball to in a tight position who could find that extra yard of space to take the pressure off the defence and spark attacks.

The way I want my Dream Team to play I want someone sitting deep, being the general in the middle of the park and there is nobody better at doing that than Jim. I played with Graeme Souness and he played a similar role to that. Jim was a Souness type without the real thunder that Souness had. There was many a time when I needed an out from defence and needed for someone to show themselves and take a pass in a tight area.

Invariably it was Jim who would show himself, keep the ball a few seconds, and then play a pass to get us out of trouble. He never hid as a player. He could also switch play effortlessly, which is a great knack. He always stood up to be counted and I want players who do that in my Dream Team. My aim is to have an Aberdeen Dream Team packed full of top footballers and Jim fits that bill as my central midfielder.

Now I know some Aberdeen fans may not agree with my choice. Neil Simpson, Neale Cooper or some other players from the past may be more to their liking, who maybe looked a bit more dynamic. Some of you may have thought Jim was a bit lazy and ambling out on the park but that was just the way he looked at times and looks can be misleading.

He was a strong boy who could hold people off so he didn't have to run about ten to the dozen all the time. When you are a great passer of the ball with fantastic vision you can do things at your own pace.

Off the park Jim had a quiet personality and did not say an awful lot. I realise that being in the centre of midfield in my Dream Team is a vitally important role and people may think you need a loud player in there to shout orders to team mates. To be honest I have always thought it was a myth that every successful team was packed with loud players who never stopped talking. Some people think all the players of yesteryear were talkers and organisers but that wasn't the way I remember things.

I talked and organised but I was captain. Not many other players did that as they wanted to simply get on with the job of playing football and getting the better of their direct opponent. I think some fans get mixed up between shouters and moaners. You've always got a lot of moaners on the pitch, in fact you get them in all levels of football, but that is a very different thing.

I would definitely say that the characters of the players were stronger back in my day and they would take no crap from anybody but that does not mean to say they were talking all the time on the park. Sorry, I digress. Getting back to Jim, all I want him to do is to make himself available and keep the ball and use it well, and he did that nine times out of ten when I played with him. On the rare occasion he would make a mistake he would be the first one chasing back to make up for his error.

Jim had been a schoolboy signing at Dundee before he moved to Airdrie and then Icelandic side Valur. At that stage his career wasn't going anywhere fast until a few good performances in Europe for Valur alerted FC Lokeren of Belgium, where he made a real name for himself.

From there John Greig paid £180,000 to bring him to Ibrox but that didn't really work out. He rejoined Lokeren from where Sir Alex signed him for £300,000 in June 1985. He was already an established Scotland internationalist when he joined us with thirteen caps under his belt. In fact he played in one of our most important World Cup qualifying games alongside me against Iceland just two weeks before he came to Pittodrie.

Spain had already won our World Cup qualification group with ease which meant it was between us and Wales for second spot. We needed to win in Iceland to keep up our chances of finishing ahead of them which would set up a showdown in Cardiff.

Iceland were all over us in the first half during the game in Reykjavik and only a great penalty save from Jim Leighton kept us on level terms. It was only with four minutes left we took the lead thanks to the Aberdeen connection. Gordon Strachan broke free on the right, former Pittodrie favourite Stevie Archibald ran over the ball and Jim slammed it home. Okay Jim hadn't signed for us but we all knew he was coming at that stage. Jim had married an Icelandic woman and I would have hated to be a fly on the wall in the marital home that night.

His first game for Scotland as an Aberdeen player came in the 1-1 draw against Wales in Cardiff that secured us a play-off match against Australia, although as everyone knows our qualification was marred by the death of Jock Stein at the final whistle.

Jim played in the first leg of the play-off match against Australia that we won 2-0 at Hampden but once Sir Alex stepped down as temporary manager after Jock Stein's death he struggled to get a starting place in the Scotland team. He was always in the squads but Andy Roxburgh didn't seem to fancy his style of play enough to name him in his starting line-up which surprised me as I thought Jim was the perfect man to play European style passing football.

When I became Aberdeen manager Jim was one of my senior players along with Alex McLeish and he was a great support to me. He also taught me a lesson in that you always should try and tell the fans when a player is carrying an injury. Because Jim was such an important player he played for us with a slight groin strain for a couple of weeks and didn't play as well as he could.

The fans started to get on his back which was a shame because they didn't know about his injury and I maybe should have told them beforehand that Jim had made a real sacrifice to play. Okay I might have alerted the opposition to the fact that one of my star players was not 100 per cent fit, and that would have given them the chance to target him but it would have saved Jim from taking unfair criticism from the supporters.

Now I thought hard, but in fairness not very long, about who to play in an attacking left sided midfield role to complement Gordon and Jim but in the end there was only one logical choice. I could have named Peter Weir as an out-and-out winger but the balance of the 4-3-3 formation I have chosen means I feel he will be better sitting in midfield and breaking up the line.

Jim Bett in the centre of midfield can spray passes to him while Gordon Strachan on the right side can link up with right back Stuart Kennedy as he usually did during matches or cut inside to help Jim if he is in trouble.

Also I felt I had to find Peter a place in my Dream Team because the three strikers I have picked would benefit from his style of play, and his service up to them would be very different to the type that Gordon will provide. Gordon will mainly play balls into them while Peter will get to the byline and cut the ball back or put in long, hanging crosses.

I remember Sir Alex used to always say to anyone who would listen that when Peter Weir played, the whole Aberdeen football team played. I certainly want a guy like that in my Dream Team!

Peter reminded me of Davie Cooper or to a lesser extent John Robertson as they used to glide rather than speed past defenders. Now that isn't just a polite way of me saying Peter wasn't quick. It is more my way of saying that you don't always have to be quick to leave your opponent on his backside as you disappear up the wing.

Peter was never the type to go past someone with a burst of speed over five yards. He would slowly rev up his engine and go past them in ten, fifteen yards which I know from experience is much more of a soul destroying thing for a defender to cope with. Just when you think you have your man covered and can cope with him he steps up a gear and you are left looking like you lack fitness.

I think a lot of people probably didn't appreciate all the hard work Peter did during matches in terms of chasing back. That is why I feel he would sit well in a midfield three, where he could work back, pick the ball up, look ahead and start attacking moves. His delivery from the left, especially when he got to the line, was always top-class and his passing was terrific.

He wasn't the type who came inside all that much like Gordon Strachan, which is fine as that will allow Jim Bett more room in the central midfield area in my Dream Team. He would hug the touchline and keep to his position.

You would never get the Aberdeen left back running past Peter like Stuart Kennedy used to do with Gordon Strachan. You sometimes got big Doug Rougvie running into Peter due to the fact big Doug was not watching where he was going but that was it.

Many people feel the best Peter ever played was in the European Cup Winners' Cup final where he was admittedly absolutely magnificent. He tortured the Real Madrid defence all evening and of course it was his pass to Mark McGhee, and Mark's cross that led to John Hewitt's famous winner. On that day Peter was world class, no question.

But in my view he had been equally world class against Ipswich in a UEFA Cup tie against Ipswich Town in 1981, the same year he joined Aberdeen. Now Ipswich were the UEFA Cup holders at the time and had just gone top of the English First Division when we played them. They had guys like Alan Brazil, Russell Osman, Paul Mariner and left back Mick Mills, who was both the Ipswich and England captain, in their ranks.

Despite all their talent we still drew 1-1 down at Portman Road with John Hewitt scoring our equalising goal. Their manager at the time was the legendary Bobby Robson who really wound us up by suggesting he thought we couldn't play any better than that and we would be beaten in the second leg at Pittodrie because the pressure on us would be too great.

It could be argued there was more pressure on Peter Weir that evening than anyone because he had had a quiet start to his Pittodrie career since his £200,000 transfer from St Mirren a few months earlier which saw Ian Scanlon, another left sided player, head to Paisley.

He had a reasonable first half against Ipswich without being outstanding, and penalties from Gordon Strachan and John Wark meant the game was deadlocked at half-time.

In the second half Peter came of age. Mick Mills may have been the Ipswich and England captain but he was made to look like an amateur by Peter. He kept going at him time and time again before the poor man was left looking like a shadow of the player he was. Peter had Mick totally confused. He turned the poor man inside out when he scored our second goal and to rub salt into the wounds got our third and final goal as well with five minutes to go. At no stage of my career have I seen a top international player getting a bigger doing. It must have been the biggest embarrassment Mick Mills had ever had to face.

In my book that result was the most significant to date during Sir Alex's time in charge and we all had Peter to thank for making it happen. We had not been taken too seriously by the English media or the rest of Europe at that stage but beating the mighty Ipswich Town made everybody sit up and take notice.

Peter gained huge confidence from that performance and never looked back from that moment. As well as the European Cup Winners' Cup success Peter was there alongside me when we won the Scottish Cup just ten days after Gothenburg. He also starred in the Super Cup win over Hamburg and helped us defend the Scottish Cup against Celtic, and he won it again when we beat Hearts in 1986. He won two League Championship medals and was one of the finest players I ever played alongside.

Also what many people may not know was that Peter was a true boyhood Aberdeen fan. I doubted his story when I first met him because he was a Glaswegian just like me, but it is absolutely true. Apparently his dad took him to the 1970 Scottish Cup final when he was twelve years old. The young Peter was so enthralled by the Aberdeen team that beat the mighty Celtic he was hooked on the spot. Little did he know that one day he would go down in history as one of the greatest players ever to play for his favourite club.

Now before I end my midfield discussions some of you may wonder why Zoltan Varga has not made my final cut or even been considered as a Dream Team candidate. My debut for Aberdeen was against Morton at Cappielow on April 28, 1973 and that turned out to be his final game for the club. I notice that in the Celebrity Dream Team selections both Buff Hardie and Jack Webster, two men who know their football and have been following Aberdeen all their lives, have named him in their Dream Teams.

Sorry boys, although I highly respect your opinion, I don't agree with you on the merits of Varga. I feel there has been a myth around Zoltan that I can't understand. Yes, he was a talented player but he only signed for Aberdeen because he had nowhere else to go after being kicked out of German football when he was at Hertha Berlin after a bribes scandal. I do not doubt he was a magnificent player but he was only at Pittodrie for less than one full one season during which time he won nothing and played just 26 league games.

Yes, he had a sublime talent and was an Olympic Gold medal winner with the Hungarian national side in 1964, and had played in two European finals against Leeds United and Juventus when he was with Ferencvaros, where he made his debut as a sixteen year old but that was long before he signed for Aberdeen and maybe he was a wee bit past his peak when he joined us.

Jimmy Bonthrone spent £40,000 on him after he had been banned from German football for two years when he was simply available to the highest bidder. To be fair Zoltan was a trooper and did his best to come to terms with the physicality of Scottish football. I remember in his first ever training session with the first team he needed stitches in a head wound after getting an elbow from someone in an aerial challenge.

Yes, I do remember he scored a fantastic goal against Celtic at Pittodrie with a lob in October 1972 but Aberdeen lost 3-2 so it was all in vain. He picked up a knee injury and left us in November 1973 with newspapers at the time stating that he felt he wasn't getting paid enough at Pittodrie.

Such was his stature in football he was recruited to Ajax to replace Johan Cruyff, but not surprisingly didn't fill the great man's shoes very well and joined Borussia Dortmund once his two-year ban for his part in the bribery scandal had ended. I accept Zoltan shone brightly at Pittodrie for a short time but to me he didn't really want to be there and left far too soon. The vast majority of players I have considered for my Dream Team have won some sort of silverware or have given great service to the club. Sorry, Jack and Buff, but that rules the late Zoltan Varga out on both counts.

8

FORWARD THINKING

At any club anywhere in the world it is the forwards, strikers, call them what you will, who are remembered the most. They write their names in the history books by scoring winning goals and not surprisingly get the most adulation from the fans.

The Aberdeen team of the 1970s and 1980s that I played in was blessed with some of the greatest front men in the history of the club, of that there is no doubt. However as I delved a bit more into the past there are other players who clearly had their shooting boots on at Pittodrie and left a lasting legacy.

Some were wingers who could swing in some great crosses and were experts at scoring from free-kicks. Others were good old-fashioned centre forwards and inside-halves who all were Pittodrie heroes.

Choosing my front three for my Dream Team was a difficult task as I had so many quality strikers to choose from. Some were tall and great in the air, others small and dumpy but deadly, others simply born goalscorers.

Can I start by considering one man who made the grade at one of Europe's greatest ever club sides. No, I'm not talking about Aberdeen in this case but the mighty Barcelona.

Steve Archibald narrowly missed out on making my starting eleven but deserves a place on the bench.

Now I know Steve was a player who split opinion. Everybody has a view on his talents and I accept that some fans found him infuriating to watch.

I can understand that his body language was probably not the best at times but come on folks. Here is a guy who played superbly for Aberdeen and whose eleven goals in the 1979/80 season – one less that top scorer Drew Jarvie – helped us win our first Scottish League Championship since 1955. He also won two FA Cups and a UEFA Cup with Spurs and a Spanish League title with Barcelona. Only world class players could have done that.

Steve was a time-served car mechanic before he became a footballer and had just finished his apprenticeship when Clyde boss Stan Anderson signed him in 1974 at the age of eighteen.

It was only when Billy McNeill took over at Shawfield that Steve started to hit the big time. Billy was only at Clyde for a few months but in that short period had been so impressed that he paid a modest £20,000 to bring Steve to Pittodrie in January 1978. It turned out to be money well spent.

He became an instant hero with the fans after he scored two goals in a 3-0 victory over Rangers at Ibrox in only his third game in Aberdeen colours. Initially he formed a good goalscoring partnership with Joe Harper, and even when wee Joe dropped out of the picture in that crucial League Championship winning season in 1979/80 Steve kept banging them in.

The most important of that whole campaign was the opening goal he scored against Hibs in our second last game of the season at Easter Road. We had to win to lift the title against all the odds, as we had been a massive eleven points behind Celtic at one stage.

We were all a bit nervous on the bus journey down to Edinburgh as we knew we were so close to securing Aberdeen's first title win since 1955. In the dressing room beforehand we talked of the need for an early goal to calm us down. It was Steve who delivered when he rose to head home an inch perfect John McMaster free-kick. At that precise moment I could feel the confidence flowing through my veins even more and knew we were on our way to victory. Sure enough, a rare goal from Andy Watson, one from Mark McGhee and two from Ian Scanlon gave us a 5-0 win which, coupled with Celtic's draw at St Mirren, meant we were league champions.

Throughout his time at Pittodrie Sir Alex rated Steve highly although he was nearly as strong-willed as the gaffer which meant they did have a few fall-outs. There was even a suggestion that Sir Alex had named a chair in his office 'Archibald' because Steve was always sitting in it as he came in to see the gaffer about something or other.

One of the assets Steve had that many other strikers didn't was that he was versatile. You could play him as an out-and-out striker or in what they call nowadays 'the hole' and he would be comfortable in either role. Wherever he played he had the sniffer's nose for a goal and for a man who wasn't that tall scored some superb headed goals

When Spurs offered £800,000 to take Steve to White Hart Lane he was on his way out of Pittodrie as Sir Alex was never one who kept a player who felt his heart wasn't at the club. He finished England's top scorer in his first season and won the 1981 FA Cup when he played his part in the famous 3-2 replay win over Manchester City, which is remembered for the fantastic solo goal from Ricky Villa. He picked up another FA Cup winners medal the following season when Spurs beat Queen's Park Rangers after a replay.

He scored seventy-seven times in 189 appearances for Spurs, and after he scored in the 4-3 penalty shoot-out second leg UEFA Cup final win over Anderlecht there was a huge demand for his services. The highest bid came in from Terry Venables, who paid £1.15m to bring him to Barcelona in August 1984 and he looked perfectly at home playing at such an exalted club.

The one claim to fame that Steve has off the pitch is that he appeared twice on the same edition of Top of The Pops back in 1982. Bet you didn't know that! The only reason I do was that on one occasion he was in the Scotland World Cup squad choir that included yours truly. We mimed our way very badly through 'We Have A Dream' which was sung by the actor John Gordon

Sinclair and the singer B.A.Robertson and was our 1982 World Cup song. Later on in the show up popped Steve again, this time on video, singing along with the Spurs team and Chas and Dave on their FA Cup final song 'Tottenham, Tottenham'. Steve always tells me he is a Top of the Pops veteran as he also appeared on it in 1981 with the Spurs team as they sang 'Ossie's Dream'.

While Steve was a prolific goalscorer at Pittodrie there was an old fashioned style centre forward called Matt Armstrong who beat his total of forty-six goals in sixty-six games hands down when he played for the club from 1931 to 1939. Overall Matt scored a remarkable 155 goals in 215 games for Aberdeen from 1931 to 1939 and he remains our second highest all-time scorer behind Joe Harper.

They used to call Matt the greyhound as he was one of the fastest players to appear at Pittodrie. He had been brought up in Port Glasgow and trained with Celtic as a schoolboy under Willie Maley but they never signed him which allowed Paddy Travers, the Aberdeen manager, to steal him from under their noses in the summer of 1931. It took the nineteen-year-old Armstrong a while to settle at Pittodrie and his success story is a case of simply sticking in and having faith in your own ability.

In his first season he played just ten times and scored twice then the following season scored just three goals in seven appearances. The same mediocre statistics continued in the 1933/34 campaign when he played just thirteen times and scored fourteen goals which was at least a bit of an improvement.

Matt was one of the most dedicated footballers of his generation and pledged to work hard to improve his goalscoring, and by heck he fulfilled his promise in style. For the four years up until the outbreak of the Second World War he was on fire and even caught the eye of the international selectors who awarded him his first Scotland cap against Wales in 1935 closely followed by another against Northern Ireland. His call-ups came in the wake of an incredible thirty-nine goals in forty-five games during the 1934/35 season which included hat-tricks against Ayr United and Queen's

Park. This in an Aberdeen team that only managed to finish sixth in the First Division.

Matt loved the big occasion and scored Aberdeen's goal in the 2-1 Scottish Cup final defeat at the hands of Celtic in front of 146,433 fans at Hampden in 1937. That game was significant as it was the only time that Aberdeen's old black and gold strip was seen in a Scottish Cup final at Hampden because two years later the club adopted its more famous red strip.

During the war Matt joined the Royal Corps of Signals and although he played a few exhibition matches for Aberdeen during the hostilities he left the club when peace broke out. He didn't hang up his boots straight away and played well into his forties at Elgin City before becoming a scout for Falkirk. He retained his close links with Aberdeen by returning to run the Pittodrie Development Association.

The man who used to supply the crosses for Matt when he was at his peak – including the one that led to his goal in the 1937 Scottish Cup final – was Welsh right winger Jack Benyon who had signed from Doncaster Rovers in 1933. He had joined as a replacement for Andy Love who had been a lightning-fast winger but was coming towards the end of his career which gave Jack his opportunity. He was a hugely popular figure at Pittodrie where he had four great seasons before tragedy struck.

Six games into a tour of South Africa he complained of severe abdominal pain and died suddenly on June 26, 1937 in a Johannesburg Hospital. He was buried in the South African city with the Aberdeen players joining Welsh exiles singing 'Land Of My Fathers' at his graveside. Jack's body was later re-interred and brought back to a permanent resting place in his beloved Wales.

Scott Booth was a player I relied on heavily when I was manager and was one of the young players who did me a turn. He scored a hat-trick in our 4-1 win over Hamilton in the first round of the Scottish Cup in 1993 and he helped us get all the way to the final where we lost to Rangers. We also finished second to the Ibrox side in the league with Scott's goals aiding our challenge. He was a superb player on his day which is shown by the fact he clocked up twenty-two Scotland caps and also played on the continent with Borussia Dortmund, Utrecht and Twente Enschede. During two spells at Pittodrie, the first under me, the second under Steve Paterson in 2003, he played 228 games for the club scoring seventy times.

For me, Eric Black must have made a pact with the devil in a previous life because he still looks as fresh-faced as when he first walked through the door at Pittodrie as a youngster fresh out of Alness Academy. He was a vital part of Sir Alex's plans and I have never before, or since, seen a player have the ability to hang in the air so well until the ball reached his head. As he matured he became an expert at reacting quicker than defenders and managing to get in front of them from close-in to score vital goals.

He made his debut against Dundee United, who were our bitter rivals at the time, on September 31, 1982 and marked his arrival with a brilliant headed goal which was to be the first of many. He also played against Hamburg that season and gave Franz Beckenbauer a real tough time. He was a deceptive player because although Eric looked slight he was very, very clever and put what muscle he had to good use.

Of all his goals the one that I will always remember best was his strike against Real Madrid in the European Cup Winners' Cup final because it gave us a belief we could go on and beat them. Eric had hit the bar after just three minutes and then two minutes later a move from a corner we had practised in training worked superbly well. Gordon Strachan took it, Alex McLeish met it with his head and Eric slammed the ball home. John Hewitt's winner in the same game may have been the most important one in the history of Aberdeen Football Club but Eric's opener was the second most important of that there is no question!

Throughout his career Eric had a knack of being in the right place at the right time. As well as scoring regularly in Europe he also hit the net in vital domestic matches like the 1984 Scottish Cup win over Celtic, and also scored twice in the Scottish League Cup final win over Hibs in 1985. In his five years he played 180 times and scored sixty-nine goals and was a vital part of our glory years before he decided to try his luck in French football.

Like Eric, Paisley-born Bobby Bruce was not incredibly tall but still incredibly good in the air. He was only five feet six inches tall but was a brave player who was also a great passer of the ball. From 1924 up until 1928 he was in magnificent form and scored forty-five goals in 110 appearances.

What makes Bobby stand out from the crowd is the fact that he was the first Aberdeen player to score a hat-trick in a Scottish Cup tie and still end up on the losing side. His moment of misfortune came away from home against Raith Rovers in a first round tie on January 21, 1928 when 8,000 fans saw his three goals count for nothing as Aberdeen lost 4-3. He left us to join Middlesbrough for £4,000 ten days later at the age of just twenty-one and his goals were badly missed.

Up until now the players I have mentioned haven't really been the bustling, rampaging centre forward type. You would not expect any of the men I have mentioned to barge goalkeepers into the net as some strikers tried to do in the old days or throw their weight around. All of them were clever players with a bit of a subtle touch about them.

You couldn't say the same about Leith-born Paddy Buckley who combined his physicality with incredible pace. I remember when I first came to Aberdeen in the early 1970s some of the older guys used to always go on about Paddy. I was a budding centre forward as a teenager and they used to say that he was the top striker of his day.

Paddy played for Bo'ness United and moved to the senior ranks with St Johnstone before arriving at Pittodrie for £7,500 in April 1952. Throughout the mid-1950s he was a prolific scorer and in thirty-eight games in the 1953/54 season he scored twenty-seven goals. During the Scottish League Championship winning campaign the following year he got twenty-eight goals in forty games. He also played in two losing Scottish Cup final sides in 1953 and 1954.

Capped three times for Scotland he made his debut in a 1-0 win over Norway in 1954, but the fact he was up against Willie Bauld of Hearts and Lawrie Reilly of Hibs meant he struggled to get a regular game at international level.

Because of his physical approach to the game he picked up a lot of niggling injuries and a knee problem cost him a place in the Scotland 1954 World Cup squad. Although he soldiered on he was forced to retire through his persistent knee injury in 1957. An indication of his standing came when, after he died in 2008, all the Aberdeen players wore black armbands to commemorate his memory as they held a minute's silence before a game against St Mirren on 12 November.

One man I must admit I wasn't too aware of before I started researching my Dream Team book was the fascinating character of Alex Cheyne who became an overnight national hero when he scored direct from a corner kick for Scotland against England at Hampden Park on April 13, 1929. His famous goal led to such loud cheering on the terraces that the press at the time said they had heard nothing like it before and at that moment the famous 'Hampden Roar' was born. His other claim to fame was that he was one of the first British players to try his luck in continental football.

Alex was born in Glasgow on April 28, 1907 and signed for Aberdeen in 1925 from Shettleston Juniors. He was a typical attacking inside-right of his day with bags of control and skill but his trademark was the Cheyne bodyswerve which would nearly always fool his opponent.

Alex's great play for Aberdeen soon had the Scottish selectors watching with interest and it came as no surprise that he was given his debut against England at Hampden. These were the days when substitutes were not allowed so when Alex Jackson, himself a former Aberdeen player, went off injured after just half an hour Alex was moved out to the wing and told to take the ball for as many walks as he could to the corner flag as his team tried to hold on for a draw.

After one such foray near the touchline he won a corner and took the kick himself. With the wind gusting down the pitch towards the

England penalty area he lobbed a vicious in-swinging corner into the box. The flight of the ball deceived their defenders who all let the ball go over their heads thinking it was going to drift way over the bar at the back post. To their horror the ball bent in and found its way into the back of the net to give Scotland an unlikely victory.

The 110,512 strong Hampden crowd roared themselves hoarse for the 'Hampden Roar'. For years later the newspapers of the time described the game as 'the Cheyne international', such was his importance to the occasion.

Overall Alex won six caps for Scotland, scoring four goals, including a hat-trick against Norway, but it will always be the goal against England direct from that corner – a feat which was only legalised the season before he did it – that he will be remembered for. By the way, Alex seems to have made scoring from corners something of a specialty after that, performing the feat twice more for Aberdeen.

After his famous goal against England it was no surprise that he became a hot property and Chelsea paid £6,000 for his services in June 1930, which was a record for an Aberdeen player at that time. After two years at Stamford Bridge he became one of the first British players to play abroad when he signed for French side Nimes Olympique where he had two successful seasons. On his return he became coach of Chelmsford City in the late 1930s and after the war was manager of Arbroath up until 1955.

Another player who ended up playing for Chelsea, albeit a few years after leaving Aberdeen, was Charlie Cooke who I bet the Aberdeen fans of his generation are kicking themselves that they did not see more of at Pittodrie. The man they called 'The Bonnie Prince' was an absolute wing wizard. Allegedly the Aberdeen fans even used to sing 'Charlie is my darling' to their new hero, although I'm not sure how many of the guys nowadays would join in that chorus.

Charlie was Fife-born but grew up in Greenock and joined us from Renfrew Juniors in October 1959 and was a real find. He scored twenty-six league goals in a four year career at Pittodrie and is remembered warmly by anyone who saw him play. Let's face it, the

Dons team in the early 1960s wasn't the best, yet Charlie still shone to the extent he won three Scotland Under-23 caps and captured the headlines wherever he played.

At best Aberdeen finished as high as sixth position when he was at Pittodrie and that lack of success proved to be a real frustration to him. He asked for a transfer and was sold to Dundee in 1964 for a record fee – the highest deal between two Scottish clubs at the time of £44,000. I still think that may have been a mistake as he was still to fulfill his potential. With top English clubs like Newcastle United and Arsenal also weighing in with offers I am sure his sale would have been more accepted by the Aberdeen fans if he had gone south straight away.

As it turned he was given his first full Scotland cap within a month of moving to Dens Park and won sixteen caps in total, mostly out wide, although he was versatile enough to drop into the right half position if injury forced him to move there.

The Dens Park board made a decent profit when they sold him to Chelsea two years later for £75,000 in 1966. At Stamford Bridge he became a superstar before moving to Crystal Palace and then to America to finish his career where he became a respected soccer coach.

Whenever the talents of Charlie Cooke are mentioned both Dundee and Chelsea are named as his previous clubs and the fact he started out at Aberdeen is sometimes forgotten. He was worth considering for my Dream Team as he was a player who showed he was a top-class performer from day one at Pittodrie. Getting him to move from the west of Scotland to Aberdeen in the first place was a real coup and showed that our scout Bobby Calder was a very persuasive gentleman.

Billy Dodds was another west of Scotland man who gave his all for Aberdeen after he came to us in 1994 when I was manager. I had always rated Billy highly and was delighted to bring him to Pittodrie. He made his debut in the 0-0 draw against Skonto Riga in the UEFA Cup which is a game I would rather forget for obvious reasons. We may have lost on aggregate to the Latvian side but Billy showed from the off the level of commitment that made him such an important player for Aberdeen.

The word tenacious was created for Billy. He just never gave up. Whether it was in training or over ninety minutes on a Saturday he gave his all. Even after I left the club to be replaced by Roy Aitken he kept scoring vital goals for us and he helped the club win the League Cup by beating his former club Dundee in the final.

He scored twenty-six goals in the 1996/97 season and overall scored sixty-eight goals in 162 games. He was sold by Alex Miller in September 1998 to Dundee United but the best from Billy was yet to come. He went on to score so many goals at Tannadice that he was snapped up by Rangers before having a short spell at Partick Thistle before he retired.

Billy was high up on my list of candidates for my Dream Team squad but at the end of the day although he did superbly well at Pittodrie he just missed out, partly because he did just as well at Dundee United and Rangers, but I forgive you for that, Billy!

Also a man I could not forget is Jim Forrest who seems to be remembered for all the wrong reasons outside of Aberdeen. Jim joined Rangers straight from school in 1960 and was a prolific scorer at Ibrox, and in 1965 won his first Scotland cap. But in the wake of Rangers' shock Scottish Cup defeat at the hands of Berwick Rangers in 1967 he never played for the Ibrox club again which turned out to be Aberdeen's gain.

He was transferred to Preston North End a few months after the game but never settled and signed for Aberdeen for £25,000 at the start of the 1968/69 season. He showed that his goal scoring prowess had not deserted him and ended his first season at Pittodrie as captain as well as top scorer with twenty-three goals from forty-seven appearances, which led to him collecting the Aberdeen Supporters' Club Player of the Year prize. It was a reward for Jim keeping us up as his goals helped the team narrowly avoid relegation by just two league places.

Despite his undoubted talent there was a new kid on the block by the name of Joe Harper, who I will talk about a lot more later, who took his place as first choice number nine. But it was a measure of Jim's talent that he simply moved to the right wing to accommodate Joe when required.

Both Joe and Jim played together in the Scottish Cup final winning team of 1970 and Jim deservedly got a Scotland recall the following year on the back of his great form. His cousin Alex Willoughby was also a professional footballer and they were team mates at Aberdeen for a while. Indeed Alex would have been involved in the Scottish Cup final win over Celtic if it had not been for a knee injury in the third last league game of the season against Kilmarnock.

In Jim's five seasons at Pittodrie he scored sixty-two goals in 191 appearances which was an impressive haul, and when he left the club at the end of the 1972/73 season I was making my mark in the first team but knew enough about him to realise he was a quality centre forward who could also play wide.

One man who made his mark straight away when I was there as a player but went off the boil a bit later in his time at Aberdeen was Hans Gillhaus who was a left-sided striker who must have had the most impressive start to an Aberdeen career ever.

On his day he was unplayable and the fact he was brought in by PSV Eindhoven from FC Den Bosch as their supposed savour after Ruud Gullit left for AC Milan in 1987 tells its own story of how highly rated he was at the time. It was only because a certain little Brazilian genius called Romario started to keep him out of the team that meant he was available for transfer. For Alex Smith to bring a man of his quality to Pittodrie for £650,000 in November 1989, was a fantastic piece of business.

I could only look on in awe as he scored two great goals on his Aberdeen debut, one a header, the other a bicycle kick in a 3-0 win over Dunfermline at East End Park on November 18.

If that wasn't enough we had a midweek fixture four days later at Pittodrie against our old rivals Rangers. And what does Hans do? Only takes the ball from twenty-five yards with four defenders in front of him and hits a dipping and swerving shot into the top corner past Chris Woods. Talk about introducing yourselves to the home fans in spectacular style. Almost instantly, the partnership between Charlie Nicholas, a man I will talk about later, and Hans looked like dynamite.

The pair of them were on fire in the run up to the 1990 Scottish Cup final and in that final Hans got the better of a physical battle with Celtic's Paul Elliot. We were under the cosh for long periods but Hans held the ball up superbly to take the pressure off our defence. To win the final on a penalty shoot-out was the perfect end to Hans' first season at the club.

The following season Charlie left to go back to Celtic but Hans led the line just as well scoring fifteen goals. His ability to hit the back of the net helped us take Rangers to the wire in the league and he was as heartbroken as the rest of us when we lost the title on the last day of the season after we lost 2-0 at Ibrox. He went to the 1990 World Cup with Holland but didn't get a game because he was kept out of the side by Marco van Basten which was no disgrace.

I must admit at times, especially as manager, it was hard to come to terms with Hans' laid-back approach but that was just the way he was. We didn't get on too badly when I was in charge despite what people might have thought at the time. I always rated him as a player and his pace, ability to run with the ball at his feet and his timing in the air made him a very special player.

Maybe he was a victim of that great start I mentioned earlier. Everyone saw in his first two games he was a world-beater on his day but he maybe lacked the consistency to show that class week after week.

We had no choice but to let him go when he refused a new contract and was very selective over where he wanted to play next. He turned down Aston Villa, Ipswich, West Ham and Sunderland, and he finally went to Vitesse Arnhem but only after a few months out of the game before starting a period of globetrotting. He played in Japan, Finland and then back at Den Bosch where it had all started for him.

For those who haven't kept up with his movements since can I just say he hasn't done half bad for himself. His Danish friend Frank Arnesen, who he played with at PSV Eindhoven, became head scout at Chelsea and took Hans on as his right-hand man. For over two years he was employed on what I can only assume was big money by Roman Abramovich before leaving in the summer of 2011 to become Feyenoord's technical director in place of Leo Beenhakker.

Hans was a great finisher. Can you imagine the service he would have got from Arthur 'Bumper' Graham, who was one of the greatest ever left wingers to play at Pittodrie, if they had ever played together?

I used to watch Arthur avidly in my early days as a schoolboy visiting Pittodrie during holidays because in those days, as I mentioned earlier, I was an aspiring striker. I used to watch Bumper in training put in cross after cross and think how great it would be to be on the end of one or two of them.

He got the nickname Bumper from the time he had one foot in plaster and was getting about on crutches. He was a sociable chap and didn't let his injury curtail his social activities. He turned up on more than one occasion at discos, never a good idea when you are on crutches and have one foot in plaster, to enjoy a few drinks. Of course he could not get his normal shoe on his injured foot so he adapted an old, oversized training shoe to fit over it so it stopped his injured foot bumping on the ground, hence the nickname 'Bumper' was born.

Arthur was a Glasgow boy like me and grew up in Castlemilk and was working in the steelworks at Cambuslang when he signed for Aberdeen. He told me the story of how Bobby Calder stopped at nothing to bring him north.

He was playing junior football at the age of sixteen for Cambuslang Rangers at the time, which must have been tough for Bumper, who was not fully physically developed, yet here he was thrown in against some absolute brutes who liked nothing better than to put him up in the air. He had played just a few games when a Celtic scout asked him to sign and being a fan of the club he was, as they say, over the moon.

The Celtic scout spoke to Bumper and promised he would meet Sean Fallon and the legendary Jock Stein the following week with a view to signing. At that time Celtic signed a lot of kids, then put them out on loan to junior clubs with players like Kenny Dalglish going to Cumbernauld United for instance.

On the same day he had been made all these promises by Celtic, Aberdeen scout Bobby Calder got wind of what was going on. He got on board the Cambuslang Rangers team bus as it made its way back from a match against Irvine Meadow and strode up to the back of the bus, where Bumper was sitting, and offered to take him to Aberdeen the next day to sign a two-year contract. Bumper said no to begin with because he wanted to meet Mr Stein and sign for Celtic.

Then Bobby said he would take him to Aberdeen the next day and pay him £50 a week for those two years. Bumper was only earning £4 a week in the steel works but still said no because of his love of Celtic. Then Bobby played his trump card and said he would pay him £50 a week and give him a £500 signing-on fee. That was the clincher and Arthur was on his way to Pittodrie.

He was seventeen when he signed for Aberdeen, and when he went up there he couldn't believe what a breath of fresh air it was living up there compared to Glasgow. Like me, it was great to know nobody bothered whether you supported Celtic or Rangers.

Bumper was an instant success and on his first visit to play at Parkhead a few weeks after he signed he scored the winner in a 2-1 victory on March 25, 1970. Because he was a Celtic supporter from Castlemilk he used to get real stick from the more passionate fans in the Jungle section of Parkhead during matches, some of whom knew him from the days he used to stand on the terraces beside them.

He was always getting pelters whenever he went there, with the funniest one he told me about being a chant that went along the lines of: 'Arthur Graham, Arthur Graham. We're gonna cut your mother's washing line.' The Celtic fans thought he was a traitor for not signing for their team but Bumper was made of strong stuff and laughed it off.

He admitted Eddie Turnbull helped him through his tough, early days as a teenage left winger and just six weeks after signing he was part of the Aberdeen team that won the Scottish Cup by beating his boyhood heroes Celtic 3-1 in that famous final. He played an absolute blinder and in his first season and at the age of seventeen he helped set up two of the Aberdeen goals. He remained at Aberdeen until July 1977, winning the Scottish League Cup in his final season before he signed for Leeds United for £125,000.

A reason I remain envious of Bumper to this day was that when he played for Scotland against Argentina at Hampden in 1979 I was stuck on the bench for the whole game. The reason that bugs me is that a certain gentleman called Maradona was playing his first game in Britain.

There were more than 62,000 in Hampden that June day to watch the reigning World Cup holders give us a football lesson. I was itching to get on but was left on the bench with Joe Jordan and could only watch events unfolding. Leopoldo Luque scored the opening two goals before Maradona scored his first ever goal for Argentina at the age of just eighteen.

It was Bumper who scored Scotland's only goal of the game with five minutes left, and because of that Maradona swapped shirts with him at the end of the 3-1 defeat, and there are famous pictures of him saluting the Hampden crowd in his Scotland shirt. Bumper could probably auction it off for a fortune and I bet he has it firmly under lock and key.

While Arthur was more a goal provider 'Gentleman George' Hamilton was one of our top goalscorers after the Second World War. The fact he had broken into the team the year before hostilities broke out and had his career disrupted suggests he could have scored a lot more. He was born in Irvine, Ayrshire on December 7, 1917 and started out with junior outfit Irvine Meadow before joining Queen of the South after Rangers told him he was too light to play up front.

He was spotted by Billy Halliday, brother of Dave Halliday who was the Aberdeen manager at the time, who convinced him to sign

George for £3,000 in April 1938. He showed his worth as an inside forward then as a centre forward with some top-class performances in the 1938 Empire Exhibition Trophy tournament in Bellahouston Park, Glasgow where the Dons lost in the semi-finals to Everton. In his first season he scored eighteen goals in forty-two matches.

At the outbreak of war he went to work at the local shipyard in Irvine before he joined the Royal Engineers. Although he was a driver in the North African campaign he still played a bit of football in an Army team alongside the legendary Tom Finney.

When he returned from active service George played for a while in the regional divisions which were set up due to war-time travel restrictions. Top players like him would guest for local sides and George was in great demand because of his talent and played for Ayr United and Rangers.

He clearly had lost none of his talent when hostilities ended and in the 1946/47 season when he made his comeback he played forty-two times scoring an incredible thirty-three goals for Aberdeen, his highest ever total at any stage of his ten years at Pittodrie. What made his scoring feats even more remarkable that year was that occasionally he had to nip back to Maryhill Barracks in Glasgow where he still had army commitments to do some work, so his football training and some of his match preparation was disrupted.

One of his finest moments came when he scored Aberdeen's opening goal in their 2-1 Scottish Cup final win over Hibernian in front of 82,140 fans at Hampden in April 1947. By the same token he was a relieved man at the final whistle as Hibs goalkeeper Jimmy Kerr had saved a penalty from him in the second half, but thankfully his team still held on to win.

In December 1947 he was transferred to Hearts for £8,000 with Archie Kelly going to Pittodrie which the Aberdeen board felt was a good deal for a thirty year old. After just seventeen games at Tynecastle an unsettled Hamilton asked for a transfer and returned to the north-east for an increased fee of £10,000.

Despite Aberdeen's erratic league results, Hamilton helped his team to two further losing Scottish Cup Final appearances, in 1953 and 1954. His form was so good that in 1954, at the age of thirty-six, he was recalled to the Scotland team for a match against Northern Ireland. He was picked for the twenty-two-man squad for the 1954 World Cup in Switzerland but Scotland decided to take only thirteen players to the finals and it looked like he was going to miss out.

By the way, can you imagine Scotland, or any team for that matter, just taking thirteen players to a World Cup? Absolutely incredible. George was one of the players due to stay at home on the reserve list with the likes of Bobby Combe and Jimmy Binning. Luckily for George, but not so for the legendary Bobby Johnstone, the Hibs front man had to withdraw through injury with George called in to replace him. However his optimism was misplaced as he sat on the bench for the whole tournament.

Having just played four league games as a young Dons side won the 1954/55 League title he was transferred to Hamilton Academical that summer before retiring in December of that year. George scored 153 goals for Aberdeen in 281 matches – but remember he didn't play during the Second World War, when he would have been at his peak.

A superb all-round footballer who had great natural ability George deserved to be considered for my Dream Team and although he doesn't make the starting eleven he deserves a place on the bench.

Tony Harris was a big, burly centre forward. He was a member of the 1947 Scottish Cup winning side that beats Hibs although he was playing on the right wing in that famous team.

He played in every single one of the Scottish Cup ties up to and including the final and was one of the main reasons his team lifted the trophy. Tony showed that all footballers' brains were not just in their feet as he was a local dentist who was the focus of some good natured banter from the Pittodrie crowd as he ran up the wing with his pearly whites gleaming.

Tony may have been from Glasgow but he was a huge Aberdeen

fan and just when I was joining the club he was trying to buy it. Tony and his former Pittodrie team mate Don Emery tried to overthrow the board in 1969 but failed to win enough support and after that he decided to move back to the west coast.

Tony was still playing for Aberdeen when Englishman Jack 'The Hare' Hather was in action out on the left wing. He signed in 1952 – the year before Tony left – from non-league club Annfield Plain in County Durham and was first choice number eleven up until 1960. During these eight years he picked up a clutch of medals at Pittodrie including a League championship badge and a League Cup winner's medal. Unfortunately for Jack he finished on the losing side in three Scottish Cup finals.

What was remarkable about him was that he played throughout his career with just one kidney after having the other removed when he was just eleven. Jack was told it would be advisable not to play a contact sport in case someone kicked the other one but he ignored such suggestions and bravely played on which was to Aberdeen's gain.

Returning to my own era there is one man who will always be remembered forever as an ace finisher and scorer of big-game goals. John Hewitt didn't make my Dream Team but he deserves a mention for his all-round ability.

It has always been a bugbear of mine that people always tag John simply a supersub for the way he used to come off the bench and score vital goals. I know that putting him on my Dream Team bench simply continues that stereotype and opens me up to accusations of not practising what I am preaching. In my defence remember John is competing with strikers from every era and I just couldn't quite find a space for him in my starting line-up although he came very close.

John started a lot of important matches for Aberdeen and had a long, successful career at Pittodrie spanning eight years. I accept that his two most famous goals were scored from the bench but that just showed his predatory instinct in front of goal and his ability to adapt to the pace of the game straight away.

No one will ever forget his match winning header against Real

Madrid in the European Cup Winners' Cup final. There is a whole generation of Aberdeen fans who can talk you through the move that led to John heading home the winning goal. It was a moment that he will never forget and for that goal alone he will always have a special place in Aberdeen football history.

John still chuckles to this day at the fact that he may not have been on the pitch to score that great, historic goal after Sir Alex blew his top at him. Some of you may not have realised that when John came on as a substitute against Real Madrid he was supposed to play up front, which he did but he also started to drift all over the place and did not follow the orders the gaffer gave him.

Sir Alex was going crazy on the touchline and was even thinking of bringing him off. Can you imagine that, a sub being subbed in a European Cup Winners' Cup final? John would never have lived it down.

While Sir Alex was trying to work out what to do with him and thinking to himself a penalty shoot-out was round the corner – one that we had not practised for – Peter Weir passed to Mark McGhee who crossed the ball which the Real Madrid goalkeeper Augustin just missed. Now players with less concentration may have been put off for that vital split second by the goalkeeper's attempted punch but not John. He was a brave, wee player and kept his eyes only on the ball which allowed him to head home and write his name in the history books.

I realise that John's goal will never be forgotten but what about all his other vital strikes through the years? For instance, it was John who scored against Dinamo Tirana of Albania at Pittodrie in the first round proper in the year we won the tournament. It gave us a 1-0 lead to take to Albania and by heck we needed it. We came away from the return leg mighty relieved after holding onto a 0-0 draw that allowed us to squeeze into the next round against Lech Poznan.

Also it was John who scored the winning goal in the quarter-final victory at Pittodrie over Bayern Munich after coming off the bench for Neil Simpson. Not that many of you would need to be reminded but it was 2-2 and time was running out fast when John McMaster put in a lob to the back post that was met by Eric Black whose header looked goal bound. Bayern Munich goalkeeper Muller did well to palm the ball away but John showed great composure to collect the ball, control it and poke it through the legs of the goalkeeper to clinch the win.

He also scored twice in our 1985/86 Scottish Cup final against Hearts, a game in which he was deservedly named man of the match. John started that game, which came just a few weeks after our win in Gothenburg, and was in fantastic form as we won 3-0 with Billy Stark getting the other goal in what was another great day for the whole team.

So remember there was a lot more to John Hewitt than the winning goal in the European Cup Winners' Cup final, although I must admit that one goal would have done most people.

John is also in the record books for another reason due to another goal that I was privileged to witness that I'll never forget. It came on January 23, 1982 when he scored in 9.6 seconds against Motherwell which remains at the time of writing the quickest goal in Scottish Cup history.

It is said that Celtic's John McPhail scored in the league in six seconds against East Fife on December 16, 1950, during a 6-2 win. Berwick Rangers' Alex Burke found the net in just seven seconds shortly after kick-off in a match against Raith Rovers at Shielfield Park on February 22, 2003.

But the record books tend to be vague where early goals are concerned, especially in circumstances where the match is not broadcast live on television or recorded for broadcast later.

There is absolutely no dubiety about John's goal. It is the fastest Scottish Cup goal televised which means it will live on forever, maybe even more than the rest of the record breakers.

John wasn't just a goalscorer and was a very unselfish player. I will always remember when we played Hibs in the Scottish League Cup final of 1985 when he set up Eric Black and Billy Stark who both scored in the first twelve minutes to put us on easy street.

The problem John had was that he played in an era when we had some terrific strikers ahead of him which was a real shame as it meant he faced a constant battle to remain in the side for any length of time.

He was only seventeen when he made his debut, which didn't surprise me as he was a huge talent even then. Manchester United boss Dave Sexton had tried to sign him beforehand but it took Sir Alex's persuasive powers to keep him in the north-east. In all, John won three championship medals, four Scottish Cup winners' medals, a Scottish League Cup winner's medal, as well as the Cup Winners' Cup and the following season's UEFA Super Cup before he moved to Celtic, then to St Mirren and Dundalk before retiring from the game to become assistant manager at Cove Rangers alongside Doug Rougvie. Now that would be a little and large managerial double-act I would have loved to have watched in action.

The next man I want to mention is Alex Jackson, a real legend of Scottish football who gained immorality after scoring a hat-trick for Scotland in the 'Wembley Wizards' team that destroyed England 5-1 at Wembley in March 1928. Now I know he had moved south to sign for Huddersfield when he played in that match but he had had his career resurrected at Aberdeen beforehand.

Alex was a great right winger who was part of an international forward line that day which included James Dunn, Hughie Gallacher, Alex James and Alan Morton. They were pocket dynamos one and all with Jackson being the tallest at just five feet seven inches tall.

Alex scored the first goal after just three minutes when he headed home a cross from Alan Morton. Alex James got the second just before half-time before the Scots put in one of the greatest ever forty-five minutes ever seen by an opposition international team at Wembley.

Although the rain was falling heavily an Alan Morton cross was headed home by Alex Jackson for his second goal of the game. Then Alex James got his second before Alex got his hat-trick to make it 5-0. A late Bob Kelly free-kick gave England a consolation goal.

Now some of you may accuse me of double-standards by not bringing in Zoltan Varga into my Dream Team considerations yet here I am mentioning Alex Jackson who spent just one season at Pittodrie. I thought long and hard whether to throw Alex's name into the mix but I felt, as I said earlier, he kick-started his career at Aberdeen and wanted to be at the club through choice, something I never really thought Zoltan did. Also Alex, in that short season at Pittodrie won three Scotland caps in what was called the British Home Countries championship, and was one of the best right wingers ever to grace not just Pittodrie, but the national team as well.

Also he helped Aberdeen stay up that season. He wasn't in the best Pittodrie team ever and going into the last day of the season they were equal bottom with five other clubs, and only an inspired performance from him, plus goals from his brother Walter and another from Jimmy Jackson – no relation – kept them up after a home win over Motherwell.

Alex's career took off after that season at Aberdeen. Born in Renton in May 1905, he was the youngest of five football playing brothers who joined Dumbarton from his local juvenile team Renton Victoria Juveniles in 1922 for the princely sum of a new ball. He went to join his brother, Walter, playing in America with Bethlehem Steel of Pennsylvania for a year but both were both homesick and signed for Aberdeen in 1924 for less than £1,000.

They returned on the recommendation of former Pittodrie full-back Jock Hume who was coaching Brooklyn Wanderers at the time. The pair of them made their debuts against Rangers on August 23, 1924 with Alex playing forty times for Aberdeen and scoring eight goals.

He was such an instant success that during that one season, 1924/25, he was picked for Scotland at the age of nineteen. His flamboyant, skilful style of wing play also earned him the nickname The Gay Cavalier. Herbert Chapman, the manager at Huddersfield Town, which was the top team in England at the time, spotted his talent at international level and brought him south. Huddersfield were in the middle of winning the English League Championship three times in succession when Alex joined them for £5,000 in 1925. It was an indication of his talent that the transfer fee was a record for both clubs.

It was while playing for Huddersfield that Alex won his remaining fourteen Scottish caps between October 1925 and May 1930. One of them was against England in 1926 at Wembley when he scored the winning goal which, although not as famous as his hat-trick at the home of English football two years later, was still celebrated in style by the Tartan Army.

He moved on to big spending Chelsea – nothing changes there then – who he signed for in 1930 for £8,500 before taking the bold move to move to France to play for Nice and Le Touquet when he was just twenty-nine years old.

In his later years the SFA made the daft decision not to pick any Anglo-Scots in the national side which meant Alex should have won more than seventeen caps, although to win fifteen, is an impressive record. Tragically Alex, who was serving as a Major in the British Army at the time after his retirement, was killed in Egypt in a road accident in November 1946, aged forty-one. He helped give a lift to Scottish football with his hat-trick at Wembley and throughout his life never failed to praise Aberdeen for giving him a lifeline after he returned to Scotland from the USA, and I would like to think after hearing his story you too feel he deserved to be considered for my Dream Team.

From Alex Jackson we come to Drew Jarvie who I have a lot to thank for. Drew was in prolific form when I was a young defender and on more than one occasion he scored a few goals to cancel out any mistakes I made at the back. The earliest time I remember that happening was when I gifted a goal to Alan Gordon of Hibs at Pittodrie just a few months into my first team career. I let him get away from me in the box to score but I need not have worried as Drew got two goals and Joe Harper another couple to help us to victory.

Drew was always among the most optimistic in our dressing room and his infectious enthusiasm rubbed off on everybody else.

For instance we were all excited and very proud that we had made the European Cup courtesy of winning the league title in 1980. After we squeezed past Austria Memphis in the first round with a 1-0 win at Pittodrie and a goalless draw away from home we were paired with the mighty Liverpool who had the likes of Kenny Dalglish, Phil Thompson, Graeme Souness and Alan Hansen in their ranks.

They had won the competition in 1977 and again in 1978 and were a class act. We lost the first leg at Pittodrie by one goal to nil and in the return at Anfield I put through my own goal to give them a one goal advantage on the night, then Phil Neal scored another before the break. When we got back to the dressing room at half-time we were all crestfallen until Drew, trying to lighten the mood, shouted: 'Right lads, three quick goals and we are back in this game.' And he meant it! Maybe his voice carried through the dressing room wall and got Liverpool angry as Dalglish and Alan Hansen scored in the second half to complete their destruction job.

Drew was a great servant to Aberdeen and joined us when Jimmy Bonthrone was coach back in 1972 around the time when I was establishing myself. He cost £70,000 from Airdrie with the cash coming out of the £125,000 the club had got from Manchester United for Martin Buchan nineteen months earlier. He formed a great partnership up front with Joe Harper but when Joe left for Everton he was left to take the responsibility of being the main striker for a few years.

He enjoyed the starring role and scored twenty-eight goals in that first season then got twenty-four the next, which included four against Falkirk, before netting thirteen times in the 1974/75 season to make him our top scorer three years in a row.

Drew, with Joe Harper back at the club, played a major part in us winning the Scottish League Cup under Ally MacLeod in 1976. He scored the equaliser two minutes after Kenny Dalglish had put Celtic ahead before Davie Robb scored the winner in extra-time. He then went on to form a great partnership with Steve Archibald when he scored twelve and Steve eleven in the year we won our first league title under Alex Ferguson.

Although he doesn't make my Dream Team it could be argued that Drew has done more for Aberdeen than most over the years. He went back to Airdrie in October 1982 with the best wishes of Sir Alex. When he retired he became assistant manager at St Mirren under Alex Miller and then went to Dundee under Jocky Scott before he arrived back at Pittodrie under Jocky and his co-manager Alex Smith in 1988, where he was very much an important part of the management team that won the Scottish and League Cups.

I always trusted and respected Drew a lot which was why I made him, along with Roy Aitken, one of my assistants when I took over as Aberdeen manager. I wished him well when he stayed on after I left as manager. He took over as the man in charge of Aberdeen's youth system before he left the club when Steve Paterson took over in 2002.

While Drew was an out-and-out goalscorer I always felt Eoin Jess was a different sort of striker who could play in midfield or make runs from deep. He was undoubtedly one of the most talented youngsters ever at Pittodrie and I am sure he won't mind me saying this that he was at his best at Aberdeen rather than anywhere else.

He was easily the most sensational new talent to breakthrough not just at Aberdeen, but in Scottish football when I was nearing the end of my career and I was impressed with him when he made his debut against Motherwell in May 1989.

He was a Portsoy boy who seemed to enjoy scoring or at the very least playing well against Rangers, from whom he had been released as a schoolboy, which gave him a special bond with the Aberdeen fans. I remember watching the Scottish League Cup semi-final of 1995 when Billy Dodds scored twice for a great win over the Ibrox side. With the game in the bag Eoin indulged in a bit of showboating down the touchline with a wee bit of keepy-uppy. It went down badly with the Ibrox fans but brought huge roars from the Aberdeen end.

Later that season he also scored a great goal at Ibrox when he broke past two midfielders and hit a great shot in the top left-hand corner that even Paul Gascoigne, who was in the Rangers team that day, admitted he would have been delighted to have scored.

Eoin played in our 2-1 Scottish League Cup final win in October 1989 but although he was given a Scottish Cup final badge after the famous penalty shoot-out win over Celtic the following year he was an unused substitute which disappointed him a lot.

He played when I was manager although a broken leg in a Scottish Cup tie against Clydebank was a huge set-back for such a naturally gifted player. Such was his dedication that I wasn't surprised that he bounced back and was in the 1995 League Cup winning team against Dundee when Roy Aitken was manager. He deserved to win that medal after having the guts to do those keepy-uppies I mentioned earlier in front of the Rangers fans in the semi-final.

A few months later he was off to Coventry City for £1.7m but was back at Pittodrie within a year in a £700,000 deal, but success didn't come too easily after that and he signed for Bradford City in 2000 and then Nottingham Forest and Northampton Town before going into coaching with Nottingham Forest.

Eoin was always a really fit guy and I was concerned to hear he had had a mild stroke a couple of years ago that was later diagnosed as a hole in the heart that needed an operation. That was a similar complaint to the one that Asa Hartford, the former Scotland internationalist who went back to playing after his treatment, had during my era. Eoin was a great talent and I wish him the best of health and with a bit of luck he could be a great manager one day.

Graham Leggat, who Aberdeen historian Kevin Stirling raves about, was a winger who both scored and provided goals. He was a member of the very first Scotland Under-23 team and won eighteen full caps for Scotland, his first coming against England at Hampden in 1956 when he scored.

Graham, who was born in Aberdeen, was a naturally fit guy who was a qualified PE teacher from Jordanhill College in Glasgow who went on to play for Fulham, Birmingham and Rotherham before he emigrated to Canada to join the Toronto Metros. After he retired he became well known as the main football presenter on Canadian television's Soccer Saturday programme.

Although he did have a glittering career south of the border for five years from 1953 the former Banks O'Dee player was also a huge success at Aberdeen. He was the most versatile forward player the club has ever seen, playing in all five positions along the front line at various times. His best position was outside right and it was from there, at the age of just twenty, he played most of the time as he helped Aberdeen to the 1954/55 League title when he played twenty-six times and scored eleven goals.

In the successful League Cup run he scored a hat-trick in a 5-3 quarter-final first leg win over Hearts and scored again in the 4-2 second leg victory. Rangers were on the receiving end in the semi-final with his goal opening the scoring in a 2-1 win. Although he picked up a shoulder injury he was fit enough to play in the final against St Mirren where he scored the winning goal with ten minutes left.

The following season when Aberdeen finished second he scored twenty-nine goals in just twenty-nine starts, and he never lost the knack of scoring goals. Against Airdrie on October 12, 1957 he scored five out of the six goals in a 6-2 win.

He took that form south of the border, and an indication of his class came during his time at Fulham who he joined for a fee of £16,000 in August 1958 where he formed a striking partnership with the legendary England internationalist Johnny Haynes.

Whilst at Fulham he scored reputedly the fastest ever hat-trick in the history of the English league. His three goals against Ipswich Town in a club record 10-1 win on December 26, 1963 were scored in just three minutes.

A year later Tommy Ross of Ross County is reputed to have scored three in ninety seconds but in terms of first class British football it is Graham's record that I believe still stands. Graham played eighteen times for Scotland, two of these caps coming in the 1958 World Cup in Sweden in the matches against Yugoslavia and Paraguay.

One man who will also always be in the Aberdeen history books is left winger Willie Lennie who has two 'firsts' to his credit. Way back in 1905, just two years after the club had joined the Scottish League, Willie moved north from Fulham to play for us in the old Scottish First Division. He had been round the block a few times before that with spells at Queen's Park, Rangers and Dundee.

Along with Charlie O'Hagan, who played inside left, he was a great servant to the club playing 227 games and scoring sixty-seven goals up until he was transferred to Falkirk for £30 in 1913.

And his claim to fame? He was the first Aberdeen player to be capped for Scotland when he got the call-up in March 1908 to play against Wales at Dens Park in the British International Championship. For that alone he deserves mentioning as a candidate for my Dream Team. He celebrated the honour of playing for his country in style, scoring the winning goal with three minutes left.

His other 'first' as it were, was that in 1910 he was the first player to ever be granted a club testimonial when 3,000 supporters turned out at Pittodrie to show their appreciation. Once all the cash had been counted the board handed him over the princely sum in those days of £150.

Of the modern day players Darren Mackie deserves a mention in my Dream Team considerations for his loyal ten years service with the club and also for scoring one of the most important goals of recent years. It came against Dnipro from Ukraine in the UEFA Cup first round in the 2006/07 season. The first leg at Pittodrie had ended goalless but in the return Darren scored the opening goal and although they equalised through Andriy Vorobey that was good enough to get us into the group section of the tournament.

We had a tough group including Atletico Madrid, Panathinaikos, Copenhagen and Lokomotiv Moscow, but the team managed to qualify for the last thirty-two where we drew Bayern Munich.

For the fans, having the great German side back at Pittodrie for the first time since we beat them on our way to the European Cup Winners' Cup final victory over Real Madrid sparked real excitement. Although they beat us over the two legs there was a great atmosphere inside Pittodrie for the first leg which ended 2-2.

Although a 5-1 defeat awaited in Munich that European run – sparked by Darren's goal against Dnipro – was still a great experience for the fans and the players at the time that included top-class pros like Darren, Jamie Langfield, Andrew Considine, Lee Miller and Barry Nicholson. In tough financial times the run in Europe also secured us a decent financial windfall which was an added bonus. Darren was given a testimonial against Villarreal in July 2011 to mark his ten years' service and it was a thoroughly deserved honour.

Next up is a man who was a huge favourite of Sir Alex and a player who was a larger than life character. Frank McDougall is on the bench for my Dream Team and came close to making the starting eleven for the simple reason he was one of the most deadly finishers I ever played with.

Frank was a really strong character as he had to be because there was huge pressure on his shoulders the minute he walked through the main door at Pittodrie. He was signed by Sir Alex as a direct replacement for Mark McGhee, and who had scored important goals for us in vital games. Knowing he had big shoes to fill did not deter big Frank. He was confident in his own ability which is always important for a striker

I hated playing against him as he was such a handful. Subtlety was not a word he understood. It was all or nothing for Frank. He was a bit like Andy Gray at his peak. He would put his head in where other players would not. He was brave and a bit crazy all rolled into one.

He came to Pittodrie in 1984 from St Mirren for £100,000 to replace Mark who had left the club at the same time as Gordon Strachan and Doug Rougvie, which was tough for the gaffer to take. But he always had a good eye for a player and knew his first priority was to make sure he got a goalscorer of proven quality. Just like he has done time and time again at Manchester United he was facing a major rebuilding job and Frank was an important part of that process.

It doesn't take a genius to work out that you need a strong spine to your side and the gaffer still had Jim Leighton, myself and Alex McLeish at the back, Neil Simpson and Neale Cooper in the middle of midfield and the missing link was a top striker to complement the ones we already had.

Frank looked the business from day one and although he looked like he was carrying a bit of weight he used it to good effect. He was simply unplayable at times using his body well to get in front of defenders and shielding the ball until his breaking midfielders linked up with him.

He became a firm fans favourite when he scored a hat-trick in a 5-1 drubbing of Rangers at Pittodrie on January 19, 1985 and for good measure on November 13 of the same year he scored all four goals at home against Celtic in a 4-1 win.

Frank played for just two full seasons but clocked up more honours than most players would win in a lifetime. As well as the League title he also lifted the League Cup after Hibs were beaten. Then he helped us destroy their Edinburgh rivals Hearts in the Scottish Cup final of the same season. It should be no surprise to anyone that he finished top scorer in his two seasons at Pittodrie, scoring twenty-four in the league winning season and getting twenty in the next.

Frank could be a bit like a bull in a china shop at times and wasn't shy in coming forward. I remember one game against Hearts when Frank had struggled with a groin strain and played when maybe he really shouldn't but it was a measure of the man he would never even admit he was injured.

The next morning he was given a real roasting by the gaffer for his poor performance and reacted badly because he felt he had played when injured and that had been a mitigating factor. Since then he has told the story to anyone who will listen that he punched Sir Alex in anger and floored him although the boss was up in seconds like a boxer trying to beat the count. I can't imagine anyone has ever done that to Sir Alex apart from Frank and lived to tell the tale.

Frank had lots of respect for the gaffer and knew the minute he threw the punch that he had made a big, big mistake. He made great efforts to stay out of the gaffer's way for as long as possible to allow him to calm down and when he did go to apologise he feared the worst.

Although he got a dressing down he wasn't kicked out of the club. The gaffer said he could make it up to him on the pitch and big Frank breathed the biggest sigh of relief of his life. Don't think the gaffer made the decision out of the goodness of his heart. Sir Alex knew that because Frank was in such great form he could not afford to sack him. Also I am sure Teddy Scott made him give big Frank a second chance as Teddy was like that and could have got a job with the United Nations, such was his ability to smooth things over.

Frank's career ended because of a serious back injury that brought the curtain down on his playing career which was a tragedy as who knows how much he could have achieved if he had remained fit.

His last game was against Hibs early in the 1986/87 season when he hobbled off the pitch with a back complaint. He tried to make it back but unfortunately for Ian Porterfield, who replaced Sir Alex as manager, it never happened and on his twenty-ninth birthday he got the bad news he was being forced to retire. Frank had played just seventy-five games for the club but in my book should still be regarded as one of Aberdeen's greatest strikers. The gaffer used to say that Frank was his greatest ever signing at Aberdeen and there is no higher praise that he can receive.

Derek 'Cup tie' McKay deserves a mention for his place in Aberdeen's football folklore. Yes he was only at the club for over a season but in that time he helped the club win their first Scottish Cup since 1947 and became a real cult hero. Derek clearly lived the dream of having success with the club he supported as a boy.

He was a Banff lad who got up to all sorts of mischief with Joe Harper. Derek was a real character and in the 1969/70 season, when he joined us on a free transfer from Dundee, he was on fire in the Scottish Cup.

Overall Derek played thirteen league matches and didn't score once. He wasn't even picked to play in any League Cup matches, but boy oh boy did he save his best for the Scottish Cup. In four incredible months he went from being a fringe player in the competition to one of our main strikers alongside his pal Joe.

It was a flu bug that downed several key players that led to Derek being drafted into Eddie Turnbull's starting team for the quarter-finals against Falkirk on February 3, 1970 in the first place.

Eddie was so concerned that he was missing so many top guys because of the flu bug he petitioned the SFA to have the game postponed, which they rejected.

Derek had been playing on the wing for the reserves and was drafted in for his first start for the club for the simple reason Eddie didn't have anyone else left standing as they were all in their beds ill.

Derek must have realised this was meant to be and he went on to play one of his greatest games, scoring the only goal of the match.

Eddie was never someone who would disregard a player in form and retained Derek for the next four league games, and also for the Scottish Cup semi-final against Kilmarnock on March 14 at Muirton Park, Perth. Lightning struck in the same place twice and he was at his goalscoring best yet again netting the winner in front of over 25,000 fans.

In the final against Celtic at Hampden he scored twice, with his pal Joe Harper getting the other from the penalty spot in the famous win. He had played just three Scottish cup ties, scored four vital goals and helped his team to victory. What a story!

As such things unfortunately happen in football Derek dropped out of the spotlight as quickly as he had arrived in it. He played only two games of the following season before having a contract disagreement with Eddie and left the club after his moment in the sun.

Derek used to say the thing that led to the rift between him and Eddie was the fact that Aberdeen were on £250 a man to win the Scottish Cup final while Celtic got £500 for getting beat.

Having a financial sense of injustice that would have made Stuart

Kennedy, who was our union rep of sorts in my day, proud he marched in to complain along with Joe Harper. The deadly duo won the argument and the Aberdeen board paid out an extra £250 per man, but he claims Eddie never liked him after that.

Derek played briefly for Forres in the Highland League and then joined Barrow before taking his talents to Hong Kong, South Africa and Australia.

I was saddened to hear of Derek's death from a heart attack when he was on holiday in Thailand in 2008 and my thoughts – like all Aberdeen fans – were with his family. Derek was only fifty-nine when he died, which was far too early but his Scottish Cup fairytale story will live on forever in the hearts of Aberdeen fans everywhere.

A similar type of forward to Derek was Joe Miller who many associate with Celtic, but who did us a decent turn in his two seasons at Pittodrie. Sir Alex gave him his debut as a seventeen year old against Dundee United just three days before Christmas in 1984. Throwing Joe in at the deep end at such a young age was a statement of intent by the gaffer who rated him highly.

Joe won his first Scottish Cup winners medal in 1986 when he came on for John Hewitt in the victory over Hearts at Hampden just before Sir Alex left for Manchester United. Unfortunately Joe left at the end of the following season to join Celtic. I brought him back to Pittodrie when I was manager and he went on to be part of Roy Aitken's team that won the Scottish League Cup in 1995 after a win over Dundee.

When the words Dream Team were mentioned in the thirties at Pittodrie it was usually in relation not to the whole side but to the striking partnership of Matt Armstrong and Willie Mills. They were the real lights of the north in the 1930s, with Mills, who was an old-fashioned attacking inside forward, providing and scoring goals.

Willie, who was from Bonhill in Dunbartonshire, was just seventeen when he made his debut in August 1932 against Motherwell at Pittodrie and within three months had scored his first hat-trick in the 8-1 win over Clyde at Pittodrie. It was in the 1934/35 season that the pair of them made such a big impression. Willie missed just two matches – against Falkirk at home and Dundee away through injury and scored sixteen goals from forty appearances. Armstrong, who was more of a straightforward number nine, also missed just two games – in his case against Patrick Thistle and Falkirk – and netted thirty-nine times in forty-three appearances.

What I find incredible is that with such a great goalscoring duo Aberdeen still finished just sixth in the league and lost in the semi-final of the Scottish Cup to Hamilton where Willie scored our consolation goal.

Willie's team did make the Scottish Cup final of 1937 when they lost 2-1 to Celtic but that was as close as he ever got to winning anything at Pittodrie. Willie was one of the most famous figures in Scottish football at the time, with Aberdeen manager Pat Travers claiming five minutes of Willie playing to his full potential could win any match for his team.

Although the short, passing game was in vogue Willie was one of the few players who was actively encouraged to play sweeping passes from one side of the pitch to the other as everybody knew he could land the ball on a sixpence.

Willie was transferred to Huddersfield for £6,500 in 1938 on the offer of a weekly wage of £8 but like so many players had his career cut short by the Second World War.

Another great entertainer at Pittodrie was left winger Tommy Pearson. Tommy is a prime example of how sometimes a player can better with age.

He joined Aberdeen for £4,000 from Newcastle United in 1948 when he was thirty-five years old. He was famous for his 'double-shuffle' which he perfected playing football for the army. He used to stand in front of a player and with his quick feet go one way and then the other, catch them off balance and head towards the byline. The patriotic Scot interestingly turned out for England as 'an emergency winger' during the war years when they were short of players.

Such was his standing in British football that for Aberdeen to get such a superstar, even at the age of thirty-five was still a huge deal. Thousands used to turn up to watch him even in reserve matches. He retired in 1953 after eighty-four games and sixteen goals spread over a six year period.

He wasn't finished just yet and returned in 1959 as manager but could not recapture the magic he showed in his playing days and resigned in 1965.

The next man I considered for my Dream Team squad was Dave 'Brush' Robb – who got his nickname because he supposedly looked like Basil Brush.

Some Aberdeen players always saw themselves as sharp dressers, as befits their reputations as superstars. Look at a picture of Dave Robb and you will see the direct opposite. A kipper tie, jackets with big lapels, wide flairs. In other words a 1970s fashion disaster, but to be fair he wasn't alone. We were all guilty of crimes against dress sense, Dave more than most.

Also did you know Bobby Clark used to dream about Dave? Not all the time, thank heaven, but after Dave's finest moment in an Aberdeen jersey the bold Bobby claimed he knew he was going to be a hero.

The pair of them had roomed together before the 1976 Scottish League Cup final where Bobby played but Dave, despite having a great season, had been left on the bench by Ally MacLeod. As things turned out Dave had the last laugh because after Kenny Dalglish had scored from the spot Drew Jarvie equalised before Dave came off the bench to score the winner during the first period of extra-time.

Dave was delighted at scoring the winner but was left a bit disconcerted when Bobby told him after the game he had been dreaming about him and the dream had ended with Dave scoring the winning goal. Bobby was such an honest gent I can only assume he didn't make up his Mystic Meg act just to spook Dave, but it certainly did just that.

Unfortunately Bobby never woke up again on the morning of any match predicting that Dave would score a goal for us because if he did we would have all been down the bookies sharp as you like to put on a tenner. Only joking, all you reading this with links to the SFA!

I have a lot to thank Dave for because when I was breaking through he was always very helpful and it was an indication of his long-standing consistency and talent that he played under Eddie Turnbull, who recruited him from junior football as well as Jimmy Bonthrone, Ally MacLeod and Billy McNeill before he reached the end of the line soon after Sir Alex took over.

The next man came closer than any other to making my Dream Team but in the end I have left him reluctantly on the bench.

I had to think long and hard over whether to include Duncan Shearer because since the glory days of the 1980s and early 1990s he has been Aberdeen's most prolific goalscorer and a big fans favourite.

What many forget is that Duncan arrived at Pittodrie the finished article after some good seasons south of the border. He started as a striker at Inverness Clachnacuddin and from the Highland League moved to Chelsea in 1983 before moving to Huddersfield, Swindon Town and Blackburn Rovers.

Although we had a great side in the 1980s under Sir Alex I rate Duncan so highly that I am sure he could have held his own and been an important member of our squad. Indeed Sir Alex had watched Duncan score five times in an Aberdeen reserve game and was thinking about signing him when he was a teenager but illness meant he missed a second trial and dropped off the radar before he moved south.

When I was manager I had tried to sign him from Swindon Town but was beaten by Kenny Dalglish at Blackburn Rovers and thought I had lost my man for good. But Duncan never settled there and I managed to bring him north for £500,000 in 1992 and it was money very well spent.

Deadly Dunc had a fantastic strike rate and was easily my best signing when I was manager. He helped improve strikers such as

Eoin Jess, Scott Booth and to a lesser extent Mixu Paatelainen and Billy Dodds.

He played 116 league games, scoring fifty-three goals. He was part of the team that lost the Scottish Cup final to Rangers in 1993 and two years later was in the side that won the Scottish League Cup where he scored along with Billy Dodds. He was still playing at thirty-five with Inverness Caledonian Thistle, which is an incredible achievement in the modern era.

He played seven times for Scotland and remains a true Aberdeen legend. Through the years we have had some top-class strikers at Aberdeen and for me Duncan can be mentioned in the same breath as all the greats. He was always on his toes and if you look closely at television footage from that era you will notice that Duncan is always in the picture waiting for a slip-up by the goalkeeper. He was incredibly quick-thinking and scored lots of what you would call poacher's goals.

With his experience it was no surprise that he turned to coaching and was part of the backroom staff when Caley Thistle beat Celtic 3-1 at Parkhead in the Scottish Cup in the year 2000. Duncan was assistant to Steve Paterson at Caley Thistle before he became Steve's number two at Aberdeen, which, as everyone knows, didn't prove a success and the pair left Pittodrie in 2004.

There were two players with the same name who I considered for my Dream Team both classy players indeed. Jimmy Smith from Ayrshire joined from Rangers as a full back in 1922 but was transformed into a left winger at Pittodrie. In nine seasons he hardly missed a match clocking up an impressive 297 appearances and scoring sixty-four times. For that alone he deserves respect as he was one of our finest servants between the wars.

The other Jimmy Smith was another class act who I just missed training and playing with at Pittodrie but heard lots about. He was a Glaswegian just like me and a top-class inside forward. Some fans called him 'Jinky' because they said he could do things on his day that was on a par with the legendary Jimmy Johnstone.

That is high praise indeed and in 1968 Jock Stein made a bid to bring him to Parkhead that failed, with Jimmy staying for one more season before he moved to Newcastle United for £80,000, where he played alongside the goal machine that was 'Supermac' Malcolm MacDonald to whom he supplied many a wonderful cross. The fact that 8,000 turned up to watch his first game for Newcastle reserves against Aston Villa's second string tells you all you have to know about his talent. Also the fact he is still revered on Tyneside shows his standing in what is a football hotbed. Anyone who saw him in action for the four seasons he was at Pittodrie where he played 103 games and scored thirty-seven goals can count themselves lucky.

Others I feel worthy of a mention include outside left Billy Strauss who was one of the unluckiest players I came across in my research. He was a South African who helped the Dons get to the Scottish Cup final in 1937 for the first time in their history with some remarkable scoring.

He netted twice in the first round 6-0 win over Inverness Thistle and followed that up with two goals in the 4-1 win over Third Lanark. The Dons got a bye in the third round and next up was Hamilton Academical when he scored the winner in a close match that finished 2-1.

In the semi-final he was on target again scoring the second of two goals in a win over Morton at Easter Road. After playing so well to get his team into the final the poor bloke picked up a serious leg injury in that match and missed the final. Many feel if Billy had been fit Aberdeen would have beaten Celtic that day rather than narrowly losing.

Another South African who will always remain part of Aberdeen history is little Stan Williams. I looked at his playing record at Pittodrie and it was impressive.

Stan was spotted on Aberdeen's tour of South Africa in 1937. He had two full seasons at Pittodrie before guesting for a variety of clubs including Millwall and Stoke City during the war.

When hostilities ended he returned north thinking he had some unfinished business and went about things the right way. He scored in the 1947 quarter-final and semi-final Scottish Cup wins over

Dundee and Arbroath respectively and went on to secure a special place in the hearts of all Dons fans by being a member of the first ever Aberdeen team to lift the trophy in April of that year.

Hibs had taken the lead in the game but it was Stan who crossed for George Hamilton to head home the equaliser. Three minutes before half-time he wrote his name into the history books by getting on the end of a Tony Harris through ball to score the goal that helped the Dons to victory.

Coming from South Africa, not surprisingly the one thing Stan hated about the north-east of Scotland was the weather. His trade-mark stance during a break in play was to hold his shirt sleeves over his hands. What he did love by all accounts was the dancing in the Palais in Diamond Street and he was also a keen golfer as well who loved to play the course at Stonehaven.

The men who concluded my Dream Team debate are Benny Yorston and Harry Yorston, who were distantly related. Benny, who signed for Aberdeen in 1927, turned out to be the second cousin of Harry's dad.

He was only five feet five inches tall, but had great timing in the air and could shoot with either foot. During the 1929/30 season he scored thirty-eight league goals in thirty-eight appearances and was capped by Scotland in 1931. Unfortunately for Benny he appears to have blotted his copybook by becoming involved in the betting scandal, 'The Great Mystery', and left under a cloud to go to Middlesbrough.

Harry seems to have been very much a different character, was always smiling and became known as 'The Golden Boy' during his time at Pittodrie. He joined from local juvenile side St Clement's in 1946 and made his debut on Christmas Day 1947. His present to the travelling Aberdeen fans that day was a goal within five minutes, although Third Lanark still won 3-2. Over a decade he played 201 times and scored 141 times making him the most consistent goal-scorer that had been at the club since its formation.

Although he appears to have split fans opinion, some of whom felt he never really fulfilled his full potential, that incredible scoring record speaks for itself. I most definitely am on the side of the folk who felt Harry, who was in the Scottish League and League Cup winning sides of the mid 1950s is up there among the best who have played at the club.

Harry quit Aberdeen in 1957, aged twenty-eight, to follow the family tradition of becoming a fish porter which was a much-prized job in Aberdeen. He played out his career with Buckie Thistle, Fraserburgh, Deveronvale and Lossiemouth.

Remember I told you he was called 'Golden Boy' during his time at Pittodrie? Well good luck never left him. In 1972 his wife, who was a local nurse, won £175,000 on Littlewoods pools, which was a huge amount of money back then and meant he gave up being a fish porter and led a life of luxury which included the odd visit or two to see his beloved Aberdeen. Wonder if he could have been the money man to have paid for my Dream Team? Certainly my front three alone would be worth a king's ransom in today's transfer market.

More than thirty years ago I described Joe Harper as meaning more to Aberdeen Football Club than North Sea oil and I stand by every word. I may have had so many great strikers to choose from for my Dream Team but it was wee Joe that was first on my list.

His contribution to the club has to be put in context. Although Eddie Turnbull had put together a decent team the brutal fact was that Aberdeen had won not a single major honour since 1955 when the team ran out to play Celtic in the Scottish Cup final of 1970.

Jock Stein's Celtic were the biggest favourites for years against an Aberdeen team that many didn't give a prayer. They needed a hero that day and 'King Joey' fitted the bill. I was an apprentice at Pittodrie at the time and watched the game on television.

I remember Celtic dominating the first fifteen minutes or so but Martin Buchan kept the Aberdeen defence rock solid. The game turned on its head when Bobby Murdoch handled a Derek McKay cross and referee Bobby Davidson pointed to the spot.

Tommy Gemmell got booked for moving the ball from the penalty spot and through it all the Celtic players did their best to put Joe off. As mayhem broke out all around him for a full nine minutes he casually played keepie-uppie. It was a supreme moment from a supreme player. It showed that Joe would not be intimidated.

When he finally stepped up to take the penalty Evan Williams in the Celtic goal didn't even move. Instead he just fell to his knees as Joe's shot hit the net. It was the breakthrough Aberdeen needed and they matched Celtic from then on in.

With seven minutes left a Jim Forrest shot fell to Derek McKay, a big mate of Joe's as I mentioned earlier, who scored. Bobby Lennox got one back but Derek scored again and the cup was heading back to Pittodrie.

Although Derek grabbed the headlines it was wee Joe's contribution that fascinated me. He showed me that it is possible to go into the zone, as they might call it, in pressure situations and keep your concentration. Lesser players would have missed that vital penalty that day but not Joe Harper.

He became a hero to a whole generation of young Aberdeen fans, some of whom I saw playing in the park, falling to their knees just like Joe did every time he scored. I used to say to him he must have skinned his knees a hell of a lot through the years as he scored so many goals.

Now I know from first-hand experience he didn't see eye to eye with Sir Alex and left, at the age of thirty-three, fairly early on during Sir Alex's time in charge on not terribly good terms but that does not detract from his talent.

As this is my Dream Team, having Sir Alex managing wee Joe again at the peak of his powers as well as Gordon Strachan for that matter would make the dressing room an interesting place.

Joe was as sharp with his tongue as he was with his boot and didn't suffer fools gladly. Once when a drunken journalist goaded his young team mate, Arthur Graham, Joe punched him in the face.

When he was carried off with a serious knee injury at Celtic Park, to the strains of 'Harper's a barrel, Harper's a barrel of shite', he sat up on his stretcher to blow kisses. He also used to occasionally grab defenders by the testicles to put them off their game to gain half a yard. He would stop at nothing to score goals.

I would say I played alongside Joe but he never ventured much into his own half and some would say my second home was within sight of Jim Leighton. He always reminded me of that prolific German striker Gerd Muller in that he was a small, barrel-chested type of player who if you passed in the street would not have given him a second look.

Indeed, I bet a lot of defenders saw wee Joe wandering out onto the pitch before kick-off and thought they would be able to keep him in their pocket. They could never be more wrong as his brain was always quicker than their feet. Even if we didn't give Joe the best of service he would still scavenge for the ball. He could live off scraps and drive defenders crazy with his constant hassling.

His mentor was Eddie Turnbull, who brought him to Aberdeen in the first place from Morton, but even that relationship was not without its problems. I remember he told me Sir Alex was like a pussycat compared to Eddie who signed him for £40,000 in 1969. Joe told me that he had once been left with a black eye after Eddie had punched him once during a disagreement.

Like me, Joe, had a debut we used to joke about. I made my debut as a left winger against Morton in 1973 after Arthur Graham was injured. He made his debut four years earlier against Ayr as a right winger, which wasn't too bad, with Jim Forrest and Davie Robb playing the two striking roles. But because you were only allowed one substitute back then an injury to Henning Boel meant he had to move back to right back which most definitely was not Joe's favourite position.

I was training with him but had never played a first team game when he left Aberdeen for Everton for £172,000 in December 1972. I had been impressed the year before he left when he scored a total of forty-two goals – thirty-three in the league, two in the Scottish Cup, four in the League Cup and three in Europe – from a total of forty-seven appearances which won him the European 'Bronze Boot' for the third highest goalscorer in Europe. That remains for me one of the most impressive modern day scoring records that I have witnessed in Aberdeen's history.

The ninety minutes I remember more than any other that season was his four goals in a 7-0 league win over Ayr which were a mixture of long range efforts, tap-ins and headers. A real tour de force for Joe that day.

After his time at Everton and Hibs he returned to the club under Ally MacLeod in April 1976, which is when I really got to know Joe. In his first season back he replaced me as captain for the first three Scottish League Cup ties as I had to sit them out because of suspension. He led Aberdeen to wins over Kilmarnock, St Mirren and Ayr United before I got the captaincy back and led us out to our League Cup final win over Celtic where Joe played a major role. He scored a total of twenty-eight goals from forty-eight appearances that season which enhanced his standing with the fans who were delighted to have him back.

Joe scored thirty-two goals in Sir Alex's first full season in charge but had fallen out of favour and also picked up a bad knee injury the year we won the championship in 1979/80. Although he played seven times in the League, that knee injury he picked up against Celtic on November 29, 1979 meant he played just eleven league games that season.

He played 364 times for Aberdeen scoring 242 goals in all competitions which includes friendlies. Two hundred and five of them came in competitive matches which was a massive forty-seven ahead of Matt Armstrong, who is the second highest scorer in the history of the club, so you can see why Joe is an Aberdeen legend and an important part of my Dream Team.

It was between Frank McDougall and Mark McGhee as to who would be my main striker but in the end Mark got the nod because of his ability to blend in with the other two front men I have chosen as well as his ability to score regularly at the top level for longer than Frank did.

Mark, at his peak, was a real street-wise player, who knew exactly how to find gaps in the opposition defence. Like Frank he was a real physical player that nobody could push off the ball very easily. He was strong, powerful, gritty, determined and fearless. All you ever wanted in a striker.

His experience will be vital in my Dream Team as even when he arrived at Aberdeen he had been at a few other top clubs beforehand and was at his peak when he arrived at Pittodrie.

He had been at Bristol City as a sixteen-year-old in 1973 before returning north to join Morton where his displays had English clubs bidding to secure his services. Newcastle United won the race to sign him for £150,000 and he scored thirty-six goals in ninety-nine appearances for them which is a decent return. In March 1979 Sir Alex had him watched a few times and brought him north to join us for £80,000 when he was still just twenty-one years old, where he was an instant success.

He was in the team that won the 1983 European Cup Winners' Cup and UEFA Super Cup and before he left us he also had two Scottish Premier Division medals and three Scottish Cup badges in his collection.

Mention Mark's name and the first thing many Dons fans will think of is his left-foot cross to John Hewitt for the winning goal in the European Cup Winners' Cup final against Real Madrid. In a way I am pleased that is continually mentioned as that one incident was a prime example of the tireless work that Mark did during matches. He wasn't one of these strikers who would never leave the six yard area.

During our successful European run he scored six goals in ten games and his double in the 5-1 first leg win over Belgian side Waterschei got us into the final in the first place.

The one domestic game I remember involving Mark more than any other was his performance in the 1982 Scottish Cup final against Rangers. He had been rampaging around the park all day putting the fear of death into the Rangers defenders and they could not cope with him.

He had gone close a couple of times and Rangers were fortunate to take the match into extra-time after it had finished 1-1 with goals from Alex McLeish and John MacDonald for Rangers.

It was fitting that it was Mark who scored with a header three minutes into the first period of extra-time which opened the floodgates as he had played superbly well.

We all took great confidence from his goal and it was Mark who set up Gordon Strachan for the third before Neale Cooper made it 4-1 for one of the most satisfying wins of all my time at Aberdeen. He also got the Scottish Cup final winner two years later when we beat Celtic in what proved to be his final game for the club. He joined Hamburg for £280,000 in the summer of 1984 after six great years and after that moved to Celtic for £200,000 and then Newcastle United.

Mark went into management as player-manager at Reading where he took over from Ian Porterfield who used to be boss at Aberdeen, after being recommended for the job by Sir Alex Ferguson. He then had time at Wolverhampton Wanderers before he became a scout at Coventry City where his big pal from his Aberdeen days, Gordon Strachan, was manager.

Two months later he was appointed manager at Millwall, and had spells at Brighton and then Motherwell before he joined us. It was a huge disappointment for me, and indeed for Mark, that his time at Pittodrie did not work out as he would have liked. We suffered some heavy defeats during his eighteen months in charge but I never once doubted Mark's professionalism or dedication.

After we were beaten by Inverness there was a meeting when we had a long and frank discussion with Mark when he came over to the board as still being as passionate as he was about taking Aberdeen forward.

Unfortunately soon afterwards results did not improve and it was with deep regret that he parted company with Aberdeen, the club he has served so well as player and as manager, in December 2010.

What happened when he was manager should not detract from his standing at Aberdeen Football Club and I have no hesitation in naming him in my Aberdeen Dream Team.

The final member of my front three is a man who I got on incredibly well with during his time at Pittodrie and who was one of my best mates at the club. You may be surprised to learn that the player in question is 'Champagne' Charlie Nicholas.

Before he arrived at Aberdeen I played against Charlie when he was at Celtic and he could be an elusive bugger. Give him an inch and he would take a mile.

I would have Mark McGhee as the main striker in my Dream Team with Charlie and Joe Harper just in behind.

Also Charlie and Joe have the ability to drift wide and I expect both men to create chances as well as score them. They are not out-and-out target men, but I like the blend of Mark through the middle and Joe and Charlie either in behind or playing off him.

I accept that some of you will be questioning the inclusion of Charlie in my Dream Team, maybe more than any other. I can understand that to a degree as a lot of football supporters think of Arsenal or Celtic when they think of Charlie.

He is in first and foremost because he is a great, great player who fits into my Dream Team formation. Secondly, as I touched on earlier, he had a seismic affect on the club when he arrived as he was a superb signing and he gave the fans something to shout about.

Thirdly the bottle he showed to take and score a penalty against Celtic in the Scottish Cup final shoot-out of 1990 showed how much Aberdeen Football Club meant to him at the time. It was an open secret before the match that he was going back to join Celtic afterwards.

So here he was playing in a Scottish Cup final against Celtic, the team he supported as a boy and was about to rejoin, and about to take the fifth and final regulation shoot-out penalty against them. Miss and Celtic would have won the final with what would be Charlie's last kick of the ball ever for Aberdeen. Score and there was every chance the Parkhead club would lose and miss out on a place in Europe for the first time in nearly forty years. That would have impacted on Charlie, who would not have European nights at Parkhead to look forward to when he returned there.

I was watching the match from the stands that day and was

praying he scored. If he missed you can guess what people would have said. As it turned out I need not have worried. Charlie stood strong and fired it home before saluting the Aberdeen fans, and he celebrated as much as the next player after we beat his boyhood heroes 9-8 when Theo Snelders saved Anton Rogan's penalty before Brian Irvine put away the winning kick. To put himself down for the fifth and final regulation penalty took guts and showed the character of the guy. I want players like that in my Dream Team.

Being a total professional Charlie enjoyed beating Celtic that day. But what I bet he enjoyed even more was when two Paul Mason goals saw us lift the Scottish League Cup with an extra-time win over a star-studded Rangers side that included the likes of Terry Butcher, Ray Wilkins, Trevor Steven, Ally McCoist and Mo Johnston seven months earlier. To say Charlie was happy as he went up to get his winners medal at Hampden that day was an understatement. He was getting terrible stick from the Ibrox faithful but that just made him play harder, and he was in great form and had the last laugh.

Charlie used to call me 'the head waiter' because I used to sit at the back observing everyone else running about daft and letting them do the dirty work. 'Buffalo' was also his other nickname for me after 'Buffalo Bill' who he thought I resembled because of my big, black moustache.

I had a bit a reputation for being a bit of a loner at times which is an accusation you could never have thrown at Charlie. He was the life and soul of the party and a man who was great fun to be with. He turned out to be one of the most exciting signings ever made by the club and was an instant hit with the fans.

Ian Porterfield brought him from Arsenal for £500,000 on New Year's Day 1988 and it was an incredible coup. Charlie had offers on the table from the legendary Brian Clough at Nottingham Forest, and Derby County were also keen to keep him south of the border.

I must admit I wasn't sure what to expect to begin with. I knew him from the time when we were in the same Scotland squads from 1983 and we had got on very well but that was a very different environment to the club game. Here we would see each other every day and as senior players would have a lot of responsibility on our shoulders.

In the past Charlie had been more used to nightclubs than cold nights in the north-east and he looked, dare I say it, a bit of a poseur, the first time he walked through the door at Pittodrie.

He arrived in a leather coat and fedora hat and looked like Bono from U2. We were all thinking here comes a big-time Charlie but he wasn't like that at all. The minute he walked into the dressing room he immediately became one of the lads, and great mates with myself and my big mate Craig Robertson.

Maybe he took one look at the likes of me in particular, who was six years older than him and thought, 'No, I can't imagine having much fun with this lot day after day.' But can I just say he did and was a great asset to our squad. Charlie never acted like he was above us and the fact he had just got married at the time maybe settled him down a bit.

More than 20,000 fans turned up to watch his debut at Pittodrie against Dunfermline on January 16, 1988, which was 6,000 up on the last visit of the Pars to Aberdeen. He scored in his second game against Motherwell but the fact that he had been out of favour with Arsenal manager George Graham and had not played for three months meant he was a bit rusty for the remainder of the season. To be fair to Charlie our championship challenge had evaporated long before he arrived and he could do little to improve our position as we finished a disappointing fourth, a massive thirteen points behind Celtic.

Charlie was a marked man from his first game in Aberdeen colours with things coming to a head in our Scottish Cup campaign of that season. We beat St Johnstone, Hamilton and Clyde but lost in the semi-final to Dundee United which turned out to be a steamy affair involving me, Charlie and Jim McLean.

The first semi-final match was a drab affair ending 0-0 at Dens Park. There was more tension off the park than on it with Ian Porterfield and his assistant Jimmy Mullen sent to the stand after a touchline row with the fourth official. The replay was very, very different and there was bad feeling from the start with tackles flying in everywhere.

Because of Charlie's talent he was getting more than his fair share of attention from the Dundee United defenders. Four minutes before half-time in the replay, that was held at Dens Park once again, Paul Hegarty brought down Charlie in a really bad challenge near the corner flag.

As captain I felt well within my rights to get down there and find out how Charlie was, and also voice my anger towards Paul and make my point to the referee Bill Crombie for the persistent fouls going in on him.

As I passed the referee on the way to check on Charlie, who was writhing in agony on the turf I noticed him take the red card out of his pocket and flash it at Paul. Thankfully Charlie was not seriously injured in the challenge, although he could have been, and he scored just before the break to put us ahead which was a bit of poetic justice.

As I headed towards the tunnel chatting to Charlie with a spring in my step, out of the corner of my eye I saw big Alex McLeish and Maurice Malpas trying to keep Dundee United boss Jim McLean away from me. Jim accused me of running seventy yards to complain to the ref about Paul's tackle and to try and get him sent off, which was a laughable accusation. It was so silly that I only knew that was what he was claiming after the game, which ended in a 1-1 draw, with Charlie scoring our goal.

It says a lot about how Charlie had matured since he arrived at Aberdeen that when Jim disgracefully tried to gatecrash the man of the match presentation at the end of the game, he kept his cool. As Charlie was being presented with a bottle of champagne, Jim was calling him for everything just off camera and had to be held back. Jim had really lost the rag and his actions led to him receiving a three-year touchline ban and a £4,000 fine from the SFA.

I could understand why the punishment was so severe as his actions at half-time could have led to crowd trouble. In the end Jim had the last laugh over me and Charlie because in the third semi-final match an Ian Ferguson goal put United into the Scottish Cup final at our expense.

So there you have it. That is my Aberdeen Dream Team, a side that I am confident would beat any other, anywhere, anytime. As I have said before in the book, you may not agree with my final choices but you can't argue with the quality of the players, both in my starting eleven and on the bench – or, for that matter, the manager and backroom staff that would put them through their paces.

I know when I played, Sir Alex Ferguson favoured a 4-4-2 but I decided to go with a 4-3-3 because, let's not forget, I had top players from every generation to try and fit into my team and felt this was the best way to get them all in.

I had great fun picking my Dream Team and I hope you have enjoyed reading about all the stars from the history of Aberdeen Football Club that made the club so great.

Willie Miller's Aberdeen Dream Team
4-3-3

Goalkeeper:
Jim Leighton
Defence:
Stewart Kennedy, Alex McLeish, Martin Buchan, John McMaster
Midfield:
Gordon Strachan, Jim Bett, Peter Weir
Forwards:
Charlie Nicholas, Mark McGhee, Joe Harper

Subs:
Bobby Clark
Stewart McKimmie
Steve Archibald
John Hewitt
Frank McDougall

George Hamilton
Duncan Shearer

Manager: Sir Alex Ferguson
Assistant manager: Archie Knox
Coach: Teddy Scott
Chief Scout: Bobby Calder
Assistant chief scout: Jim Carswell
Chairman: Dick Donald

9

THE MAN IN THE MIDDLE

Now I have my Aberdeen Dream Team, manager and back room staff in place we are ready to face all comers but we need someone to referee our matches. Some opposition fans suggested I did my best to ref matches when I played but I always maintained that was just sour grapes on their part because they had to blame somebody for Aberdeen being better than their team.

While the north east of Scotland has produced many top whistlers over the years, they all followed on from one of the most famous in Scottish football, who I have chosen to be our Dream Team referee.

Peter Craigmyle was one of the best known referees in an age when sporting fervour was just as heated as we see today, but respect was always given to the officials in charge. He spent thirty-one years as a whistler after first hitting the big time when taking charge of an Old Firm match at the age of just twenty-three.

He was brought up in Aberdeen and it was a terrible accident that made him turn to refereeing. It was in August 1916 that Peter broke both his legs in an accident in a naval dockyard in Invergordon. Back then young Peter played in goal for Aberdeen side Linksfield but his accident put paid to that.

It was after a chance meeting with Aberdeen manager Jimmy Philip, who was a former referee, in 1918 that persuaded him to pick up his whistle. The following year, after progressing through the ranks, Jimmy asked him to take charge of Aberdeen friendly matches against Albion Rovers, Third Lanark, Partick and Hearts. Reports of how well he had officiated in these matches went down well with the SFA as up until that moment there were no top-class whistlers in the north-east of Scotland.

Later that year he was accepted as a referee by the SFA and Scottish League. Peter asked Aberdeen for use of their training facilities and not only did Jimmy Philip agree, he insisted on Craigmyle training with the rest of the Aberdeen team which included the likes of Jock Hutton and Bobby Hannah.

After 'serving his time' in the Highland League, Craigmyle took charge of a top flight game at Tynecastle between Hearts and Albion Rovers in 1920. Two years later he was due to take charge of a game in the south when a rail strike wrecked his travel plans. The call came from Pittodrie as a referee was required for the Dons match against Morton because no officials could make it north due to the same rail strike. Refereeing an Aberdeen game in front of 25,000 supporters was a tough task for a local boy but he showed enough quality to suggest that he was destined for a lengthy career as a referee.

In December 1921 Peter sent off his first player; Celtic's Joe Cassidy after he threw a punch at Falkirk defender Tommy Scott; a blow that effectively knocked him out and split his jaw. Ten days later his first Old Firm match beckoned and it was after that Celtic sending off that Craigmyle was asked whether it would be better if he called off from taking charge of the fixture. Typically Peter refused and at the age of twenty-three he took charge of his first Celtic v Rangers match.

Three years later he took charge of his first full international, at Liverpool where England played Ireland. In 1931 he took charge of the Scottish Cup final between Celtic and Motherwell.

In 1933 Peter created a 'first' by becoming the first referee ever to fly to a game. It was from Inverness to the Orkney Isles where he took charge of an inter-island game against Shetland. Peter had been taking charge of these games since 1928 but always made his way there by ferry up until then.

When he finally hung up his whistle, he went with a fitting testimonial from the legendary Arsenal boss Herbert Chapman who declared that Peter Craigmyle was 'as efficient and business-like an official as I have ever seen in the game'.

With such an impressive track record Peter is my choice as Dream Team referee and I bet he would never get a decision wrong.

10

CAPTAIN'S LOG

Being named Aberdeen captain was one of the proudest moments of my football career. It still sends a shiver down my spine when I think of when Ally MacLeod told me that I would follow in the footsteps of all-time great captains like Martin Buchan, Jimmy Mitchell and Archie Glen in leading the team. Since I retired, players of the calibre of Alex McLeish, Jim Leighton, Russell Anderson and Paul Hartley have all worn the armband with pride.

For every well known Aberdeen captain like the ones I have mentioned, there are others who have maybe been forgotten in the midst of time. As this is my Aberdeen Dream Team book can I use its pages to fulfil my own little dream which is to pay a personal tribute to all the Aberdeen captains of the past by telling you a little bit about them one by one.

Willie MacAulay will certainly not be a name that many Aberdeen fans will be familiar with, but it was Willie who had the distinction of being the first Aberdeen Football Club captain back in 1903 when Aberdeen made their first appearance as a club following the amalgamation of the original Aberdeen, Orion and Victoria United some months earlier. He was an obvious choice to lead the first Aberdeen side in their Northern League campaign for season 1903/04. His other claim to fame is that he scored the club's first ever competitive goal against Stenhousemuir on August 15, 1903. An injury and loss of form meant that he gave up the captaincy to

Duncan McNicol a year later. Duncan had been at Pittodrie since October 1903 and he arrived with a proven track record from Woolwich Arsenal. He was a classy full-back who went on to be widely accepted as the best player at the club in those days. After a long-term injury forced him to give up the professional game he went on to take up hockey in the Aberdeen area. There was no doubt that Aberdeen suffered in his enforced absence and the club came under increasing pressure from the support to rectify matters.

Former Scotland keeper **Rab MacFarlane** was one of the club's greatest characters and he took over the captaincy after re-signing for the club following a dispute over terms in 1906 but his ability to lead the team was perhaps not best served while playing in goal. While Rab's career was coming to a close another one was about to flourish.

Donald Colman was hardly a big name signing for the club when he arrived from Motherwell on a free transfer in 1907. Looked upon as too small for a defender, he enjoyed the best part of his career at Aberdeen and he went on to become one of the club's most distinguished captains. Donald was capped for Scotland at the age of thirty-three; the oldest Aberdeen player to be capped and he took over as Aberdeen captain from **Ecky Halkett** in 1908.

Colman was still around when football resumed after the First World War but **Bert MacLachlan** had taken over as captain by then. Bert served the club in two spells after joining from Aston Villa in 1914. He went on to represent the Scottish League and was the driving force behind the Dons in the immediate post war years. He was eventually allowed to join Hearts in 1927 after a succession of injuries had taken a toll at Pittodrie.

Aberdeen had a ready-made replacement as captain in former Rangers player **Bob McDermid** who joined Aberdeen in June 1925. He became a 'father figure' at Pittodrie in the aftermath of the bribes scandal known as 'The Great Mystery' in 1931.

Bob Fraser also emerged in the Aberdeen side after several first team players lost their places in 'The Great Mystery' and was appointed captain of the Dons side that performed well in the mid 1930s. Injury deprived Bob of leading the Dons out at Hampden in their first Scottish Cup Final in 1937, and it was Irishman **Eddie Falloon** who deputised. Aberdeen stalwart **Willie Cooper** also filled the captaincy role around the same time but was never made the regular captain at Pittodrie.

It was during the Second World War that **Frank Dunlop** emerged as the next Aberdeen captain and he had the distinction of leading Aberdeen to their first successes on the national stage. While the club had success during wartime football, it was in 1946 that Frank was captain of the Aberdeen side that beat Rangers 3-2 in the Southern League Cup Final before a 153,000 Hampden crowd. A year later the Scottish Cup followed after a win over Hibernian.

Former Aberdeen manager **Davie Shaw** was signed from Hibernian in 1950 and was immediately installed as captain at Pittodrie. Davie had a wealth of experience and was the Hibernian captain in direct opposition to the Dons in the 1947 Scottish Cup final. When he retired Aberdeen found a replacement in **Jimmy Mitchell**, a record club buy from Morton in 1952. He went on to lead Aberdeen through a successful period and was captain for Scottish Cup finals of 1953 and 1954. He was also the captain who led Aberdeen to their first League Championship in 1955 and also the League Cup success later that year. Jimmy was famed for his television interview after the final when he invited all Aberdonians to a party in Aberdeen to celebrate their win. More than 15,000 took him up on his offer as the Aberdeen Joint Station was swamped late into the night as the victorious Aberdeen side returned with the cup.

As the success of the 1950s evaporated, Aberdeen turned to **Archie Glen** as their next captain to guide the club through a difficult spell. Glen had been with the Dons since 1948 and was part of the famed Allister, Young and Glen half back line that was pivotal to the Dons success in the fifties. After Archie retired in 1960, Aberdeen appointed **Jimmy Hogg** as captain.

Jimmy had been around Pittodrie since 1952 and had to bide his time before becoming a regular in the first team following his move from Preston Athletic. The Dons released him in April 1965 as Aberdeen entered a new era with Eddie Turnbull at the helm. **George Kinnell** was a natural leader for the Dons in the early sixties and his tenacious approach was ideally suited in his role as club captain before he was sold to Stoke City in 1963. Turnbull later turned to **Ally Shewan** to lead the Dons in what were exciting times for the club. Ally had been the epitome of consistency in the Aberdeen side since joining in 1960. He was replaced by **Harry Melrose** who was signed from Dunfermline in 1965 and he had the distinction of leading Aberdeen to Hampden in the 1967 Scottish Cup Final against Celtic.

After Harry left, Danish international **Jens Petersen** stood in as captain until Turnbull turned to the Dons youngest captain at that point in local lad **Martin Buchan.** His first game as captain was certainly an eventful one as the Dons were jeered from the Pittodrie pitch after scraping past Clydebank in a Scottish Cup tie. Two months later Martin became the youngest player to captain a cup winning side when Aberdeen defeated Celtic 3-1 at Hampden to lift the Scottish Cup. Following Buchan's £125,000 transfer to Manchester United in February 1972, former Dundee captain **Steve Murray** was handed the captain's role at Pittodrie. Steve eventually left in 1974 after a contract dispute and joined Celtic. Former Scotland U-23 player **Jim Hermiston** took over as captain under Jimmy Bonthrone as the Dons were going through a period of transition. **Willie Young** was an emerging talent and he too would captain the side on occasion. Young's career at Pittodrie was effectively over when he threw his shirt at the Pittodrie management team after being taken off in a game against Dundee Utd in 1975. While Young was soon on his way to Tottenham, manager Jimmy Bonthrone left shortly after and made way for Ally MacLeod.

Bobby Clark was made captain at the start of season 1975/76 under Bonthrone, but when MacLeod arrived he wanted an outfield player to lead his side. He chose me and I joined the long list of men who had the honour of leading Aberdeen Football Club. The period when I was captain was the most successful in the Dons history and

I served under MacLeod, Billy McNeill, Alex Ferguson, Ian Porter-field, Alex Smith and Jocky Scott.

My first success was the League Cup in 1976 and there followed three Premier League titles, four Scottish Cups, two more League Cups and of course success in the European Cup Winners' Cup in 1983 and also the European Super Cup of the same year. My last honour as captain came in 1989 when we defeated Rangers 2-1 at Hampden, my third League Cup win.

Later that season, after I had sustained an injury that effectively ended my playing career, **Alex McLeish** took over as captain and led Aberdeen to a Scottish Cup win in 1990 over Celtic. Big Eck wound down a memorable Pittodrie career in 1994 when I was manager and handed the captaincy to **Stewart McKimmie**. Signed from Dundee in 1983, McKimmie won forty Scotland caps and he was the logical choice to lead the Dons at that time. Stewart became the last Aberdeen captain to lift a major trophy when Aberdeen won the League Cup in 1995. After Stewart moved to Dundee Utd in 1997, **Brian Irvine** took the armband on a temporary basis, then **Eoin Jess** was given a run as captain before **Jim Leighton** returned to Pittodrie in 1997 and was installed as captain.

When Alex Miller took over he brought in **Derek Whyte** from Middlesbrough and shortly after made the former Celtic defender the Dons captain. Derek remained in that role long after Alex Miller left and was captain under Ebbe Skovdahl. **Darren Young** was then the choice to lead the Dons, becoming the youngest player to captain the side since my good self.

After Ebbe left Aberdeen in 2002, Steve Paterson took over and when Derek moved to Dunfermline in 2003, **Russell Anderson** was the outstanding candidate to take over. Russell went on to lead Aberdeen back into Europe.

When he was sold to Sunderland for £1m in the summer of 2007 the manager at the time, Jimmy Calderwood then turned to his first signing, **Scott Severin** to take over as Aberdeen captain. Scott took Aberdeen through to the last thirty-two of the UEFA Cup in 2008 which ended in defeat to Bayern Munich. Severin followed

Anderson down south by signing for Watford in June 2009. When Scott left **Mark Kerr,** who had come from Dundee United, took over as captain for a season before leaving to play in Greece. **Paul Hartley** was given the captaincy by Mark McGhee and retained it under Craig Brown before he retired at the end of the 2010/11 season. At the start of the next season **Richard Foster** was given the honour of leading the team.

CELEBRITY DREAM TEAMS

ALLY BEGG

Ally Begg is from Newburgh in the north-east of Scotland and trained with Aberdeen as a schoolboy. He is currently one of ESPN's main worldwide sports anchors.

Ally Begg's Aberdeen Dream team (formation 4-4-1-1)

Manager: Sir Alex Ferguson
It would border on the ridiculous to select anybody else, not just Aberdeen's greatest ever manager but football's greatest ever manager. I have personal reasons for choosing Sir Alex as many moons ago the former St Mirren Chairman Willie Todd phoned my late grandfather (freelance football journalist, John Begg) and asked him for his advice on whom he thought would make an excellent manager. My grandfather gave Mr Todd one name, Alex Ferguson and he got his first job at Love Street. By the way, Sir Alex once told me never to change my broadcasting style; it's the best compliment I am ever likely to receive.

Goalkeeper: Theo Snelders
I was torn between Theo Snelders and Jim Leighton but I opted for Theo for one reason. His penalty shoot-out save from Anton Rogan

against Celtic in the 1990 Scottish Cup was the greatest save I have witnessed live.

Defence:
Stewart McKimmie. This was a simple choice, as he epitomized everything a full-back should be. He was great going forward had superb positional sense and defended like his life depended on it.
Alex McLeish. Simply Aberdeen's greatest centre back, no argument and a true gentleman.
Willie Miller. Aberdeen's greatest ever player, no argument. My hero!
Doug Rougvie. Unconventional and at times a little clumsy but a brilliant defender, who, coupled with his toothless grin and scowl scared most opponents into submission.

Midfield:
Gordon Strachan. An absolute genius. His vision, drive and bravery has not been matched since. Great on the ball, cool under pressure, supported the front men and chipped in with the odd goal. The fact that I got to know him well during my days with Setanta Sports confirmed that's he's not just a great player but a great man too.
Scott Severin. I felt deserved his place in my team as his leadership during some tough times shone through. I have yet to see a better player in an Aberdeen shirt since the early nineties.
Neil Simpson. He was Aberdeen's rock in midfield, his unforgiving style coupled with astonishing levels of fitness dragged the Dons through many a game. He went about his job without fuss or complaint, a truly great midfielder.
Peter Weir. There has been no better winger in the history of Aberdeen. His dazzling runs and pin-point crosses were the stuff of dreams; his left foot possessed nothing but pure magic. As for his ranking in my hero stakes he came a very close second behind Mr Miller.

Forwards:

Eoin Jess. In my opinion Eoin is the last of the great youth products, an outstanding attacking midfielder who in my formation is at his most affective playing in the hole behind the lone striker. A player who could readily slip into any position, his skill, range of passing and uncanny knack of scoring spectacular goals has been sorely missed.

Frank McDougall. His predatory instincts in front of goal, his ability to hold the ball up and his physical presence tipped the scale in his favour. If his injuries had not prematurely ended his career I have no doubt Joe Harper's goal-scoring record would have been in serious trouble! His impact in less than sixty games will never be seen again.

Ally says: 'I toyed for many an hour over who to make my lone striker. Eric Black, Hans Gillhaus, Charlie Nicholas were all in the mix but I think with Eoin Jess in the hole behind Frank and with such a strong midfield this is an attacking side that would score a lot of goals.'

Willie says: 'I can understand Ally's thinking playing Frank up front on his own with Eoin in behind and I think that would work. Scott Severin was a good captain for Aberdeen and although he did come into my consideration for my Dream Team I found stronger candidates.'

CHRIS CUSITER

Chris Cusiter is a proud Aberdonian who has won more than fifty rugby caps for Scotland, and who has also played for the British and Irish Lions. He is a former Aberdeen Grammar School pupil whose whole family have followed the Dons through the years.

Chris Cusiter's Aberdeen Dream Team (formation 4-3-3)

Manager: Sir Alex Ferguson
Far and away the greatest manager Aberdeen has ever seen. The

glory years were just a bit before my time but for Sir Alex to lead the team to so many honours including the European Cup Winners' Cup singles him out as one of the greatest of all time.

Goalkeeper: Theo Snelders
Definitely **Theo Snelders**. That may sound a bit harsh on Jim Leighton but Theo was a firm favourite with me and my pals.

Defence:
Stuart McKimmie. A class act who was the captain when I was growing up. A lot of people have told me that Stuart Kennedy may have been a better all-round player but he must have been going some to be better than Stuart.

Alex McLeish. One of the greatest players Scotland, never mind Aberdeen have ever produced.

Willie Miller. Easiest pick of the lot. What can you say? A true Aberdeen legend.

Kevin McNaughton. I was always impressed by Kevin's ability to get up and down the pitch and he was a great loss when he left us to join Cardiff City.

Midfield:
Gordon Strachan. One of the players who was just a bit before my time as well but his reputation carries him through and gets him in my team.

Eoin Jess. Probably the first name on my teamsheet. A fantastic player and at the peak of his form when I was watching the team regularly.

Jim Bett. A real class act who never looked like he was under pressure. A great passer of the ball and a fantastic link man between defence and attack.

Forwards:
'Champagne' Charlie Nicholas was a superb striker who helped us win the Scottish Cup in the famous penalty shoot-out against Celtic in 1990.

Hicham Zerouali. I was always impressed by Hicham and it was a tragedy that he died that at the age of just twenty-seven in a car crash in his native Morocco back in 2004. The fans used to call him 'Zero' and he was a real cult hero. Hicham was so popular that fans sported fezzes in tribute to his Moroccan heritage. Also he had an impressive goal celebration when he did a somersault. Sadly missed.

Joe Harper. Joe was another before my time but every single person I spoke made it clear he had to be in my Dream Team. I was too young to see him play but his goal scoring record is phenomenal.

Chris says: 'I like the look of my Dream Team and we could easily win the SPL with that line-up. There were a few other players I considered like Russell Anderson and Brian Irvine but when you have McLeish and Miller in the centre of your defence you are never going to lose many goals. I'm afraid Russell and Brian will have to settle for places on my Dream Team bench.'

Willie says: 'As a forward line goes I think Chris has picked the most entertaining. Can you imagine how much excitement would be generated by Hicham, Joe and Charlie all playing together at their peak? I would have loved to have seen that. He has also chosen an exciting pair of full-backs as both Stewart and Kevin were always keen to get forward. I like Chris's formation and there looks fluency about his Dream Team.'

RICHARD GORDON

Richard Gordon is a highly respected sports broadcaster and presenter and a lifelong Aberdeen supporter. He writes a column in the Aberdeen match day programme and follows the fortunes of the club avidly.

Richard Gordon's Aberdeen Dream Team (formation 4-4-2)

Manager: Sir Alex Ferguson

I would be astonished if any fan selected anyone other than 'Sir

Alex' to manage their Dons Dream Team. His Pittodrie roll of honour was breathtaking as he took the club by the scruff of the neck and, aided and abetted by a carefully assembled group of players, dragged the Dons to unparalleled and unimaginable success.

Goalkeeper: Jim Leighton

Not only the best goalkeeper to play for Aberdeen, but to my mind the best keeper Scotland has produced in my lifetime. Razor sharp reflexes and good handling, big Jim played a massive role in the club's glory years – his overall contribution on the pitch and behind the scenes should never be overlooked.

Defence:

Stuart Kennedy. Epitomised everything that was good about the magnificent team I saw come together and grow together from the late 1970s through to the early 1980s. A determined competitor with a startling turn of pace and an excellent tackler. His only flaw was his inability, at times, to cross the ball, but I will forgive him that.
Alex McLeish. A commanding old-fashioned central defender who was prepared to take the knocks while maintaining impressive levels of consistency throughout his career. Seventy-seven caps for his country and a richly deserved place in the Scottish Football Hall of Fame. I was there for his debut against Dundee United in January 1978 and followed his career closely thereafter. A committed professional and one of the game's good guys.
Willie Miller. The all-time greatest Aberdeen player and an absolute must for any Dons compilation. Injury ended his career prematurely, but by then he had scooped up every honour the game had to offer and set standards most players can only dream of. Without doubt the best penalty box defender I have ever watched.
Jim Hermiston. The one non-Gothenburg hero in my back line was one of the first Dons players I remember and part of the 1970 Scottish Cup Final winning side. He was hard and tough-tackling and could also move up comfortably into midfield. Left back has

been a problem position for Aberdeen managers down the years, but Jim gets the nod for his overall defensive qualities.

Midfield:

Gordon Strachan. Boundless energy, an almost unmatched will-to-win, and a highly impressive goal return are just some of the reasons why Gordon makes my side. His dribbling skills and his undoubted ability to wind up the opposition are two others. The team of the early 1980s never quite seemed the same if he was out injured or suspended.

Neil Simpson. One of the most gifted from the crop of youngsters ever to move through to the Dons first team, Neil became one of the cornerstones of our most successful side, allowing more gifted colleagues the freedom to roam while he anchored midfield. A hard but fair competitor, he also weighed in with some memorable goals in vital matches.

Jim Bett. An imperious midfielder who always played with his head up and had a superb range of passing. He joined the club as the Gothenburg side was beginning to be dismantled and was a driving force in the successes that followed, collecting both League Cup and Scottish Cup winner's medals in 1989/90, the year in which he was deservedly voted SPFA Player of the Year. In full flow he was a joy to watch.

Peter Weir. The left wing position was really tough for me, but Peter just edges out my first Dons hero, Arthur Graham, and the mercurially talented Ian Scanlon. Peter shared Scanlon's skills, but was more consistent over a number of years despite injury problems. The Ipswich UEFA Cup-tie at Pittodrie was his signature game, but I saw him destroy many a defence at home and abroad during his Aberdeen career.

Forwards:

Joe Harper. The club's record goalscorer and the most lethal finisher ever to pull on an Aberdeen shirt. The iconic pose of him on his knees, arms outstretched in front of the Beach End after hitting the net yet again, is one of the most enduring images of my early days as a Dons fan. It was a crime that he only ever played four times for his country.

Eric Black. This was another really difficult decision with John Hewitt and Duncan Shearer the other genuine candidates, but I went for Eric mainly because I think he and Harper would, at their peak, have formed an irresistible partnership. His career was cruelly shortened, but his class shone through, and he scored some spectacular and important goals.

Richard says: 'There are so many others that I could have selected, some of whom are club legends like Bobby Clark, Drew Jarvie, Derek McKay, Zoltan Varga, Neale Cooper, Mark McGhee, Martin Buchan and John McMaster; others that became personal favourites for a whole variety of reasons such as Henning Boel, Brian Grant, Paul Mason, Charlie Nicholas, Billy Dodds, Arild Stavrum and Davie Robb. It is a joyous exercise for any football fan to pick a Dream Team and it really is not about who makes the starting eleven – the actual fun is in recalling all the greats (and not so greats) you have watched and supported down the years, and revelling in those delicious memories.'

Willie says: 'Richard has put together a top-class side here. The only question mark I have is over playing Jim Hermiston at left back. Don't get me wrong Jim was a very good player but more a hard-tackling defender rather than a guy that would get up and down the park and ping passes all over the place, which is the template as to the sort of play I want in my Dream Team. Partnering Eric Black and Joe Harper would really work and there would not be a defence in Dream Team land that wouldn't be quaking in their boots when the pair of them started buzzing all over the place.'

BUFF HARDIE, MBE

Buff Hardie, MBE, was a member of the highly successful three-man comedy revue act titled *Scotland the What?* that played to sell-out crowds all over the world. An Aberdeen University graduate he is one of the best known faces in the north-east of Scotland and one of Willie's favourite performers.

Buff Hardie's Aberdeen Dream Team (formation 4-4-2)

Goalkeeper:
Peter Kjaer
Defence:
Stuart Kennedy, Alex McLeish, Willie Miller and Martin Buchan
Midfield:
Gordon Strachan, Zoltan Varga, Archie Glen and Charlie Cooke
Strikers:
Graham Leggat and Joe Harper

Buff says: 'I have picked a Dream Team from all the Aberdeen players I have seen in seventy plus years of watching the Dons, on the assumption that all are alive and in peak fitness and form.

'There is of course a difficulty in that positions and formations have changed over the years. In selecting Peter Kjaer, I feel disloyal towards Bobby Clark and Jim Leighton, but what a class act Kjaer was! Martin Buchan at left back? Well, he has to get into the team somewhere, and I think he did once play at full-back for Scotland.

'Of the outfield players whom I saw, the one whom I most regret having to miss out is striker George Hamilton. Of those whom I never saw, because they were before my time, I guess my Dad, if he had been participating in the selection process, would have been pushing for Alex Jackson, presumably in place of Graham Leggat. He would I'm sure have advocated Jackson and Hamilton up front. Come to think of it!'

Willie says: 'I have great respect for Buff as a performer and Aberdeen expert and he has picked a very interesting team but there are a couple of picks I would disagree with. One is Zoltan Varga who was a great player but not Dream Team material and of course

Peter Kjaer. He was a Danish internationalist but I would rank Jim Leighton, Bobby Clark and Theo Snelders above him.

For me Buff and the *Scotland the What?* team always provided fantastic entertainment and with Charlie Cooke and Graham Leggat in the side there would be no shortage of the same sort of stuff out on the pitch. I'm glad Buff has managed to get Martin Buchan into his Dream Team as he was one of the greatest captains Aberdeen ever had and deserves to be given a spot. The left back was always a problem area to Aberdeen managers through the years and I am sure Martin could slot in there easily.'

PAUL LAWRIE, MBE

Paul Lawrie, MBE, won The Open at Carnoustie in 1999 and was a member of the European Ryder Cup team in the same year. He was born and bred in Aberdeen and lists his hobbies as Aberdeen Football club and cars, with his sporting heroes being Sir Alex Ferguson and Sandy Lyle. Paul is a regular attender at Pittodrie when his busy schedule allows.

Paul Lawrie's Aberdeen Dream Team (formation 4-4-2)

Manager: Sir Alex Ferguson
Goalkeeper:
Jim Leighton
Defence:
Stuart Kennedy, Alex McLeish, Willie Miller, Doug Rougvie
Midfield:
Gordon Strachan, Neale Cooper, Neil Simpson, Peter Weir
Forwards:
Eric Black, Mark McGhee

Paul says: 'There might have been some better players who played before my time but this team I watched as a teenager at Pittodrie in the old stand with my father and brother. We were also in Gothenburg for European Cup Winners' Cup final which was a great night. I like to think my Dream Team would be very difficult to beat and as for my favourite player in my starting eleven I would pick Willie Miller just ahead of Gordon Strachan.'

Willie says: 'Paul has picked the nucleus of the side that brought such success to Pittodrie. In fact ten of his eleven played in the European Cup Winners' Cup team with only Stuart Kennedy missing the final through injury. I know for a fact that Paul's whole family have been loyal Aberdeen fans through the generations and he clearly has great memories of watching this side in action. His formation is spot on and his team includes some of the greatest football players I ever shared a pitch with.'

JAMES NAUGHTIE

Jim Naughtie is a respected journalist and broadcaster who is one of the main presenters on Radio Four's *Today* programme. A life-long Aberdeen fan, he was brought up in Milltown of Rothiemay near Huntly and was in Gothenburg to witness his favourite team win the European Cup Winners' Cup.

Jim Naughtie's Aberdeen Dream Team (formation 4-3-3)

Goalkeeper:
Jim Leighton
Defence:
Henning Boel, Alex McLeish, Willie Miller, Ally Shewan
Midfield:
Zoltan Varga, Tommy Craig, Gordon Strachan
Forwards:
Joe Harper, Peter Weir, Drew Jarvie

Jim says: 'My perfect team is post-sixties. I do ask myself how it is possible to come up with a team that doesn't include Charlie Cooke from the sixties (dazzling, in his lazy way), Dave Smith from the following period (elegance personified, despite a Beckhamish ability in the tackle), Derek Mackay or Eric Black (for very sentimental reasons). But there we are. I had to wrestle a long time about Bobby Clark vs Jim Leighton, about leaving out Jim Hermiston and Jens Petersen, though not – I confess – about Davie Robb. Ally Shewan, I admit, would not normally appear in a team of world-beating defenders . . . but what a servant! I'm a little worried about midfield, because I'm not sure if Varga-Craig-Strachan makes much tactical sense. But I couldn't leave any of them out. And because Joey Harper is, shall we say, on the short side, I wanted Drew Jarvie's gleaming pate beside him. And Peter Weir? Alex Ferguson says that when he played well, so did the team. That's good enough for me. They speak for themselves. This lot would be very hard to beat. I think.'

Willie says: 'Jim has come up with a very interesting starting eleven that would be very difficult to beat as he suggests. Although I like the look of his 4-3-3 set up I can't agree with his midfield in particular. Zoltan Varga wouldn't make my team despite his undoubted talent. Tommy Craig was a fine player but because I feel he peaked during his time at Newcastle United rather than at Aberdeen, I believe there are others who deserve consideration in the middle of the park ahead of him.

'I can fully understand why he has put Peter Weir in his team as on his day he was one of the greatest players in the history of Aberdeen. I did consider naming Drew Jarvie on my Dream Team bench because he was a great servant to the club both as a player and a coach, but although he missed out in my team I am pleased he is being recognised by such a big Aberdeen fan as Jim.'

JACK WEBSTER

Jack Webster is one of Scotland's foremost writers and broadcasters. Such is his knowledge of the club and journalistic skills he was selected to write the definitive history of Aberdeen Football Club.

Jack Webster's Aberdeen Dream Team (formation 2-3-5)

Goalkeeper:
Leighton
Full-backs:
Cooper, Colman
Half-backs:
Miller, McLeish, Varga
Forwards:
Strachan, Hamilton, Harper, Mills, Pearson

Jack says: 'As you can guess, picking my Aberdeen Dream Team has been a really tricky but enjoyable task. Like Buff Hardie, I go back a long time. When I wrote the first Dons history in the 1970s I was able to interview players right back to the First World War, virtually to the origins of 1903.

'I originally drew up three Dream Teams, which gives you an idea of my dilemma, showing the wealth of talent that has passed Pittodrie's way. Remember I stuck to the old 2-3-5 formation and have moved one or two players from their normal positions, if only to get them in my Dream Team.

'Some would rage that I haven't even mentioned memorable names like Stan Williams, the brilliant South African from that first Scottish Cup winning team of 1947 or Matt Armstrong, he of the film-star good looks and great partner up front of Willie Mills. Also what about Alec Jackson or Benny Yorston? It was a tough decision to leave these guys out but there was a balancing job to be done.'

Willie says: 'With his vast knowledge of the history of Aberdeen Jack has put together a fine team in an old-style formation. From my era apart from myself, he has Jim Leighton, Alex McLeish, Gordon Strachan, Joe Harper and Zoltan Varga. Like I mentioned when commenting on Buff Hardie's choices I can't agree with Varga's selection. He was a top player but didn't do enough for Aberdeen to deserve a Dream Team selection. Jack has picked the cream of the crop from the past which helps reflect all the great players we have had at the club since its formation in 1903, and also his vast knowledge of everything to do with the club makes this a well-informed choice of players.'

BIBLIOGRAPHY

Aberdeen: A Complete Record 1903–1987. Jim Rickaby. Breedon Books Sport.

Aberdeen: Champions of Scotland 1954/55. Kevin Stirling. Desert Island Books.

Aberdeen A Centenary History 1903–2003. Kevin Stirling. Desert Island Books.

Aberdeen FC Miscellany: Aberdeen Trivia, History, Facts and Stats. Kevin Stirling. Pitch Publishing.

Managing My Life: My Autobiography. Alex Ferguson. Hodder and Stoughton.

Behind The Goal. James Addison. Mainstream Publishing.

In the Firing Line: The Jim Leighton Story. Jim Leighton and Ken Robertson. Mainstream Publishing.

In Where It Hurts: My Autobiography. Bryan Gunn. VSP.

King Joey: Upfront and Personal. Joe Harper with Charlie Allan. Birlinn Ltd.

Pittodrie Idols: The Story of Aberdeen's Cult Heroes. Paul Smith. Black & White Publishing.

Strachan: My Life in Football. Gordon Strachan with Jason Thomas. Sphere.

Strachan: An Autobiography. Gordon Strachan with Jack Webster. Stanley Paul.

Ten Days That Shook Scotland. Hugh MacDonald, Allan Patullo, Rob Robertson. Fort Publishing.

The Don: The Willie Miller Story. Willie Miller with Rob Robertson. Birlinn Ltd.

The King. Denis Law with Bob Harris. Bantam Books.

The Legends of Aberdeen. Paul Smith. Breedon Books.

The Management: Scotland's Greatest Football Bosses. Michael Grant and Rob Robertson. Birlinn Ltd.

What A Difference A Day Makes: The Autobiography of Brian Irvine. Brian Irvine and Stuart Weir. Mainstream Publishing.